T0320271

'This book is very timely, given the fact that the world is currently experiencing the third wave of environmentalism: the environment and climate emergency. Zaman and Ahsan propose an alternative zero-waste approach to tackle the critical waste problems we have in our society. We cannot continue to deplete our global natural resource in the name of consumerism. The book argues an alternative circular design and systems thinking where zero-waste practice is a central approach to solving the core challenge of global waste.'

– **Greg Morrison**, *Professor of Sustainable Cities,*
Director of Curtin University Sustainability Policy (CUSP) Institute,
Curtin University, Australia

'The opportunity presented by striving for zero waste and building a circular economy shouldn't be underestimated by businesses wanting to improve their triple bottom line or governments seeking jobs growth and a better environment. This book documents examples and gives hope that we can achieve these goals.'

– **Vaughan Levitzke**, *PSM, Chief Executive,*
Green Industries SA, Adelaide, Australia

'The global waste crisis has made the issues addressed in this book ever more urgent: we need a clear waste reduction and elimination goal to aim for, a mix of "hard and soft" strategies to reshape systems towards this goal, and ways of measuring progress towards its achievement. This valuable book addresses all three essentials together, showing how they depend upon each other, and does so in an accessible yet scholarly and balanced way. This is a substantial achievement.'

– **Robert Crocker**, *DPhil (oxon), Deputy Director,*
China Australia Centre for Sustainable Development,
University of South Australia, Australia

'This book is in response to the enormous waste problem plaguing the planet's ecosystems from urban settlements to landfills and contaminated sites, and severely impacting the once pristine marine environments. We need a drastic change in the way "waste" is perceived. Zaman and Ahsan offer the zero-waste approach as an alternative to the current practices and management systems. They tackle the challenges of plastics use, e-waste, consumerism and planned obsolescence through zero-waste strategies and solutions. The readers will find insights and examples which help understand better the essence and solutions of the problem created by industrial society and human behaviour.'

– **Dora Marinova**, *Professor of Sustainability,*
Curtin University Sustainability Policy (CUSP) Institute,
Curtin University, Australia

ZERO-WASTE

This book analyses 'zero-waste' (ZW) as an emerging waste management strategy for the future, which considers waste prevention through innovative design and sustainable consumption practices.

Drawing on a diverse range of case studies from Australia, Bangladesh, Japan, New Zealand, Sweden, and the USA, this book explores why urban waste management systems still remain a major challenge for almost all cities around the world. Rejecting waste as an 'end-of-life' problem, Atiq Zaman and Tahmina Ahsan instead consider waste prevention through the ZW model, in which resources are utilized and consumed with minimum environmental degradation. In addition, the authors give extended discussion on why embracing the ZW concept will be beneficial for the circular economy (CE).

Providing a strategic zero-waste framework and an evaluation tool to measure waste management performance aimed towards ZW goals, this book will be of great relevance to students, scholars, and policymakers with an interest in waste management, sustainable consumption, urban planning, and sustainable development.

Atiq Zaman is a Lecturer at the School of Design and the Built Environment and an early carrier researcher at the Curtin University Sustainability Policy Institute, Curtin University, Australia. He has more than eight years of research experiences in the area of sustainable waste management and environmental assessment. He is an active advocate for ZW philosophy, activities, and practices. His research interests include sustainable waste management, collaborative consumption, circular economy, and sustainability in the built environment.

Tahmina Ahsan is a casual academic at the School of Design and the Built Environment, Curtin University, Australia. She is an architect with a master's in environmental engineering and sustainable infrastructure from KTH, the Royal Institute of Technology, Sweden; and a PhD degree from the University of Adelaide, Australia. She has a keen interest in sustainable practices and design.

Routledge Studies in Waste Management and Policy

For more information about this series, please visit: www.routledge.com/Routledge-Studies-in-Waste-Management-and-Policy/book-series/RSWMP

ZERO-WASTE

Reconsidering Waste Management for the Future

Atiq Zaman and Tahmina Ahsan

LONDON AND NEW YORK

First published 2020
by Routledge
2 Park Square, Milton Park, Abingdon, Oxon OX14 4RN

and by Routledge
52 Vanderbilt Avenue, New York, NY 10017

Routledge is an imprint of the Taylor & Francis Group, an informa business

British Library Cataloguing-in-Publication Data
A catalogue record for this book is available from the British Library

Library of Congress Cataloging-in-Publication Data
Names: Zaman, Atiq, author. | Ahsan, Tahmina, author.
Title: Zero-waste : reconsidering waste management for the future / Atiq Zaman and Tahmina Ahsan.
Description: Abingdon, Oxon ; New York, NY : Routledge, 2020. | Includes bibliographical references.
Identifiers: LCCN 2019033579 (print) | LCCN 2019033580 (ebook) | ISBN 9781138219083 (hbk) | ISBN 9781138219090 (pbk) | ISBN 9781315436296 (ebk)
Subjects: LCSH: Source reduction (Waste management) | Refuse and refuse disposal. | Sustainable living. | Waste minimization—Case studies. | Recycling (Waste, etc.)—Case studies.
Classification: LCC TD793.95 .Z36 2020 (print) | LCC TD793.95 (ebook) | DDC 628.4—dc23
LC record available at https://lccn.loc.gov/2019033579
LC ebook record available at https://lccn.loc.gov/2019033580

ISBN: 978-1-138-21908-3 (hbk)
ISBN: 978-1-138-21909-0 (pbk)
ISBN: 978-1-315-43629-6 (ebk)

Typeset in Bembo
by Apex CoVantage, LLC

CONTENTS

FIGURES

TABLES

PREFACE

Sustainable waste management is one of the greatest challenges of the twenty-first century. Almost all countries around the world are currently struggling to manage waste sustainably. Unfortunately, the urgently needed waste infrastructure has not been regarded with the same priority as energy and water, especially in the developing countries and in many developed countries. Therefore, waste infrastructure in developing countries lacks the very basic sorting and collection capacities.

According to the World Bank's recent report, only 44% of waste is collected in the South Asia and sub-Saharan Africa regions and 93% of the collected waste in the low-income countries is managed through open dumping Kaza et al. (2018). Most of the developed countries in North America and Europe still rely on landfill and incineration of waste. Australia is also no different from many other developed countries around the world. Due to a lack of local waste processing infrastructure, many developed countries, such as Australia, rely on exporting waste to overseas countries (mainly to China). Since the China waste ban in 2018, the global waste sector is in turmoil, as China, along with Malaysia, Indonesia, Philippines, India, and many other developing countries are not accepting waste from any foreign countries anymore. Therefore, local waste management solutions have emerged as an urgent contemporary issue.

We believe this book will contribute to better understanding the core problem of addressing the waste management system (WMS) in an urban setting. The book opens up the discussion that waste is not an engineering problem to be solved with advanced technology alone, but it is also a social problem that needs social technology (effective recycling and community involvement) to tackle the issue entirely.

The book introduces the contemporary idea of 'zero-waste (ZW)', which is 'the conservation of all resources by means of responsible production, consumption, reuse, and recovery of products, packaging, and materials without burning and with no discharges to land, water, or air that threaten the environment or human health' (ZWIA, 2018). The authors argue that ZW does not mean 100% recycling or achieving a 100% diversion rate but rather creating 0% unwanted waste from the production and consumption activities through improved cradle-to-cradle (C2C) design and sustainable consumption behaviour.

The authors suggest the following three fundamental strategic action plans that need to be implemented simultaneously for moving towards ZW societies: (i) sustainable production through a C2C design and product stewardship, (ii) collaborative and responsible consumption of natural resources, and (iii) ZW management through conservation of resources.

References

Kaza, S., Yao, L. C., Bhada-Tata, P., & Van Woerden, F. (2018). What a waste 2.0: A global snapshot of solid waste management to 2050. *What a Waste 2.0: A Global Snapshot of Solid Waste Management to 2050*. Urban Development; Washington, DC: World Bank. © World Bank. Retrieved from https://openknowledge.worldbank.org/handle/10986/30317 License: CC BY 3.0 IGO

ZWIA. (2018). *Zero waste definition*. Retrieved June 14, 2019, from http://zwia.org/zero-waste-definition/

FOREWORD

Who wouldn't want to see zero-waste (ZW)? It's a no brainer isn't it? Actually, it's not, as there has been a long-held view by many scientists that it's not actually possible. The problem is entropy.

Entropy is the characteristic of all matter in the universe to tend towards greater chaos and dispersal. It's a fundamental of the second law of thermodynamics and it's part of all engineering calculations and design predictions. Waste always wins, eventually. Everything in the universe, according to physics, is crumbling into chaos. So is it possible to even imagine a world where we contemplate ZW in our cities and settlements?

Professor Paul Davies, an Australian physicist and philosopher who is now a professor at Arizona State, has found a way through this dilemma. In his 2019 book *The Demon in the Machine: How Hidden Webs of Information Are Solving the Mystery of Life*, Professor Davies examines how Maxwell who was one of the inventors of quantum mechanics spent 30 years trying to understand how life actually happens when the laws of thermodynamics suggest it's not really possible – he gave up and thus the dilemma is called Maxwell's demon.

Davies has now suggested that the secret is to understand webs of information that are inherent to life rather than just chemicals and physical processes. These are expressed in DNA that organizes cells and in the systems of information that are part of how ecosystems control life. I remember being fascinated by how ecosystems actually become more and more organized and elaborate as they mature after disturbance from fire or flood or human impacts and are indeed able to eventually create a highly resource efficient and ZW system. I then suggested that perhaps cities could follow the same patterns of creating such webs of information to solve the resource and waste problems of our time (Newman, 1975).

The fundamental idea is that unless we create intensely developed webs of information that waste will simply grow as the second law takes over. So, what do we need to do to emulate life in our cities and create ZW? We can start by reading this book!

Information needs to be linked into self-supporting systems at all levels from what individuals consume and how they manage their waste, how products are made and packaged, how waste is collected and processed, how we use smart systems to monitor the flows of materials from product through to waste and back to product, how we regulate all this, how we educate and inform people, how we design the metabolism of our cities, and what we do to improve such matters constantly . . .

Let's work with Atiq and Tahmina to see if we can create these new information systems needed for ZW.

Peter Newman AO
John Curtin Distinguished Professor of Sustainability
Curtin University and Western Australia Scientist of the Year 2018–2019

References

Davies, P. (2019). *The Demon in the Machine: How Hidden Webs of Information Are Finally Solving the Mystery of Life*. London, UK: Penguin.

Newman, P. W. G. (1975). An ecological model for city structure and development. *Ekistics*, *40*(239), 258–265.

ACKNOWLEDGEMENTS

A major part of this book is a result of the PhD research project "A Strategic Waste Management Framework and Tool for the Development of Zero Waste Cities", which was conducted by Dr Atiq Zaman at the Zero Waste SA Research Centre for Sustainable Design and Behaviour, School of Art, Architecture and Design, Division of Education, Arts and Social Sciences, University South Australia.

The authors would like to thank Professor Steffen Lehmann, Dr Robert Crocker, and Associate Professor Christine Garnaut for their support and guidance. It would have not been possible to complete the book without the support from the School of Design and the Built Environment, Curtin University.

I (Atiq Zaman) would personally like to thank my co-author Dr Tahmina Ahsan who has been a constant support throughout my life as my wife. Without her support and contribution to this book, I was just about to say 'no' to the publisher because of two unsuccessful extensions as the soul author of this manuscript.

We would like to thank our parents, friends, and extended family members for their prayers and almighty God for guidance. Finally, we would like to thank numerous scholars and organizations who permitted us to use their images for our book.

Atiq Zaman
Tahmina Ahsan

INTRODUCTION

Zero-waste and beyond

Existing and emerging challenges of waste management

Sustainable waste management is one of the biggest challenges for almost every city authority around the world. Since 2015, around 193 countries have been implementing sustainable development goals (SDGs) as part of their development agenda[1]. According to WasteAid UK[2] (2017), waste management will directly contribute to 12 out of 17 SDGs and indirectly to all SDGs. Till now, waste sector and waste infrastructure have not been regarded with the same priority as energy, water and transport sector.

Waste generation, as well as its management practices, vary according to the differences in social, economic, environmental, geographic, political, and legal systems (El-Haggar, 2007, p. 1) and thus waste management system (WMS) and its techniques vary between developed and developing countries. Even the management practices can differ within countries (Wilson, 2007). In the developed countries, such as Australia, WMS based on an integrated management system primarily relies on technology-based formal waste collection, management, and treatment systems. By contrast, WMS in developing countries, such as Bangladesh, is characterized by an informal management system with very little formal waste management facility (Matter, Dietschi, & Zurbrügg, 2013).

Global waste generation has increased, and it will continue to increase in the future, despite the fact that waste imposes environmental burdens and huge expenses for its management. According to World Bank's study, the world's cities generate about 1.3 billion tonnes of solid waste each year, and the volume is expected to increase to 2.2 billion tonnes by 2025 (Hoornweg & Bhada-Tata, 2012). The study also found that developing countries only collect around 41% of the waste generated, and the rest, 59%, remains uncollected at the points of generation (Hoornweg & Bhada-Tata, 2012). The collection rate in developed countries is around 98%. The study also showed that an estimated 133.82 million tonnes or only 10.29% of waste (excluding composting) is recycled globally, and the rest of the waste is mostly used in landfills or remained uncollected.

The traditional landfill-based solid WMSs without sufficient support, governance, and financing can compound environmental problems in the developing world. A recent study conducted by the Waste Atlas (2014) identified that around 64.3 million people live less than 10 kilometre from the world's 50 biggest dumpsites, and most of these dumpsites are very close to the natural resources, such as rivers, lakes, etc. (D-Waste, 2014). This indicates that the possibility of nearby environments being polluted and poses severe health impacts to the residents.

Waste-to-energy (WTE) technology, such as incineration, which is a common alternative for waste disposal, has the advantage of 'solving' an immediate problem efficiently but ignores the long-term problems of overconsumption and depletion of natural resources. Incineration is considered to be a quite controversial technology and opinions vary as to where and if it should be used (Halkos & Petrou, 2016). Incineration might appear to work in a regulated and developed nation like Sweden, where there seem to be few alternatives as a result of the climate and the higher energy needs of the country, but in developing nations, it is often introduced as a last resort: a 'modern' high-tech solution to deal with overflowing landfills. Incineration of waste (WTE) is beneficial compared to landfills because it produces electricity and heat and less environmental burdens (emissions, contaminations), compared to landfills (Assamoi & Lawryshyn, 2012). Incineration of household and industrial waste requires centralized management and efficient systems and is essentially a further development of the concept of WMS. However, it can lead to a greater demand for waste (e.g. in Sweden, waste has imported from neighbouring countries for incineration), thus encouraging more consumption.

The recent turmoil in the waste industry around the world since China waste ban (stopped accepting 24 categories of solid waste) in 2018 shows the feebleness of countries' domestic waste processing capacities and the ineffectiveness of global waste management practices (Kilvert & Smith, 2018). Before the ban, China was importing and processing a notable amount of the global recycled waste (e.g. 56% of the world's plastics garbage) mainly from developed countries including Australia. By putting a 0.5% contamination threshold for accepting waste from overseas countries into China eventually severely impacts the management of the global recycled waste. Australia alone has been facing challenges of processing around 1.3 million tonnes of recyclable waste locally (Cansdale, 2019). Similar to Australia, many other countries also need to find local solutions for managing and processing recycled waste domestically. It is predicted that the development of a local waste processing industry in Australia would create three times more jobs (9.2 jobs for every 10,000 tonnes) than the waste export to overseas countries (2.8 jobs for every 10,000 tonnes recycled waste). Local solutions need to be underpinned by enforcing the principles of circular economy (CE) and by prioritizing waste hierarchy into practices.

The waste hierarchy was proposed by experts to choose the most favourable waste management policy actions (avoid, reduce, reuse, and recycle) over the least favourable options (treatment and landfill). Undoubtedly, a major part of the WMS in the world still relies on the least favourable options in this waste hierarchy due to lower operation and management costs. However, prevention would result in the least environmental and economic life-cycle costs because it avoids collection, recycling, and processing of materials' costs (Sharp, Stocchi, Levistzke, & Hewitt, 2015).

Still, in the twenty-first century, waste is primarily managed by using various treatment technologies and disposal methods, despite having a waste management hierarchy. Waste prevention and avoidance will not be possible if we do not seek alternative and innovative product design, an efficient manufacturing process, sustainable and collaborative consumption practices, and, finally, managing the waste in a closed-loop material flow system wherein resources can be recycled and reused within the consumption process.

We have finite natural resources, and we cannot continue with our current consumption practices based on a linear resource consumption model, which is extract, manufacture, consume, and dispose. It is important and obligatory to recover as many resources as possible from the waste that we produce every day. Sustainable WMSs is now one of the prime concerns for all developed and developing countries. Zero-waste (ZW) could be an alternative solution, as it considers a 'whole system' perspective on resource consumption and resource recovery from waste.

Why ZW?

In the last few decades, many cities around the world have embraced the 'ZW' philosophy as a solution for tackling waste problems. The term 'ZW' was first used by Paul Palmer in 1973 for recovering resources from chemicals (Palmer, 2004), and later, the concept was taken up and integrated into the WMSs in many places around the world. ZW is defined by the Zero Waste International Alliance (ZWIA) as 'designing and managing products and processes systematically to eliminate the waste and materials, conserve and recover all resources and not burn or bury them' (ZWIA, 2013). Thus ZW is about waste prevention through sustainable design and consumption practices and not about managing waste by incineration or landfills. ZW is not a utopia but a realistic goal to guide sustainable WMS. The visionary ZW goals cannot be achieved through existing production and consumption practices and require the long-term application of ZWS.

The concepts encompassed by the goal of 'ZW' directly challenge the common assumption that waste is unavoidable and has no value by focusing on waste as a 'misallocated resource' that has to be recovered (Lehmann, 2010b, p. 232). In this book, the concept of ZW is extended from the conventional goal of diverting waste from landfills to encompassing the conservation of resources, optimum production, and recovery of all resources from waste. Therefore, the ZW concept not only includes maximizing the socio-cultural and economic value of 'waste' by enhanced environmental stewardship, more ethical production, and mindful consumption of goods but also incorporates efficient management of waste and optimum resource recovery from waste. Optimum resource recovery and efficient management of waste ensures environmental and social benefits, as well as economic growth.

This implies that ZW – as a concept – is a means of transforming WMSs towards a 'CE', where extraction, production, and consumption become increasingly waste-free (MacArthur, 2013). The European Commission defines circular economies as 'approaches that "design out" waste and typically involve innovation throughout the value chain, rather than relying solely on solutions at the end of life of a product' (European Commission, 2014). A similar emphasis rendered by Ken Webster also suggests that the CE is grounded on a regenerative model, and its advantage lies in designing out waste and enabling access over ownership to reduce environmental burdens (Webster, 2015).

A CE is beneficial for both the economy and the environment and promotes ZW activities. A recent study shows that business in Europe alone could potentially save €600 billion and reduce annual greenhouse gas (GHG) emissions by 2%–4% through implementing a CE that include the measures of waste prevention, reuse, and eco-design (AMEC and Bio-Intelligence, 2013). Even though the concepts of industrial ecology and C2C design are multidisciplinary, all these concepts are interlinked with one other. These theories are fundamentally supportive to the ZW concept. The theory of industrial ecology is based on material and energy flows in an industrial system and C2C design is based on an eco-effective product design that maintains a closed-loop material flow in the system. The core principle of these theories is underpinned by environmental stewardship and the conservation of resources.

ZW is a pragmatic goal, made necessary by the current universal problem of over-consumption and a consequent growth in waste, including toxic waste categories. In recent years, cities in the developed world, including Adelaide in Australia and San Francisco in the USA, have aspired to achieve a state of 'ZW' by ending the practice of landfilling municipal solid waste (MSW). As this suggests, a better understanding of waste as a resource and part of a closed-cycle urban ecology is important (Lehmann, 2010a, p. 233).

The notion of a ZW city

Many cities, such as Adelaide in South Australia and San Francisco in California, have developed the 'zero-waste strategy' (ZWS) in order to become a 'zero-waste city' (ZWC). The concept of the 'ZWC' is inspired by that of the 'eco-city', where urbanization (including urban planning and management) is comprehensively integrated with ecological management to enhance the well-being of the city's citizens and natural ecosystems. The notion of the 'ZWC' refers to an urban system where resources are utilized by producers and consumers who see themselves as, and act as, ecological stewards to minimize environmental degradation (Zaman & Lehmann, 2011).

Empirical evidence suggests that a ZWC is possible, and the concept is found in the lean production practices of Japanese industries where an integrated systems approach is applied in the production cycle to eliminate waste by ensuring multi-stakeholders' involvement (Fujita & Hill, 2007; Womack, Jones, & Roos, 1990). The urban systems and networks of a ZWC are designed and operated in keeping with the principles of industrial symbiosis. Here, industries exchange materials, energy, water, and by-products (Chertow, 2007) to manufacture products based on nature's 'no-waste' principles. In a ZWC, 'waste' will not be banished from society; instead, all 'waste' will be utilized as products, and thus no waste will be lost in a ZWC. The ZWC concept aims to transform our current over-consuming cities into sustainable ones and essentially follows the same principles outlined in a CE.

Even though the emphasis of ZWC is placed directly on the end of the waste problem, it acknowledges that it is an entire system's problem, including consumption and manufacture. Population, infrastructure, and regulatory systems are the core components of ZWC. Infrastructure and regulatory systems in a ZWC guide both producers and consumers to achieve ZW goals by optimizing resource use with minimal environmental depletion. Another way to understand this goal is to consider the ZWC in terms of its 'metabolism', including the physical flows of matter and energy within urban infrastructure and systems (Baccini & Brunner, 2012). This view of the city as a metabolic system of energy and material flows provides an essential condition for the development of a ZWC.

The content and scope of the book

One of the key focuses of this book is to examine various socio-economic and environmental challenges of current waste management practices. The main argument is given around the context why almost all cities are facing various waste management challenges despite our advancement in waste treatment technology and management practices. The book argues that the waste problem is not only an engineering problem to be solved with the help of modern technology but also a social and environmental problem which needs a systemic change of resource consumption and waste management philosophy.

In traditional WMSs, an engineering 'end-of-pipe' solution has usually been applied to solve waste problems. This needs to change by considering an alternative waste management philosophy: 'ZW'. This book expands on the discussion of 'ZW management' in the light of sustainable production, consumption, waste management, resource recovery, and sustainable waste treatment technologies. The authors argue on different perspectives of ZW management: that waste is a 'by-product' of our urban system, and to solve this problem, we need a systemic change which considers the whole life cycle of resource consumption in urban systems. This systemic change is urgently needed in every phase of resource consumption and management, viz. resource extraction, manufacture and production, resource consumption, waste management, resource recovery, and treatment.

This book contains three parts. In Part 1, Chapter 1 provides the key concepts and principles of waste management and opens up the discussion around the challenges of WMS in regard to waste generation, its management, and treatment.

Chapter 2 extends the discussion of the existing challenges of waste management and provides an empirical analysis in relation to plastic waste, as plastics seem to be the most problematic household waste stream. One of the biggest knowledge gaps in waste management is not considering production and consumption and their impacts on overall management of waste (studied in Chapter 3). Waste management has often been considered an engineering problem, and this chapter tries to integrate the missing link by bring the discussion of production and consumption and their roles in overall management of waste. Chapter 4 provides a detailed analysis of the emerging concept of 'ZW' and setting the background of ZW as an innovative solution for WMS. The first part of this book will try to provide a critical analysis on why the consideration and appropriate policies on sustainable production and consumption are the prerequisites of combating the war on waste.

The second part (Part 2) provides ZW case studies in the context of families, communities, and business (Chapter 5); problematic waste types (electronic waste – Chapter 6, construction and demolition waste – Chapter 7); and urban settings (Chapter 8). The second part of this book provides an insight of ZW by scrutinizing the current practices from the micro-level (family) to the macro-level (city) and understanding the key challenges and opportunities for moving towards the ZW world.

The third part (Part 3) of this book outlines the key ZWSs (Chapter 9) and the roles of smart technologies in ZW management system (Chapter 10). Chapter 11 introduces a new tool called the 'zero-waste index' (ZWI) as a performance measurement tool used to assess the progress towards ZW goals. Chapter 12 applies the proposed ZWI to quantify the environmental and economic benefits of ZW management system in selected cities.

In conclusion, the book tries to broaden our understanding of waste problems in the context of resource utilization, consumption in our everyday life, and resource recovery from waste. It is important to properly recognize the core waste problem, which is not an engineering problem to be solved with the help of advanced treatment technologies alone; rather, it is a systemic problem which includes social, economic, political, and environmental aspects. ZW considers a whole system approach which is often ignored in the traditional WMSs, and thus the authors argue that ZW goals can be achieved through systemic changes in traditional manufacturing processes, consumption behaviours, waste management, and treatment and disposal practices.

Notes

1 SDG Index. (2018). SDG Index and Dashboards Report 2018. Retrieved from https://s3.amazonaws.com/sustainabledevelopment.report/2018/2018_sdg_index_and_dashboards_report.pdf
2 WasteAid UK. (2017). Making Waste Work: A Toolkit Community Waste Management in Low- and Middle-Income Countries. Retrieved from https://wasteaid.org/toolkit/summary/

References

AMEC and Bio-Intelligence. (2013). *The Opportunities to Business of Improving Resource Efficiency*. Retrieved from Brussels: http://ec.europa.eu/environment/enveco/resource_efficiency/pdf/report_opportunities.pdf

Assamoi, B., & Lawryshyn, Y. (2012). The environmental comparison of landfilling vs. incineration of MSW accounting for waste diversion. *Waste Management, 32*(5), 1019–1030.

Baccini, P., & Brunner, P. H. (2012). *Metabolism of the Anthroposphere: Analysis, Evaluation, Design* (2nd ed.). Cambridge and London: MIT Press.

Cansdale, D. (2019). What's changed one year since the start of our recycling crisis? *ABC News*. Retrieved from www.abc.net.au/news/2019-01-11/australias-recycling-crisis-one-year-on-whats-changed/10701418

Chertow, M. R. (2007). "Uncovering" industrial symbiosis. *Journal of Industrial Ecology, 11*(1), 11–30.

D-Waste. (2014). *Waste Atlas: The World's 50 Biggest Dumpsites*. Retrieved from www.atlas.d--waste.com/Documents/Waste-Atlas-report-2014-webEdition.pdf

El-Haggar, S. (2007). *Sustainable Industrial Design and Waste Management: Cradle-to-Cradle for Sustainable Development*. Burlington, MA: Elsevier Academic Press.

European Commission. (2014). *Towards a Circular Economy: A Zero Waste Programme for Europe*. Retrieved from Brussels: http://eur-lex.europa.eu/resource.html?uri=cellar:aa88c66d-4553-11e4-a0cb-01aa75ed71a1.0022.03/DOC_1&format=PDF

Fujita, K., & Hill, R. C. (2007). The zero waste city: Tokyo's quest for a sustainable environment. *Journal of Comparative Policy Analysis: Research and Practice, 9*(4), 405–425. doi:10.1080/13876980701674225

Halkos, G. E., & Petrou, K. N. (2016). Moving towards a circular economy: Rethinking waste management practices. *Journal of Economic and Social Thought, 3*(2), 220–240.

Hoornweg, D., & Bhada-Tata, P. (2012). *What a Waste: A Global Review of Solid Waste Management*. Retrieved from Washington, DC: http://go.worldbank.org/BCQEP0TMO0

Kilvert, N., & Smith, C. (2018). "The demise of kerbside recycling"? China ban disrupts rubbish removal and fills warehouses. *ABC News*, 8 February. Retrieved from www.abc.net.au/news/2018-02-08/the-demise-of-kerb-side-recycling/9407650

Lehmann, S. (2010a). *The Principles of Green Urbanism: Transforming the City for Sustainability* (1st ed.). London: Earthscan.

Lehmann, S. (2010b). Resource recovery and materials flow in the city: Zero waste sustainable consumption as paradigms in urban development. *Sustainable Development Law and Policy, 11*(1), 28–38.

MacArthur, E. (2013). *Towards the Circular Economy, Economic and Business Rationale for an Accelerated Transition*. Cowes, UK: Ellen MacArthur Foundation.

Matter, A., Dietschi, M., & Zurbrügg, C. (2013). Improving the informal recycling sector through segregation of waste in the household: The case of Dhaka Bangladesh. *Habitat International, 38*(April), 150–156.

Palmer, P. (2004). *Getting to Zero Waste*. Portland, Oregon: Purple Sky Press.

Sharp, A., Stocchi, L., Levistzke, V., & Hewitt, M. (2015). *Measuring the Waste Management Hierarchy*. Paper presented at the Unmaking Waste, Adelaide. Retrieved from http://unmakingwaste2015.org/wp-content/uploads/2015/09/UMW_Session_13.pdf

Waste Atlas. (2014). *The World's 50 Biggest Dumpsites*. Retrieved from www.atlas.d-waste.com/Documents/Waste-Atlas-report-2014-webEdition.pdf

Webster, K. (2015). *The Circular Economy: A Wealth of Flows*. Cowes, UK: Ellen MacArthur Foundation.

Wilson, D. C. (2007). Development drivers for waste management. *Waste Management & Research, 25*(3), 198–207. doi:10.1177/0734242x07079149

Womack, J. P., Jones, D. T., & Roos, D. (1990). *The Machine That Changed the World.* New York: Rawson Associates.

Zaman, A. U., & Lehmann, S. (2011). Urban growth and waste management optimization towards "zero waste city". *City, Culture and Society, 2*(4), 177–187. http://dx.doi.org/10.1016/j.ccs.2011.11.007

ZWIA. (2013). *Zero Waste Communities.* Retrieved from http://zwia.org/news/zero-waste-communities/

PART 1

The anatomy of zero-waste

Zero-waste and beyond

1

BACKGROUND OF WASTE MANAGEMENT SYSTEM

What is 'waste'?

Waste is an integral part of our society, being a by-product of economic and consumption activity, it originates from households, institutions, businesses, and industries. The term 'waste' can be defined in different ways based on our understanding and perception of resource value. Based on its physical composition, waste can either be liquid, solid, or gaseous. However, in this book, the term 'waste' refers to solid waste. The US Code of Federation Regulations (2004) defines solid waste as garbage, refuse, sludge, and other discarded solid materials resulting from industrial and commercial operations and community activities. Waste is defined by the United Nations as

> materials that are not prime products for which the generator has no further use in terms of production, transformation or consumption and thus the generator wants to dispose of. Waste may be generated during the extraction, processing of raw materials into products, the consumption of products and other human activities.
>
> *(GRID-Arendal, 2004)*

Waste also refers to 'any trash, garbage, refuse or abandoned materials (US-EPA, 2011) which has "no economic value" or function for anybody'(Pichtel, 2005).

The definition of 'waste' by local authorities varies as they are based on local perceptions and understanding of waste. The government of South Australia defines waste as 'any discarded, rejected, abandoned, unwanted or surplus matter' (Government of SA, 2010), emphasizing personal behaviour and choice. Stockholm uses the same definition of waste as used in the European Commission Directive on waste, which defines waste as 'any substance or object which the holder discards or intends or is required to discard' (European Commission, 2012). Whereas the government of California defines waste as 'objects or materials for which no use or reuse is intended' (Cal-Recycle, 2010), primarily focusing on the usability of the materials or objects, and the waste authority in Dhaka defines waste as 'those residual materials that have no economic value' (DoE, 2009).

All the aforementioned definitions of waste summarize three significant points: (i) anything that appears as valueless (both subjective and objective value) to its producer, (ii) not functional to users, and (iii) requires to be discarded. Simply, when a valuable material or product loses both its subjective value (which is the value in the judgements of the owner, not in the object itself) and objective value (which is inherent in the object itself – price or materialistic value) at any point of production and consumption process, it becomes a waste, and thus the owner intends or requires to discard it. In most of the developed countries, even a newly purchased product becomes refuse, rubbish, or garbage very quickly because the owner of the product does not see any value (subjective) and function in it after a certain period of time. However, the same 'waste' may be a valuable product or resource in many developing countries; for example, old electronic 'waste' from developed countries is sold to developing countries as the so-called waste has value to the people in the developing countries. Thus 'waste' from the developed countries is seen as an opportunity in many developing countries.

Amongst various waste types, the discussion will be limited to the following waste categories in this book:

MSW

MSW is one of the most common and largely generated waste products that every city and country needs to manage. Definitions of MSW vary between countries and geographical jurisdictions. Generally, MSW is defined as 'waste generated by households and waste of a similar nature generated from commercial and industrial process' (UN-HABITAT, 2010, p. 6). MSW is defined by the Organization for Economic Co-operation and Development (OECD) as waste that is

> collected and treated by, or for municipalities. It covers waste from households, including bulky waste, similar waste from commerce and trade, office buildings, institutions and small businesses, yard and garden, street sweepings, contents of litter containers, and market cleansing. Waste from municipal sewage networks and treatment, as well as municipal construction and demolition, is excluded.
>
> *(GRID-Arendal, 2004)*

Construction and demolition (C&D) waste

C&D waste consisting of cement, bricks, asphalt, wood, metals, and other construction materials that are typically inert and are generated regularly as a result of new construction, demolition of old structures and roadways, and regular maintenance of buildings (UNEP, 2005). Very large volumes of demolition waste are generated during natural disasters (earthquakes, floods, typhoons, and others) and during wars.

Waste Electrical and Electronic Equipment (WEEE)

There is no globally agreed definition of WEEE. The European Union (EU) Directive 2002/96/EC defines WEEE as 'electrical or electronic equipment which is waste. . . ., including all components, subassemblies and consumables which are part of the product at the time of discarding' (European Commission, 2002). Some of the most common electronic waste include personal computers, printers, monitors, television sets, and cellular telephones. As the usage of these and similar products increases, many of them are replaced and disposed of each year.

Types and composition of MSW

Waste can be broadly categorized as municipal, institutional, industrial, medical, universal, C&D, radioactive, mining, and agricultural depending on the source of generation (Hartln, 1996; Pichtel, 2005). Although, MSW refers to the types of waste that are commonly managed by local waste authority, in many jurisdictions around the world, MSW can be broadly categorized as domestic or household waste, commercial, and institutional waste.

Household waste is created by various domestic consumption activities, such as cooking and eating. Besides that, a significant proportion of MSW consists of various consumer products, such as clothes, electronic items, and white goods. According to physical and chemical composition, MSW can be categorized as organic and inorganic, hazardous and non-hazardous, and combustible and non-combustible waste.

The constituents of waste composition are highly dependent on resource consumption patterns. As the consumption activities vary in different countries and locality, the composition of MSW also varies. The waste composition has changed significantly over time, as the consumption patterns have evolved from a very simple form to a highly complex form. In nomadic societies, humans produced bones and other parts of the animals as they hunted for their food (Reddy, 2011). Nature managed these wastes, and, literally, there were no waste at all as they decayed over time.

When we moved from nomadic societies to agricultural societies and started living in wooden shelters, we started to produce other types of waste, such as wood. Waste composition has been associated with human consumption cultures; for example, the ancient cultures of the east and gulf coasts of the US left huge piles of marine molluscs they had eaten (Kangas, 2003). During the fifth century BC, garbage in Greece normally consisted of food waste, faecal matter, potsherds, and abandoned babies (e.g. malformed or illegitimate) (Kelly, 1973). The composition of London's solid waste in 1888 mainly consisted of fine dust and cinder (81.7%) and vegetable, putrescible, and bone (13.2%) (Pichtel, 2005). Paper and plastic were not present as widespread consumer products during that time; however, less than a century later, paper constituted the highest (34%) waste composition in 1967.

During the Industrial Revolution (in the eighteenth to nineteenth century), people started to move from a predominantly agrarian or rural society to an urban society. New products and product categories were developed in a short period of time due to innovative manufacturing processes and efficient machineries, motorized vehicles, new construction materials, innovative spinning, and weaving technologies are some examples. Along with products, various urban services were also introduced to meet the ever-growing demand of human needs. In the modern era, lifestyles changed, and people embraced new products and gadgets in a daily basis, which resulted in producing a varied and complex waste composition over time.

From Table 1.1, it is evident that in the pre-industrial era, solid wastes mainly constituted biological and non-hazardous components. Later in the industrial era,

TABLE 1.1 The key inventions and influence in the waste composition over time

Tentative time	Human inventions	Waste types	Waste characteristics
2.5 million years BC	Hunting animals	Bones, leftovers	Organic and biodegradable
1 million years BC	Use of fire	Ash	Non-hazardous and inert
170,000 years BC	Clothing	Leather, textile	Non-hazardous
10,000 years BC	Agriculture	Straws/organic	Organic and biodegradable
3,000 years BC	Writing	Writing materials	Predominantly organic and non-hazardous
3,000–6,000 years BC	Metals	Metal	Recyclable and non-hazardous
1781	Steam engine	Metal	Predominantly recyclable, non-hazardous
1808–1870	Car	Mixed waste	Recyclable, non-recyclable, and hazardous
1911	Petroleum	Plastic	Non-biodegradable, recyclable, and non-recyclable
1915	Glass	Glass	Non-biodegradable, recyclable
1927	Television	Mixed/complex	Non-biodegradable, recyclable, non-recyclable, and hazardous
1951	Tetra pack	Composite	Non-biodegradable and difficult to recycle
1981	Computer	Electronic	Mixed waste with recyclable, non-recyclable, and hazardous waste
1981	3D printing	Highly composite	Varies, depends on material use
1987	Mobile	Electronic	Non-biodegradable, recyclable, non-recyclable, and hazardous
1999	Smartphone	Electronic	Non-biodegradable, recyclable, non-recyclable, and hazardous
2000s	Modern electric cars	Mixed waste	Non-biodegradable, recyclable, non-recyclable, and hazardous

non-biodegradable and hazardous materials were used in the manufacturing process to generate more of non-biodegradable and toxic wastes. We are now in the era of electronics where more than 62 different materials or composite materials are used in a simple gadget or mobile phone that leads to create the most complex, hazardous, and environmentally damaging waste compared to the past. Over the past, waste composition evolved from biological, biodegradable, and non-hazardous characteristics during the pre-industrial time to more non-biological, non-biodegradable, and toxic hazardous characteristics at the post-industrial modern time.

A brief history of WMS

Waste is truly a human intervention. In nature, there is no 'waste'; everything that is produced as 'waste' is recirculated in the natural system. Despite being a part of the natural system, we create waste products which are not suitable for the natural recirculating process. The day we started to consume, we also started to produce waste, and thus WMS is a part of human history, which has developed long before the development of our modern civilization. Ever since the birth of agricultural or non-nomadic societies, around 10,000 years BC, humans have been producing solid waste (Worrell & Vesilind, 2012). It is believed that when humans began inhabiting caves, wastes were piled near entrances, and when the heap became too large, inhabitants would simply move on to another dwelling (Pichtel, 2005, p. 21). Thus, at the beginning of human civilization, waste was thrown away and disposed to the adjacent habitat.

When people began to create permanent communities in the early 8,000 to 9,000 years BC, dumps were established away from settlements, probably located so that wild animals, insects, and odour would not migrate to the populated areas (Bilitewski et al., 1997, as cited in Pichtel, 2005, p. 21). As communities began to grow in this ancient period, people started to build cities and urban areas. Archaeological studies show that waste was generated by Native Americans in Colorado about 6,500 years BC (Young et al., 2010, p. 1). It was predicted that each day, the average Native American produced around 5.3 pounds of waste (Barbalace, 2003), merely organic. As the organic waste started to decompose and create odours, people covered them periodically with layers of soil to reduce the odour from waste pits (Priestley, 1968; Wilson, 1977). People made bucket-like trunks to collect waste (Melosi, 1981; Vesilind et al., 2002, as cited in Pichtel, 2005, p. 21) from cities to remote areas in the early 2,100 years BC and the collection of waste was considered as part of 'elite and religious' living (Melosi, 1981).

The first recorded regulations for the management of solid waste were established during the Minoan civilization from 3000 to 1000 BC (Tammemagi, 1999). The ancient recoded pits (landfills) were believed to be in the capital of Knossos where solid wastes were placed with layers of earth at intervals (Wilson, 1977). It is evident from archaeological studies that many cities in Europe were eventually buried due to a steady accumulation of waste and subsequently; cities were rebuilt either on the same site at a higher level or at another site (Wilson, 1977).

Street dumping was the most common practice before establishing any organized method of waste disposal system in Europe (Kelly, 1973). The residents of Athens in 320 BC were required by law to sweep the streets daily and transport the waste beyond the city walls (Bilitewski et al., 1997). Romans were the first civilization to create an organized waste collection workforce in 14 AD (Vesilind et al., 2002). Horse-drawn wagons were used to carry waste to a pit located at a distance from the community.

The city authority in London issued an order for its tenants in 1297 to maintain clean pavement in front of their dwellings (Pichtel, 2005, p. 23). According to Wilson (1977), inhabitants of London were instructed to keep their refuse indoors until rakers could carry it away in 1407. During this period, two urban features were introduced in London (Bilitewski et al., 1997): one was paving the street and the other was the introduction of a garbage can, which is similar to garbage bins in modern days.

The waste collection system appeared as public service in 1950s, when markets squares were cleaned four times in a year at public taxes in Germany (UNEP/GRID-Arendal, 2006). Early in the nineteenth century, street sweeping and the sale of horse manure for sanitation departments had become a source of income in London (Wilson, 1977). In the year 1870–1871, around 57,737 tonnes of city manure were sold in Edinburgh, Scotland, which generated around £8,097. However, the income declined drastically due to the introduction of synthetic fertilizers. Incineration was regarded as a solution to manage waste, and thus in 1874, England built waste incineration plants. Incineration become very popular, and by 1914, a total 200 incineration plants were built and operated in England, and 65 of them produced electricity (Wilson, 1977).

As civilization advanced, WMSs developed and evolved based on available knowledge, technology, social, cultural, and religious beliefs. Up until the present time, there have been six major waves of innovation in WMSs, using different methods, tools, techniques, and technologies.

The first WMS to be used was open dumping. Despite various problems of open dumping, it is still one of the main methods for waste management in many low-income countries around the world due to low-to-no cost. Open dumping can take place at roadsides, adjacent lowlands, drainage systems, and unprotected land areas. The second wave of waste management was uncontrolled landfills. The uncontrolled landfills are specific areas within a proximity of cities where people can dump waste. Since there is no control over its design and disposal method, uncontrolled landfill pollutes surrounding areas very severely. Despite global economic growth, many cities and countries still rely on landfills because of low waste management cost.

Waste composting, the third wave of innovation, has been used since 2000 BCE in China and still remains a common waste management practice (UNEP/GRID-Arendal, 2006). Composting of organic waste, including agricultural waste and waste from food industries is increasingly used worldwide as a means of managing organic waste. The fourth wave was recycling and controlled landfill. Recycling other than organic waste composting was first recorded in Philadelphia in 1690, where paper was made from the fibre recycled from waste (UNEP/GRID-Arendal, 2006). Since the global oil crisis in the 1970s, resource recovery and waste recycling has been spreading worldwide.

The fifth wave of innovation in WMSs is twentieth-century, WTE technologies, such as incineration, pyrolysis-gasification, and plasma-arc advanced biological treatments – for example, anaerobic digestion (AD) and advanced recycling and resource recovery facilities. ZW can be understood as the sixth wave and the most holistic innovation in waste management, capable of achieving a truly sustainable WMS. ZW management systems include C2C design, closed-loop production systems, sustainable resource consumption, and resource recovery from waste (Barber, 2007; Braungart et al., 2007; Ball et al., 2009). A detailed discussion of ZW is presented in later chapters.

The resource recovery from waste varies depending on the regulatory policies and methods (more details of each method are presented in the following section) that apply to manage waste. 'Up-cycling' methods, such as waste avoidance technique saves more resources than the 'down-cycling' approaches, including reuse, recycling, and treatment. Advanced waste treatment technologies, such as incineration, recover more resources than the traditional waste disposal method, such as landfills.

The waste hierarchy

The waste hierarchy was introduced in the EU's Waste Framework Directive in 1975, and it stated (in Article 3.1) 'member States shall take appropriate steps to encourage the prevention, recycling and processing of waste, the extraction of raw materials and possibly of energy therefrom and any other process for the re-use of waste' (European Union, 1975).

The 'waste hierarchy' is the classification of waste management options in hierarchical order to choose the most favourable waste management policy actions (avoid, reduce, reuse, and recycle) from the least favourable options (treatment and landfill). It aims to reduce environmental impacts by prioritizing prevention, reuse, recycling, and recovery over landfill (Hultman & Corvellec, 2012). In the US, pollution prevention became a priority in the '70s, and waste management cost, liability, and public opposition to landfills are the reasons for waste reduction and popularizing the hierarchy in the '80s (National Research Council, 1985; Overcash, 2002). Figure 1.1 shows the various waste management options in a hierarchical order.

The waste management hierarchy comprises prevention or avoidance of waste, minimization, or reduction of waste, reuse of wasted product, recycle of waste, recover of energy from waste, and disposal of waste to landfill. Undoubtedly, a major part of the WMS in the world still relies on the least favourable options due to lower operation and management costs. However, prevention would result in the least environmental and economic life-cycle costs because it avoids collection, recycling, and processing of materials costs (Sharp et al., 2015). All the socio-economic and

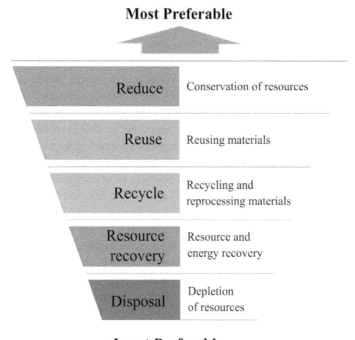

Most Preferable

Reduce	Conservation of resources
Reuse	Reusing materials
Recycle	Recycling and reprocessing materials
Resource recovery	Resource and energy recovery
Disposal	Depletion of resources

Least Preferable

FIGURE 1.1   The waste hierarchy

Source: Adapted from DEFRA (2011) under Open Government Licence

environmental concerns that culminated in the waste hierarchy can be summarized as a desire to divert waste from landfill, because the diversion of waste from landfill reduces management costs and protects the environment from pollution.

The 3R principles, which refer to reduce, reuse, and recycle, are considered the founding principles of sustainable WMS. The idea was proposed by the Department of Environment and Welsh Office in 1995 (Jiang, 2006). The 3R principles are considered to be the core strategy for sustainable WMS. The extended 7R rules were adopted based on the 3R concepts by including regulation, reduction, reuse, recycling, recovery, rethinking, and renovation as the basic tools for zero pollution (El-Haggar, 2007, p. 12).

A brief description of the waste hierarchical options

Prevention and reduction of waste is a source reduction, firstly, by changing the design and production process (minimization of waste volume) of goods, and, secondly, by moving from disposable consumption behaviour to long-lasting responsible consumption behaviour (reduction of per capita waste generation rate). Waste prevention by avoidance is the ultimate ZW goals and has the highest point on the hierarchy (US–EPA, 2002; ZWSA, 2012). Waste prevention is the first line of

defence to avoid waste creation at the beginning of product supply chain. Generation of waste is related to consumption of resources, and producers and consumers
are the major players who drive the global consumerism. On one hand, an ecological
product design can prevent waste because it considers the environmental impact of
products at the beginning of the design stage and thus the design process follows the
necessary planning and design decisions to prevent and minimize adverse impacts.
Products' durability is very important in avoidance of waste – for example, whether
designers design their products based on a longer-lasting philosophy (products can
be used for a longer period) or design their products based on a 'planned obsolescence' (designed to throw away) could make huge difference in whole waste supply
chain. On the other hand, consumes' consumption behaviour could play a vital role
in preventing waste creation at the beginning of the consumption process – for
example, not buying unnecessary products and goods.

The reuse of waste is using any wasted materials without changing its structural
property or modifying its form (Hansen et al., 2002; El-Haggar, 2007). Reuse is
defined in the European Council Directive 2008 as 'any operation by which products
or components that are not waste are used again for the same purpose for which they
were conceived' (European Council, 2008). Reuse of a waste product often involves
an extended use of the product for different purposes – for instance, the reuse of containers, such as bottles for vertical gardening and many other reuse options.

Waste recycling is a series of activities, including sorting, collecting, and the 'process
of converting wastes to raw material that can be reused to manufacture new products' (Hansen et al., 2002; El-Haggar, 2007; US-EPA, 2015). Recycling is defined in
the European Council Directive 2008 as 'any recovery operation by which waste
materials are reprocessed into products, materials or substances whether for the
original or other purposes' (European Council, 2008). Recycling is one of the key
social technologies that are influenced by the cultural habits and by which people
separate secondary materials (paper, plastic, metal, etc.) from MSW (World Bank,
2011). Recycling as we see it today generates the illusion of progress towards waste
reduction and place responsibility for increasing volumes of waste on consumers
and local government (MacBride, 2012, p. 49).

Energy recovery from waste in the form of gas, heat, or electricity can be done
before sending waste to landfill or at landfill sites. Various waste treatment technologies are available to recover energy from waste. The treatment of waste can differ
depending on waste types (organic, combustible, or non-combustible, etc.).

Disposal/waste landfill is one of the most common techniques that many developed
and developing countries use for managing MSW. Waste is buried in uncontrolled
(unsanitary), controlled, and protected (sanitary) areas, and sometimes landfill gas
(mostly methane gas) is recovered. Landfill not only occupies valuable landmass but
also emits GHG to the atmosphere. In addition, there is risk of water contamination
associated with landfill technologies.

Waste treatment technologies are important as they act as 'end-of-pipe' solutions.
Rapid population growth and urbanization generates a significant amount of waste
every day; therefore, it is almost certain to deploy advanced treatment technologies

to manage waste swiftly. Some of the advanced treatment technologies, such as incineration and sanitary landfills, are mature technologies, and these technologies are implemented in different countries around the word. A considerable amount of research and development efforts have been deployed to improve existing waste treatment technologies and to develop emerging waste treatment technologies, such as pyrolysis and gasification. The waste treatment technologies can be broadly categorized into four groups (El-Haggar, 2007):

- Physical treatment (using screening, sedimentation, centrifugation, etc., mostly for liquid or semi-solid waste);
- Chemical treatment (using chemical to reduce volume and toxicity);
- Thermal treatment (using thermal combustion to convert waste to ash); and
- Biological treatment (aerobic or anaerobic processes).

For MSW both biological treatment and thermal treatment are the most applied technologies in many developed and developing countries.

Biological treatment (including AD and mechanical biological treatment – MBT) is a treatment technology that uses bacteria to decompose organic waste fractions (World Bank, 2011) and produce compost (humus-like material). MBT is used to process only biodegradable organic waste. Biological treatment technologies are important for managing waste and recovering resources in the form of soil conditioners and biofuels. AD is used to produce biogas from biodegradable organic waste. Biogas can be used as biofuel or be converted to electricity depending on the local needs.

Thermal treatment (including incineration, pyrolysis, gasification, and plasma-arc) is a waste treatment technology that uses controlled high temperature in the presence (direct burning) and absence of oxygen (endothermic) to decompose carbon-based MSW and produce syngas and solid ash (Halton, 2007; World Bank, 2011). Syngas is used to produce heat and energy from waste. Thermal treatment technologies are very efficient in generating energy and electricity from waste. The key advantages of waste incineration are that it manages all kinds of waste, significantly reduces the waste volume, and produces energy from waste. The key disadvantages of incineration are that it requires high capital and operational costs and the emissions and ash resulting from incineration can be extremely dangerous without sophisticated technological controls in place (El-Haggar, 2007).

Table 1.2 shows a catalogue of major emerging waste treatment technologies. The strength, weakness, opportunity, and threats (SWOT) analysis has been done to understand how technologies can be retrofitted for safe launch in the near future.

The technologies are analysed in the context of potential SWOT. Technologies are assigned higher or lower values giving importance to its criteria and its qualitative data (in Table 1.3). Different technologies have different waste-handling capacity, while most of the thermal waste treatment technologies can treat all types of waste fractions, biodegradable waste fractions are handled by biological waste treatment technology. Therefore, while some technologies require higher sorting efficiency for better performance, others can manage in lower sorting systems. Emerging technology can be new or under the process of getting developed, or it can also be a

TABLE 1.2 The key features of the emerging waste treatment technologies

Methods	Strength	Weakness	Opportunity	Threats
Dry Composting	A biological process in a confine or open area. Possibility of getting nutrient-rich organic fertilizer and soil conditioner from the waste. Dried material can be extracted biogas via AD.	Only biodegradable waste can be managed by this process. Emission control from the system is difficult.	Opportunity of resource recovery and making bio-fertilizer. Biogas can be generated from the dry waste.	Potential threat to water and soil contamination for poor management. Emissions to the atmosphere are a great threat for environmental degradation.
Sanitary Landfilling	A natural decomposition process that can handle different types of waste with larger volume. Waste can be managed in controlled environment.	Huge land area is needed, and emission control is difficult and costly. Long time is required to reclaim the landfill land restoration.	Opportunity to recover biogas from the landfill. Opportunity to manage waste more environmentally friendly way if sanitary landfill fully functioned.	Potential environmental threat due to air, water and soil contamination for weak liner or management system.
Anaerobic digestion (AD)	A biochemical process with energy recovery facilities. Final residue is also used as fertilizer.	Only organic waste can be managed with AD. Higher investment cost is required.	Opportunity to retrieve biogas/fuel and manure from the AD facilities.	Potential threat of emissions to the environment.
Gasification	Almost all types of waste fractions can be treated with gasification process. Low final residue is generated from the processes.	High investment cost and still developing technology for MSW.	Energy and heat can be recovered from the gasification of MSW.	Environmental impact through emission to the atmosphere.
Pyrolysis	Different waste categories can be treated by the pyrolysis process with lower volume of final residue.	Higher investment cost and technology not yet matured enough for MSW.	Opportunity of resource and energy recovery.	Potential environmental threat from emissions.

(*Continued*)

TABLE 1.2 (Continued)

Methods	Strength	Weakness	Opportunity	Threats
Plasma Arc	Almost all types of waste categories can be treated with lower disposable residue.	New technology for MSW management and high investment cost.	Opportunity of higher energy and heat recovery option.	Threat to environmental impact from the emission.
Bio-chemical Conversion of MSW	Integrated waste treatment process with MBT with AD.	Limited waste treatment capacity. Organic waste can be treated by this technology.	Energy and resource recovery can be possible.	Potential environmental threat from emissions to the atmosphere and water.
Pyrolysis-Gasification	Hybrid thermal process with large volume of different waste treatment capabilities.	Emerging technology with higher investment cost.	Opportunity of energy and resource recovery.	Potential environmental threat from air and water emissions.
Refuse-derived fuel (RDF)	High resource value. Regular MSW can be managed by this technology.	Desire moisture content is required for getting higher energy potentials.	Energy recovery options.	Threat of the environment, pollution.
Bio-reactor	Landfill with MBT facilities. Higher waste volume can be managed by this process compare to traditional landfill	Pre-processing of waste is required.	Higher volume of biogas can be recovered from the bio-reactor.	Environmental threats due to emissions from the technology.
Hydrolysis Process	Chemical processes of food/fruit waste to ethanol production.	Very new technology with limited problem-solving capacity.	Opportunity of ethanol production.	Water contamination.
Conversion of Solid Wastes to Protein	Conversion of waste to nutrient.	Experimental stage with lower problem-solving potentials.	Opportunity of having nutrient recovery from waste.	Unknown
Hydro-pulping	Resource recovery and reuse in paper and pulp industry.	Only paper waste can be managed by this process.	Resource recovery.	Threat of environmental pollution from chemicals that are used.

TABLE 1.3 Qualitative evaluation of the selected emerging technologies

Method	Process type	Waste-handling capacity	Development stage	Problem-solving capacity
Dry composting	Biological process	★★★	★★	★★★
Sanitary landfilling	Biological process	★★★★★	★★★	★★★★
Anaerobic digestion (AD)	Biological process	★★★	★★★★	★★★★
Gasification	Thermal process	★★★★★	★★★	★★★★★
Pyrolysis	Thermal process	★★★★★	★★	★★★★★
Plasma-arc	Thermal process	★★★★★	★★	★★★★★
Pyrolysis-gasification	Thermal process	★★★★★	★★★	★★★★★
Mechanical biological treatment (MBT) and aerobic fermentation	MB processes	★★★	★★	★★★★
Hydrolysis	Biological process	★★★	★★	★★
Bioreactor	Biological process	★★★★★	★★★★	★★★
Solid wastes to protein	Biological process	★★	★	★
Hydro-pulping	Thermo-chemical	★★	★★	★★
Slurry curb process	Thermo-chemical	★★★	★	★★

technology with retro fittings. Therefore, development stage of the technology is one of the vital factors for emerging technology selection process and based on its efficiency and adaptability, development of technology has moved from the lab scale to the large-project scale. Criteria problem-solving capacity is not only the main focus in sustainable WMS but also enabling factor. Economical as well as environmental performance must be considered in the overall WMS. Environmental performance of the technology gives the high priority in the problem-solving capacity.

Integrated sustainable waste management (ISWM)

ISWM was widely adopted in developing countries in the 1990s (Marshall & Farahbakhsh, 2013). The concept of ISWM comes directly from the concept of sustainable development proposed by the Brundlandt Commission in 1987 (WCED, 1987) and the commission's proposed objectives for the framework of environmentally sound management of solid waste (United Nations, 1992) were

- Minimizing waste;
- Maximizing environmentally sound waste reuse and recycling; and
- Promoting environmentally sound waste disposal and treatment.

However, little progress has been made towards the commission's proposed objectives in the last three decades. On the contrary, the generation of waste has significantly increased globally in the same period of time. A higher waste generation means greater resource depletion and GHG emissions to the atmosphere and thus contribution to the global warming. Currently, the potential threats of climate change represent one of the main environmental concerns worldwide (Mondini et al., 2008).

According to the United Nations Environment Programme-UNEP (2009), ISWM refers to the strategic approach to sustainable management of solid wastes covering all sources and all aspects, covering generation, segregation, transfer, sorting, treatment, recovery, and disposal in an integrated manner, with an emphasis on maximizing resource use efficiency. The ISWM concept is built upon four basic principles (Van de Klundert & Anschütz, 2001):

- **Equity:** the allocation of resources, services, and opportunity to all segments of the population according to their needs. In waste management, this means that everyone has a right to be served by a WMS that protects their health and the environment.
- **Effectiveness:** the waste management methods used must meet the overall aims of any waste plan and meet the needs of the people. At the very least, effectiveness means that all the waste is collected and disposed of in a safe way. Once this has been achieved, higher-level aims, such as maximizing waste recycling and composting, should be addressed.
- **Efficiency:** in general, efficiency means increasing output for a given input or minimizing input for a given output. An efficient WMS is one that is equal and effective while making the best use of the resources available (staff effort, use of equipment, and cost).
- **Sustainability:** sustainability of the WMS can be achieved if it is appropriate to the local conditions and can continue in the long term by using the human, financial, and material resources available in the area. It should also be environmentally sustainable in that it minimizes the use of non-renewable natural resources (such as oil) and does not lead to long-term environmental problems that will be left for later generations to address.

The core concept of ISWM has been developed out of experience to address certain common problems with municipal waste management in low-and middle-income countries in the south and in countries in transition. ISWM recognizes three important dimensions in waste management: (i) stakeholders, (ii) waste system elements, and (iii) sustainability aspects. The waste management hierarchy – a policy guideline that is part of many national environmental laws and policies – is also a cornerstone of the ISWM approach.

Waste management in the developing and the developed countries

Waste management is not only managing waste sustainably; it has also become a vital urban service for the citizens of the modern world. Even in least-developed countries, people expect to have very basic waste management services, such as collection and disposal of waste on a day-to-day basis. As waste management is a costly service and often very little attention and priority is given to it when it comes to funding, most of the developing countries lack a functional waste management service for their inhabitants. As a result, two distinct types of waste management services have evolved: (i) informal WMS and (ii) formal WMS.

Informal WMSs

Rapid urbanization, population growth, migration to urban areas, lack of sufficient funds, and affordable services often force city authorities to offer unreliable, inefficient, and poor waste management services (Wilson et al., 2006). Waste collection rates range from a low 41% for low-income countries and 98% for high-income countries (Hoornweg & Bhada-Tata, 2012), which means that around 59% of waste remains uncollected in developing countries, and 2% remains uncollected in developed countries. Wilson et al. (2001) described informal WMSs as labour intensive, largely unregulated, and unregistered.

Wilson et al. (2006) identified that at least four main categories of informal waste recycling can be observed in cities, such as itinerant waste buyers, street waste picking, municipal waste collection crew, and waste picking from dumps. A significant number of urban poor are engaged with informal waste recycling activities due to the lack of formal waste management facilities in the cities of many developing countries, such as Bangladesh. Despite a high dependency on informal recycling in Bangladesh, its WMS is regarded as a market failure (Matter et al., 2015). There is a demand for recycling materials in Bangladesh and many other developing countries; however, the poor people who manually collect waste from roadside collection points or dumpsites are deprived from getting the proper economic value of their recovered materials by the middle man or small-to-medium business entities.

Two distinct types of informal WMSs exist in our world. In the first type, waste is sorted, separated, recycled, and sold by people to earn extra money (often seen in developed counties, such as Australia and Denmark) where economic incentives are available for the recyclable waste – i.e. plastic bottles and cans. In the second type, waste is sorted, separated, and recycled from bins and disposal sites to earn a living. Therefore, informal recyclers can be found in two groups – i.e. one that recycles voluntarily to earn extra money and one that recycles obligatorily to earn money for living expenses. Figure 1.2 shows the informal recycling in Dhaka and Adelaide. Informal recyclers in Adelaide belong to the first group, while those in Dhaka are in the second group.

Informal waste recyclers in developing countries belong to the lowest income group, and informal waste recycling is their only source of income. In developed countries, with the exception of homeless people (Gowan, 1997), informal recycling is usually not the primary source of income for recyclers. It has been estimated that up to 2% of the population in Asian and Latin American cities depends on waste picking to earn a living (Medina, 2000).

FIGURE 1.2 Informal waste recycling in Dhaka (left) and Adelaide (right)

Due to a lack of effective WMSs and resources, SWM in many developing countries is driven by the informal sector (Nzeadibe & Chukwuedozie, 2010; Scheinberg et al., 2011; Katusiimeh et al., 2013). In many developing cities, the informal waste sector is dominant and plays a more significant role in WMSs than the formal sector. For instance, metal recovery in 2007 by the formal and informal waste sectors in Cairo was 13% and 30%, in Lima 0.3% and 19%, and in Pune 0% and 22%, respectively (CWG & GTZ, 2010).

Recycling activities in developed countries are driven by mostly environmental policies and regulations (UN-HABITAT, 2010); however, informal recycling in developing countries is predominantly economy driven due to cheap labour costs and a lack of employment opportunities.

Informal waste collection in developed countries is driven by economic incentives and legislative policy and is supportive of the existing formal WMS. In the city of Adelaide, after the introduction of container deposit legislation (CDL) and a 10-cent return policy, many informal waste recyclers have been encouraged to recycle packaging to earn additional income. On the other hand, informal waste recycling in San Francisco from the 1990s has had a different story. Homeless people and undocumented immigrants (who are excluded from a shrinking formal labour market) are the most immediately visible group of San Francisco's recyclers (Sassen, 1988; Portes et al., 1989; Gowan, 1997). During the prolonged and severe recession of 1990–2002 in California, new full-time scavengers started recycling as a last resort after failing to find better-paying work (Gowan, 1997). Informal waste recycling in the cities of developed countries is integrated with the formal WMSs. However, in cities of developing countries, the informal sector is still excluded and at some point not acknowledged by the existing formal WMSs.

Formal solid WMSs

Formal waste management means a post-industrial WMS where local government is responsible for the collection, transportation, processing, and disposal of waste materials. Most modern WMSs are part of a formal waste sector. The formal waste sector is an integrated WMS with different stakeholders participating, including local government, citizens, community organizations, non-government organizations, business organizations, international donor organizations, and so on. In general, 'waste management' usually refers to formal waste management.

Sustainable WM is not only important as an urban service but also essential from the global resource recovery perspective. The resource scarcity of the past, once due to limited techniques, has now appeared as a reality in the twenty-first century due to a continuous expansion of demand for many scarce resources. After the global economic crisis, the scarcity of some resources became a subject of concern, and the world suddenly became aware of this source of economic fragility because of its rarity and higher cost (Veolia, 2011). Because of globalization and technological development, different complex products and packaging are manufactured today with a variety of composite materials. Consequently, the waste that we generate is growing multifaceted and becoming very challenging to manage. Waste authorities who once dealt with household solid waste (mainly organic waste) are now having to manage a diverse range of waste, including hard waste, electronic waste, hazardous waste, etc. Hence, today's waste management not only requires the application of advanced treatment technology but also a proper integration of multidisciplinary management techniques.

Challenges of current WMS

With a growing interest and awareness on sustainability, waste has become one of the focal points of sustainable urban development, yet it is still one of the least priority areas when it comes to allocation of resources to the city authorities in many countries. Once waste was regarded as a problematic by-product of our modern lifestyle, it is now considered an opportunity and valuable resource. In fact, millions of peoples' livelihoods in various parts of the world depend on the collection of the valuable materials from waste.

Waste is not only a complex anthropogenic problem; it is also an expensive problem to be managed sustainably. It is important to take proper consideration of the environmental and economic benefits of WMS, as it often involves high investment and operation costs in providing effective waste collection and management systems to the citizens. According to World Bank's report, around US$205 billion was spent on waste management worldwide in 2010 and the cost will increase to US$375 billion by 2025 (Hoornweg & Bhada-Tata, 2012).

The current trends of urbanization and over-consuming lifestyle are the biggest challenges of sustainable waste management (SWM). Cities attract people for the various opportunities they can provide to their inhabitants in terms of income and services. Cities expand both horizontally and vertically to accommodate a huge number of people every year (Ahsan & Zaman, 2014). In 1950, only one-third of the world population lived in cities, and the reverse distribution of the population can be observed within a century, as the urban population is projected to be 68% by 2050 (UN-DESA, 2018). At the same time, global consumption of natural resources could almost triple to 140 billion tonnes a year as predicted by the United Nations (SMH, 2011). This means more people will consume an increased amount of natural resources and generate an ever-increasing volume of waste in the future. According to Hoornweg et al. (2015), even with a more aggressive sustainability growth scenario and a drastic waste reduction by 30%, the global 'waste peak' will occur after 2075.

In the globalized world, we can easily shift our problem to another part of the world. In Australia, a significant amount of waste, around 1.27 million tonnes (30%) of the recycled metals, paperboard, and plastics, were exported to China in 2016–2017 (Blue Environment, 2018). Like Australia, many other developed nations have waste-exporting policies to get rid of their problems. In early 2018, due to China's restriction to waste import, Australia faced significant challenges in managing waste locally (Downes & Dominish, 2018). The contamination rate of Australia's kerbside recycling averages between 6%–10%, and even after sorting at a recycling facility, it is generally well above China's 0.5% acceptable threshold. This means Australia needs to reduce the contamination level in recycling even if it wants to export waste but also needs to seek solutions for managing waste domestically. Despite technological advancement and formal waste collection systems in place, waste management in Australia and many other developed countries is far from the future proofing sustainable solution.

The potential threat of climate change represents one of the main environmental concerns worldwide. Currently, scientists are certain about the causes of global climate change. One of the main causes of global climate change is the GHG emissions by humans into the atmosphere due to urbanization and resource consumption. Waste contributes GHGs (such as carbon dioxide and methane) and enhances global climate change.

According to a study, the 'end-of-life' solid waste contributes only 5% of a product's overall environmental impacts (Hoornweg & Thomas, 1991). However, the overall environmental impact would be greater if the considerations of the environmental impacts during the resource extraction are considered. It is estimated that around 71 tonnes of 'upstream' materials are used for every tonne of MSW (Liss & Christopher, 2012).

Despite technological advancement and engineering solutions, disposal of waste to landfills is considered one of the cheapest and most widely applied waste management options (Hoornweg & Bhada-Tata, 2012). Globally, around 84% of the waste is collected, and the rest of 16% remains uncollected and littered to the natural environment, and only 15% of the collected waste is recycled; the remaining 85% is disposed in landfills, including uncontrolled landfills and open dumping (Zaman, 2016). The true environmental cost of pollution often ignores the traditional market-driven economic system; however, landfills can be an expensive option if the cost of environmental pollution and depletion of resources are considered.

References

Ahsan, T., & Zaman, A. (2014). Household waste management in high-rise residential building in Dhaka, Bangladesh: Users' perspective. *International Journal of Waste Resources*, 4(1), 1–7.

Ball, P. D., Evans, S., Levers, A., & Ellison, D. (2009). Zero carbon manufacturing facility: Towards integrating material, energy, and waste process flows. *Proceedings of the Institution of Mechanical Engineers, Part B: Journal of Engineering Manufacture*, 223(9), 1085–1096.

Barbalace, R. C. (2003). *The History of Waste*. 12 July. Retrieved from https://environmentalchemistry.com/yogi/environmental/wastehistory.html

Barber, J. (2007). Mapping the movement to achieve sustainable production and consumption in North America. *Journal of Cleaner Production*, 15(6), 499–512.

Bilitewski, B., Härdtle, G., & Marek, K. (1997). *Waste Management*. Berlin: Springer.

Blue Environment. (2018). *Data on Exports of Recyclables from Australia to China*. Retrieved January 18, 2019, from https://blueenvironment.com.au/wp-content/uploads/2018/05/Exports-of-recyclables-from-Aust-to-China-v2.pdf

Braungart, M., McDonough, W., & Bollinger, A. (2007). Cradle-to-cradle design: Creating healthy emissions: A strategy for eco-effective product and system design. *Journal of Cleaner Production*, 15(13–14), 1337–1348.

Cal-Recycle. (2010). *Waste Prevention Terms and Definitions.* San Francisco, CA: Government of California.

CWG & GTZ. (2010). *The Economics of the Informal Sector in Solid Waste Management.* CWG and GIZ, Frankfurt: Klarmann-Druck GmbH.

DEFRA. (2011). *Guidance on Applying the Waste Hierarchy.* Retrieved February 20, 2018, from https://assets.publishing.service.gov.uk/government/uploads/system/uploads/attachment_data/file/69403/pb13530-waste-hierarchy-guidance.pdf

DoE, B. (2009). *National 3R Strategy for Waste Management: Department of Environment.* Dhaka: Ministry of Environment and Forests, Government of the People's Republic of Bangladesh. 2nd draft.

Downes, J., & Dominish, E. (2018). *China's Recycling "Ban" Throws Australia into a Very Messy Waste Crisis, Published by the Advertise on 27 April 2018.* Retrieved July 12, 2018, from https://theconversation.com/chinas-recycling-ban-throws-australia-into-a-very-messy-waste-crisis-95522

El-Haggar, S. (2007). *Sustainable Industrial Design and Waste Management: Cradle-to-Cradle for Sustainable Development.* Burlington, MA: Elsevier Academic Press.

European Commission. (2002). DIRECTIVE 2002/96/EC of the European Parliament and of the Council of 27 January 2003 on waste electrical and electronic equipment (WEEE). E. P. a. o. t. Council. Brussels European Commission.

European Commission. (2012). *Guidelines on the Interpretation of Key Provisions of Directive 2008/98/EC on Waste.* Retrieved November 22, 2013, from http://ec.europa.eu/environment/waste/framework/pdf/guidance_doc.pdf

European Council. (2008). *DIRECTIVE 2008/98/EC of the European Parliament and of the Council.* Retrieved March 16, 2015, from http://eur-lex.europa.eu/LexUriServ/LexUriServ.do?uri=OJ:L:2008:312:0003:0030:en:PDF

European Union. (1975). *Council Directive, Document no 75/442/EEC.* Retrieved May 20, 2018, from http://eur-lex.europa.eu/legal-content/EN/TXT/PDF/?uri=CELEX:31975L0442&from=EN

Government of SA. (2010). *South Australia: Environment Protection Act 1993.* Adelaide: Government of South Australia.

Gowan, T. (1997). American untouchables: Homeless scavengers in San Francisco's underground economy. *International Journal of Sociology and Social Policy, 17*(3–4), 159.

GRID-Arendal. (2004). *What Is Waste: A Multitude of Approaches and Definitions.* Retrieved November 12, 2012, from www.grida.no/publications/vg/waste/page/2853.aspx

Hansen, W., Christopher, M., & Verbuecheln, M. (2002). EU waste policy and challenges for regional and local authorities. Ecological Institute for International and European Environmental Policy: Berlin, Germany.

Hartln, J. (1996). Waste management in Sweden. *Waste Management, 16,* 385–388.

Hoornweg, D., & Bhada-Tata, P. (2012). What a Waste: A Global Review of Solid Waste Management. *Knowledge Papers No. 15.* U. d. series. Washington, DC: World Bank.

Hoornweg, D., Bhada-Tata, P., & Kennedy, C. (2015). Peak waste: When is it likely to occur? *Journal of Industrial Ecology, 19*(1), 117–128.

Hoornweg, D., & Thomas, L. (1991). *What a Waste: Solid Waste Management in Asia.* Retrieved August 13, 2015, from www.worldbank.org/urban/solid_wm/erm/CWG%20folder/uwp1.pdf

Hultman, J., & Corvellec, H. (2012). The European waste hierarchy: From the sociomateriality of waste to a politics of consumption. *Environment and Planning A, 44*(10), 2413–2427.

Jiang, S. (2006). The Practical implementation of the 3Rs of Sustainable Waste Management in the Norfolk and Norwich University Hospital. *School of Environmental Sciences.* Norwich, UK: Norwich University of East Angila. MSc.

Kangas, P. (2003). *Ecological Engineering: Principles and Practice.* Boca Raton, FL: CRC Press.

Katusiimeh, M. W., Burger, K., & Mol, A. P. (2013). Informal waste collection and its coexistence with the formal waste sector: The case of Kampala, Uganda. *Habitat International, 38*(April), 1–9.

Kelly, K. (1973). *Garbage: The History and Future of Garbage in America.* New York: Saturday Review Press.

Liss, G., & Christopher, L. (2012). Intro to zero waste and zero waste community planning. *PowerPoint Presentation.* Retrieved November 11, 2015, from www.grrn.org/nowst/uploads/assets/conf2012/Intro%20to%20ZW%20%26%20%20ZW%20Community%20Planning%202012.pdf

MacBride, S. (2012). *Recycling Reconsidered: The Present Failure and Future Promise of Environmental Action in the United States.* Cambridge, MA and London: MIT Press.

Marshall, R. E., & Farahbakhsh, K. (2013). Systems approaches to integrated solid waste management in developing countries. *Waste Management, 33*(4), 988–1003.

Matter, A., Ahsan, M., Marbach, M., & Zurbrügg, C. (2015). Impacts of policy and market incentives for solid waste recycling in Dhaka, Bangladesh. *Waste Management, 39*, 321–328.

Medina, M. (2000). Scavenger cooperatives in Asia and Latin America. *Resources, Conservation and Recycling, 31*(1), 51–69.

Melosi, M. V. (1981). *Garbage in the Cities.* College Station, TX: Texas A&M Press.

Mondini, C., Sánchez-Monedero, M. A., Cayuela, M. L., & Stentiford, E. (2008). Soils and waste management: A challenge to climate change. *Waste Management, 28*(4), 671–672.

National Research Council. (1985). *Reducing Hazardous Waste Generation: An Evaluation and a Call for Action.* Washington, DC: National Academies Press. ISBN: 978-0-309-03498-2

Nzeadibe, T. C., & Chukwuedozie, K. A. (2010). Development impact of advocacy initiatives in solid waste management in Nigeria. *Environment, Development and Sustainability, 13*(1, February), 163–177.

Overcash, M. (2002). The evolution of US pollution prevention, 1976–2001: A unique chemical engineering contribution to the environment: A review. *Journal of Chemical Technology & Biotechnology: International Research in Process, Environmental & Clean Technology, 77*(11), 1197–1205.

Pichtel, J. (Ed.). (2005). *Waste Management Practices: Municipal, Hazardous, and Industrial.* Boca Raton: Taylor & Francis Group, LLC.

Portes, A., Castells, M., & Benton, L. A. (Eds.). (1989). *The Informal Economy: Studies in Advanced and Less Developed Countries.* Baltimore: Johns Hopkins.

Priestley, J. J. (1968). Civilization, water and wastes. *Chemistry and Industry,* 353–363.

Halton. (2007). *The Regional Municipality of Halton, Step 1B: EFW Technology Overview.* Ontario, Canada: URS.

Reddy, P. J. (2011). *Municipal Solid Waste Management: Processing Energy Recovery Global Examples.* Hyderabad: BS Publications.

Sassen, S. (1988). *The Mobility of Labor and Capital.* Cambridge: Cambridge University Press.

Scheinberg, A., Spies, S., Simpson, M. H., & Mol, A. P. (2011). Assessing recycling in low- and middle-income countries: Building on modernized mixtures. *Habitat International, 35*(2), 188–198.

Sharp, A., Stocchi, L. Levitzke, V., & Hewitt, M. (2015). *Measuring the Waste Management Hierarchy.* Unmaking Waste 2015, Adelaide, Zero Waste SA Research Centre for Sustainable Design and Behaviour, University of South Australia.

SMH. (2011). *Global Resource Consumption to Triple by 2050: UN.* 13 May. Retrieved June 12, 2018, from www.smh.com.au/world/global-resource-consumption-to-triple-by-2050-un-20110513-1el3q.html

Tammemagi, H. (1999). *The Waste Crisis: Landfills, Incinerators, and the Search for a Sustainable Future*. New York: Oxford University Press.

UN-DESA. (2018). World urbanisation projects: The 2018 revision. *Department of Economic and Social Affairs*. Retrieved June 20, 2019, from https://population.un.org/wup/Publications/Files/WUP2018-KeyFacts.pdf

UNEP. (2005). *Solid Waste Management*. Retrieved June 20, 2018, from www.unep.or.jp/ietc/publications/spc/solid_waste_management/Vol_I/Binder1.pdf

UNEP. (2009). *The Environmental Food Crisis: The Environment's Role in Averting Future Food Crises*. New York: UNEP Rapid Response Assessment.

UNEP/GRID-Arendal. (2006). *A History of Waste Management*. Retrieved May 10, 2011, from http://maps.grida.no.go/graphic/a-history-of-waste-management

UN-HABITAT. (2010). *Solid Waste Management in the World's Cities: Water and Sanitation in the World's Cities*. London: Earthscan.

United Nations. (1992). Agenda 21: Environmentally sound management of solid wastes and sewage-related issues (Chapter 21). *Rio Declaration*. Volume 2, 13 August 1992.

US-CFR. (2004). *Guidelines for the Thermal Processing of Solid Wastes*. Washington, DC: US Code of Federal Regulations. 40, Part 240.

US-EPA. (2002). *Solid Waste Management: A Local Challenge with Global Impacts*. Washington, DC: US Environmental Protection Agency.

US-EPA. (2011). *Wastes-Non-Hazardous Waste*. Retrieved March 17, 2011, from www.epa.gov/osw/nonhaz/index.htm

US-EPA. (2015). *Recycling Basics*. Retrieved March 12, 2015, from www2.epa.gov/recycle/recycling-basics

Vande Klundert, A., & Anschütz, J. (2001). *Integrated Sustainable Waste Management: The Concept*. Gouda, The Netherlands: Waste. SBN Number 9076639027.

Veolia. (2011). *From Waste to Resource: An Abstract of World Waste Survey 2009*. Paris: Veolia Environmental Services

Vesilind, P. A., Worrell, W., & Reinhart, D. (2002). *Solid Waste Engineering*. Pacific Grove, CA: Brooks and Cole.

WCED. (1987). *Our Common Future*. Oxford: Oxford University Press.

Wilson, D. C., Whiteman, A., Tormin, A., & Mundial, B. (2001). *Strategic Planning Guide for Municipal Solid Waste Management*. In Strategic planning guide for municipal solid waste management. Banco Mundial. Retrieved June 7, 2018, from www.worldbank.org/urban/solid_wm/erm/start_up.pdf

Wilson, D. C., Velis, C., & Cheeseman, C. (2006). Role of informal sector recycling in waste management in developing countries. *Habitat International*, *30*, 797–808.

Wilson, D. G. (Ed.). (1977). *Handbook of Solid Waste Management*. New York: Van Nostrand Reinhold Company.

World Bank. (2011). *Urban Solid Waste Management: Glossary*. Retrieved November 18, 2011, from http://web.worldbank.org/WBSITE/EXTERNAL/TOPICS/EXTURBANDEVELOPMENT/EXTUSWM/0,contentMDK:20241717~pagePK:148956~piPK:216618~theSitePK:463841,00.html

Worrell, W. A., & Vesilind, P. A. (2012). *Solid Waste Engineering*. Stamford, CT: Cengage Learning.

Young, C.-Y., Ni, S.-P., & Fan, K.-S. (2010). Working towards a zero waste environment in Taiwan. *Waste Management & Research*, *28*, 236–244.

Zaman, A. U. (2016). A comprehensive study of the environmental and economic benefits of resource recovery from global waste management systems. *Journal of Cleaner Production*, *124*, 41–50.

ZWSA. (2012). *Waste Management Hierarchy*. Retrieved November 12, 2013, from www.zerowaste.sa.gov.au/About-Us/waste-management-hierarchy

2
PLASTICS AND THE THROWAWAY SOCIETY

Plastics as a 'magical' material

Recently, plastics have gathered attention due to their low recycling and recovery rates and significant impacts and threat to the marine environment and human health. However, the history of plastics is different from what we are currently experiencing. The story of plastics is more than 100 years of innovation. In the early 1900s, plastics were seen as a 'magical' material because of their extraordinary material properties. Plastics consist of a wide range of synthetic or semi-synthetic organic compounds, which can be easily given any form and shape. Even scientists were surprised by the versatile characteristics of plastics. Victor Yarsley and Edward Couzens wrote in 1941 in *Plastics*,[1] 'Let us try to imagine a dweller in the "Plastic Age". . . . a world in which man, like a magician, makes what he wants for almost every need' (p. 3). However, the history of plastic is not so long. Just 112 years ago in 1907, the synthetic plastic Bakelite was invented in New York by Leo Baekeland (ACSNHCL, n.d.). It took almost five decades for scientists to discover the massive potentials of plastic materials by investing polyvinyl chloride (PVC), polyethylene (PE), nylon, polystyrene (PS), polypropylene (PP), polyethylene terephthalate (PET), high-density polyethylene (HDPE), and so on (Habbu, 2017).

Before the invention of plastics, elephants were and may be still in grave danger of being 'numbered with extinct species' because of humans' insatiable demand for ivory for various uses from buttonhooks to boxes, piano keys to combs (Freinkel, 2011a). Therefore, soon after the invention of plastics, they replaced a numerous number of conventional materials, such as ivory, due to their versatile properties. In the early plastics' era, the materials were used mainly in military purposes, and during the World War II, plastic production in the US increased by 300% due to alternative use of conventional materials; for example, plastics replaced glass for aircraft windows and solders received plastic combs in their hygiene kits (Nicholson & Leighton, 1942).

Plastics were used as a tool for reviving the global economy from the Great Depression and post-World War II crisis with the aim of 'planned obsolescence'. The planned obsolescence is a purposeful implementation of various strategies to design single-use products and to get a customer to buy similar products again and again within a short period of time. Plastics fit nicely with the purpose of designing and producing short-lasting and single-use products. Thus the mass application of plastics in consumer products started in 1950s to create jobs and increase economic growth. Plastics massively replaced the use of steel in cars, paper and glass in packaging, and wood in furniture (Freinkel, 2011b).

The technological innovation (especially in the polymer technology) made it possible to offer cheaper and better products to the consumers. At one time, the concept of throwaway living was only reasonable for the wealthy people of the society, but now, due to the availability of plastic products, throwaway living is now affordable to the common people. 'Throwaway living' was promoted in the 1950s because one did not need to worry about cleaning plates or dishes, and household plastic products were so inexpensive due to the plastic innovations that everyone could afford a throwaway lifestyle (Cosgrove, 2014). In August 1955, *Life* magazine published an article titled 'Throwaway Living' with a picture showing the dad, mom, and a small kid throwing away tableware, which would otherwise take a considerable number of hours to clean. The article emphasized that no housewife needed to bother with cleaning, as the products are meant to be thrown away after use (Cosgrove, 2014).

Types of plastics

Based on thermal properties, plastics are broadly placed in two categories:

a) **Thermoplastics** are defined as polymers that can be melted and recast almost indefinitely. They are molten when heated and harden upon cooling. The curing process is completely reversible, and this characteristic allows thermoplastics to be remoulded and recycled without negatively affecting the material's physical properties. Therefore, thermoplastics are mechanically recyclable. The most common types of thermoplastics are PP, PE, polyvinylchloride, PS, PET, and polycarbonate.

b) **Thermoset plastics** which contain polymers that cross-link together during the curing process (heating, pressure, and adding catalysts) to form an irreversible chemical bond. The cure may be induced by heat, generally above 200°C (392°F), through a chemical reaction or suitable irradiation. This eliminates the risk of the product re-melting when heat is applied, making thermosets ideal for high-heat applications, such as electronics and appliances. The most common types of thermoset plastics are melamine, bakelite (saucepan handle), etc.

According to the Society of the Plastics Industry resin and recycling code, plastics are categorized into seven types:

i   PETE or PET
ii HDPE
iii PVC
iv Low-density polyethylene (LDPE)
v   PP
vi PS or styrofoam
vii Other plastics (polycarbonate, polyctide, acrylic, acrylonitrile butadiene, styrene, fiberglass, and nylon)

Plastics production and waste management

Natural resources have been extracted and used up in the production process at a massive pace to meet consumer demand. One of the main reasons for the rapid growth of plastics production and use are the unique properties of the materials; e.g. they can be easily shaped into a wide variety of forms, are impermeable to liquids, and are highly resistant to physical and chemical degradation (OECD, 2018).

Plastic packaging is the largest application by weight, but plastics are also used widely in the textile, consumer goods, transport, and construction sectors. According to the *New York Times*, in 2015, packaging accounted for 36% of non-fiber plastic produced (Schlossberg, 2017). Figure 2.1 shows primary plastics production by industry in 2015 (in million tonnes) and their lifespan.

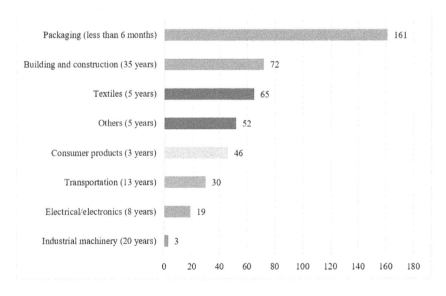

FIGURE 2.1   Primary plastics production in 2015 and their lifespan by industrial sectors

Source: Adopted from Geyer, Jambeck, and Law (2017), with permission

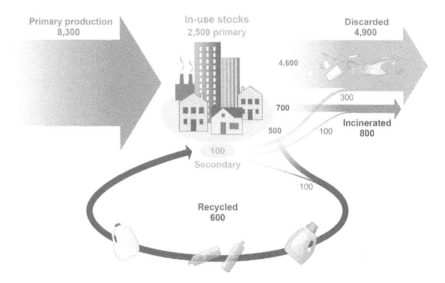

FIGURE 2.2   Global plastic production to fate (1950 to 2015; in million metric tonnes)

Source: Used with permission from Geyer et al. (2017)

The average usage time of plastics in different purposes varies before they are discarded and become waste. On average, plastics used in the building and construction industry last around 35 years before they become waste, and the usage time for transportation and consumer products are approximately around 13 years and 3 years, respectively. One of the largest uses of plastics is in the area of packaging, and it consists of 36% of global plastics use. Unfortunately, around 161 million tonnes of plastic packaging become trash within six months of their production (Parker, 2018).

Global production of resins and fibres increased from 2 Mt in 1950 to 380 Mt in 2015, with an annual growth rate of 8.4%, whereas the global gross domestic product (GDP) increased roughly 2.5% during that period (Geyer et al., 2017; PlasticsEurope, 2016). The study done by Geyer et al. (2017) found that approximately 8,300 Mt of plastic waste had been generated as of 2015, as shown in Figure 2.2, of which around 9% of had been recycled, 12% was incinerated, and 79% was accumulated in landfills or the natural environment. It is predicted that if these trends continue, then by 2050, 12 billion metric tonnes of plastic waste will enter landfills or the environment (Earth Day Network, 2018).

Key challenges of plastic recycling

When it comes to the recycling of plastic waste, we often refer to PET recycling schemes, such as take–back or container deposit scheme, as one of the best practices for recycling plastics because PET bottle recycling would be one of the easiest ways to recycle and recover resources from waste plastics. However, the reality tells a different story. According to Euromonitor, around 480 billion plastic bottles were sold globally in 2016, and less than 50% of the bottles were recycled; only 7% were used to make new bottles (BBC, 2017). There are various reasons for current poor recycling practices around the world. The key reasons are briefly described in the following sections.

Confusion around recycling codes of plastics

Although all seven categories of plastics are recyclable, the actual recycling practices vary in different jurisdictions depending on available recycling and resource recovery technologies. Figure 2.3 shows the level of difficulties in different types of plastics. Among various types of plastics, PET and HDPE are considered to be easily recycled, LDPE and PP are manageable, PS is difficult to manage and PVC and other types of plastics are very difficult to recycle (Parker, 2018).

A variety of technologies and infrastructure capacities are required to manage all plastics types locally. As a result, plastics recycling infrastructure vary in different location, thus local people need to know about the local infrastructure capacity and acceptable recyclable plastics types. Often, it creates confusion around correct recycling types, as it is very difficult for people to remember which plastics are acceptable in their local council.

Extremely slow decomposition rates

The slow decomposition rates are the major challenges for managing plastics. The current poor recycling rates are not only severely damaging the natural environment; the discarded plastics will keep polluting and deteriorating the marine environment for hundreds of years due to their poor decomposition rates. Simple plastic PET bottles, straws, or even single-use plastics would take 450 years, 200 years, and 20 years, respectively, to completely degrade to the environment. Table 2.1 shows the time taken to biodegrade for different common plastics items (NOAA, n.d.).

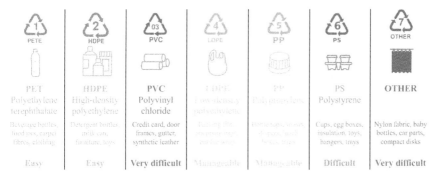

FIGURE 2.3   The level of difficulties of recycling different plastics

TABLE 2.1 Decomposition rates of various marine debris

Items	Time to biodegrade
Fishing lines	600 years
Six-pack beer holder	450 years
PET bottles	450 years
Disposable nappy	450 years
Aluminum can	200 years
Straws	200 years
Styrofoam cup	50 years
Single-use plastic bags	20 years
Cigarette butts	1.5–10 years
Waxed milk carton	3 months
Cardboard box	2 months
Cotton rope/shirt	1–5 months

Design issues

Design flaws are significantly contributing in the generation of waste. Since plastics are used in almost every single consumer good, the selection of materials and the design of products' packaging needs to consider the whole products' life cycle. It is important to consider both manufacturers' profitability and consumers' convenience; at the same time, it is also important to take responsibility and stewardship of the waste that is generated after consumption of goods. Unnecessary packaging and inappropriate design need to be omitted to avoid creating any undesirable waste.

Unnecessary plastic packaging is used significantly in the supermarket, especially in grocery items. Moreover, most often, lightweight plastic films create problems in the recycling system.

Technological limitations

Recycling of all types of plastics requires a combination of several advanced technologies, and the technology often comes with a huge price tag. Consequently, most often, even in developed countries, waste recycling technologies mainly cover the activities of sorting and recycling of selected waste categories, such as mainly PET and HDPE and somewhat LDPE and PP, which are considerably easy and low cost to recycle.

Another aspect of technological limitations is reduction of contamination, which is the reduction of undesirable items from a particular waste stream – for example, reducing the mixing of plastics in paper and cardboard stream or vice versa. A recent survey on Western Australia's waste recycling performance shows design flaws mainly in the product packaging, incorrect recycling behaviour, and lack of sophisticated waste-sorting technologies are the key reasons for a higher level of contamination in

TABLE 2.2 Plastic commodity prices before and after China waste ban

Items	AU$/tonne: pre-China ban (2015–2017)	AU$/tonne: post-China ban (2018)
Plastic – PET	$575	$375
Plastic – HDPE	$575	$500
Plastic – mixed	$325	$75

the region. Despite having the most advanced technologies, it may not be possible to reduce the level of contamination due to our packaging design fault.

Recycling cost verses market value

The waste market is one of the biggest influential drivers to effectively recycle plastics. Waste collection in developed countries often operate through the local government service systems. Although the waste collection system in many developing countries relies on an informal waste collection system, the recycling activities cost a significant amount of money. Without appropriate waste market and market value, overall performance of recycling and resource recovery is not possible.

The recycling of plastics bags cost approximately US$4,000 per ton[2] in the USA. A recent report showed that in Victoria, Australia, kerbside collection costs of recyclables in 2016 was AU$115 for each tonne (APCO, 2018). The market value of recovered mixed-plastics of each tonne of kerbside waste recycling was only AU$2, and the market value of all recyclables (including aluminum, glass, plastics, paper, cardboard, etc.) was AU$82, which is significantly low compared to the collection costs. Table 2.2 shows the value change of the waste commodity market before and after the China waste ban (APCO, 2018).

The 'Amazon effect' in the waste management

The term 'Amazon effect' describes the impact created by the digital marketplace on the traditional forms of commerce. Although the term refers to the disruptive nature of the innovative business model, it has a predominant link and influence in the WMS. Often, Amazon is criticized for the unnecessary packaging in the shipment, but due to the rapid increase of online businesses, local waste management practices are dramatically impacted by the packaging induced through online shopping from overseas countries.

Environmental pollution and health risks

Plastics pollution is the biggest waste-related environmental concern. According to the US Environmental Protection Agency (EPA), the production of plastic products account for an estimated 8% of global oil production (Earth Day Network,

2018). Therefore, plastic waste emits a significant amount of GHG emissions into the atmosphere. Recent discoveries indicate that the biggest impacts of plastics pollution are in the marine environment due to our poor waste management. Plastic wastes are accumulated in the oceans and, currently, there are five massive patches of marine plastic, and one of them is the size of the state of Texas, USA. The studies done by Van Houtan et al. (2016) and Young, Vanderlip, Duffy, Afanasyev, and Shaffer (2009) indicate that there are 180 times more plastics at the surface of the Great Pacific Garbage Patch than biomass, and 84% of plastic samples had at least one chemical pollutant in excess of acceptable limits. This high concentration of plastics pollutants was also found in the stomachs of common North Pacific subtropical gyre surface feeders. Scientists also predict that if nothing changes in our plastic consumption habits, by 2050, there will be more plastic in the oceans than there are fish (by weight) (Earth Day Network, 2018). The biggest contributions to the marine pollution are through shoreline and recreational activities (64%) and smoking-related activities (25%), followed by ocean or waterway activities (8%), dumping activities (2%), and medical or personal hygiene (1%) (NOAA, n.d.).

Plastic debris can come in different shapes and sizes, and microplastics are small plastic pieces less than 5-millimetres long, which can be harmful to our ocean and aquatic life (NOAA, 2018). The scientists from the Coastal Ocean Research Institute at Vancouver Aquarium Marine Science Centre (VAMSC, 2015) discovered that the marine zooplankton are ingesting microplastic particles, which means microplastics are propagating through the marine food chain. The scientists have discovered another very concerning issue that the ingestion of microbes is not limited to marine species; they have also been found in human waste for the first time (Quackenbush, 2018). It is estimated that 'more than 50% of the world population might have microplastics in their stools' (Harvey & Watts, 2018), which means half of the world population is under the health risk of gastrointestinal diseases.

This chapter has identified plastics as one of the rapidly growing household waste streams as nearly all consumer products use some form of plastics, which, eventually, ends up in the environment and threatens our health and well-being. We need to be able to find a strategic and holistic approach to provide sustainable solutions to manage plastic waste. The strategic approach needs to link production and consumptions of resources in relation to waste generation and management, which is often ignored in the traditional waste management solution.

Notes

1 Victor E. Yarsley and Edard G. Couzens, 1941. *Plastics*, Allen Lane, Penguin Books.
2 1 US ton (short ton) is equal to 907.185 kg.

References

ACSNHCL. (n.d.). *Bakelite: The World's First Synthetic Plastic*. Retrieved from www.acs.org/content/acs/en/education/whatischemistry/landmarks/bakelite.html
APCO. (2018). *Market Impact Assessment Report Chinese Import Restrictions for Packaging in Australia*. Retrieved from www.packagingcovenant.org.au/documents/item/1224

BBC. (2017). Seven charts that explain the plastic pollution problem. *Science and Environment.* Retrieved from www.bbc.com/news/science-environment-42264788

Cosgrove, B. (2014). *"Throwaway Living": When Tossing Out Everything Was All the Rage.* 16 May 2014. Retrieved from https://time.com/3879873/throwaway-living-when-tossing-it-all-was-all-the-rage/

Earth Day Network. (2018). Plastic pollution primer and action toolkit: End plastic pollution. *Earth Day.* Retrieved from http://160g7a3snajg2i1r662yjd5r-wpengine.netdna-ssl.com/wp-content/uploads/Plastic-Pollution-Primer-and-Action-Toolkit.pdf

Freinkel, S. (2011a). A brief history of plastic's conquest of the world. *Sci Am.* San Francisco, CA: Springer Nature America. Retrieved from www.scientificamerican.com/article/a-brief-history-of-plastic-world-conquest/

Freinkel, S. (2011b). *Plastic: A Toxic Love Story.* Boston, MA: HMH.

Geyer, R., Jambeck, J. R., & Law, K. L. (2017). Production, use, and fate of all plastics ever made. *Science Advances, 3*(7), e1700782.

Habbu, V. G. (2017). *Plasticwaste: Best technologies & global practices.* Paper presented at the ASSOCHAM National Conference on "Waste to Wealth". Retrieved from https://slideplayer.com/slide/12169085/

Harvey, F., & Watts, J. (2018). *Microplastics Found in Human Stools for the First Time.* 23 October. Retrieved from www.theguardian.com/environment/2018/oct/22/microplastics-found-in-human-stools-for-the-first-time

Nicholson, J. L., & Leighton, G. R. (1942). Plastics come of age. *Harper's Magazine, 1942,* pp. 300-307.

NOAA. (2018). *What Are Microplastics?* Retrieved from https://oceanservice.noaa.gov/facts/microplastics.html

NOAA. (n.d.). *Marine Debris Is Everyone's Problem.* Retrieved from www.whoi.edu/fileserver.do?id=107364&pt=2&p=88817

OECD. (2018). Improving Plastics Management: Trends, Policy Responses, and the Role of International Co-Operation and Trade. *Environment Policy Paper. No. 12.* Retrieved from www.oecd.org/environment/waste/policy-highlights-improving-plastics-management.pdf

Parker, L. (2018). *Planet or Plastics: We Made Plastic, We Depend on It, Now We're Drowning in It.* June. Retrieved from www.nationalgeographic.com/magazine/2018/06/plastic-planet-waste-pollution-trash-crisis/

PlasticsEurope. (2016). *Plastics: The Facts 2016: An Analysis of European Plastics Production, Demand and Waste Data.* Retrieved from https://www.plasticseurope.org/application/files/4315/1310/4805/plastic-the-fact-2016.pdf

Quackenbush, C. (2018). Researchers have found microplastics in human waste for the first time. *Science-Environment.* Retrieved from https://time.com/5431668/microplastics-human-waste-study/

Schlossberg, T. (2017). *The Immense, Eternal Footprint Humanity Leaves on Earth: Plastics.* 19 June. Retrieved from www.nytimes.com/2017/07/19/climate/plastic-pollution-study-science-advances.html?mtrref=www.google.com&gwh=89525DBCE85046E32B115A06582007E6&gwt=pay

VAMSC. (2015). *Microplastic in Aquatic Food Webs.* Retrieved from www.reef2rainforest.com/2015/07/28/microplastic-in-marine-food-webs/

Van Houtan, K. S., Francke, D. L., Alessi, S., Jones, T. T., Martin, S. L., Kurpita, L., . . . Baird, R. W. (2016). The developmental biogeography of hawksbill sea turtles in the North Pacific. *Ecology and Evolution, 6*(8), 2378–2389.

Young, L. C., Vanderlip, C., Duffy, D. C., Afanasyev, V., & Shaffer, S. A. (2009). Bringing home the trash: Do colony-based differences in foraging distribution lead to increased plastic ingestion in Laysan albatrosses? *PLoS One, 4*(10), e7623.

3

PRODUCTION, CONSUMPTION, AND WASTE MANAGEMENT

The missing link

Urbanization, production, and consumption

One of the biggest challenges of progressing towards SWM is to restrain our thoughts on the end-of-life waste phase. It is also evident from various scholarly works, publications, and conferences that a significant proportion of waste discourse often focuses on waste collection from households, resource recovery at transfer stations, recycling, composting, incineration, and landfills. However, this is only half of the issue, and we should not ignore the other half of the whole lifecycle of waste from extraction of resources, manufacturing, packaging, retail, and consumption. For example, the use of smartphones has increased significantly in recent years, and this has resulted in a higher volume of electronic waste. A smartphone contains around 62 types of various finite materials, and almost all of them are non-replaceable, which means we will continue to extract all these materials from nature and perhaps deplete all available materials as well. Since all these materials are non-renewable, there will be no chance for the next generation to utilize these metals to support and enhance their livelihoods. How often as consumers and users of smartphones do we think of the consequences of our consumption activities, and how often do we truly understand that our stewardship behaviour with correct recycling practices would significantly conserve the nature and reduce the GHG emissions, as all upstream activities from extraction of resources to the use phase contribute GHG emissions and global climate change?

Global climate change is the biggest threat to our very existence on this planet. We are now at a determining moment in the future of humanity. Whether humans will become extinct depends on the path we take today. Living within a finite planet, our demand for natural resources is accelerating. Over seven billion people use rising quantities of natural resources, destroy the global ecosystem, dump billions of tonnes of waste, and add irreversible pollution to the global atmosphere

(Worldwatch Institute, 2010). More than half of the world's population (3.3 billion) lives in urban areas (UN-HABITAT, 2010). No matter where on Earth people live, in the northern or southern hemisphere, in developed cities or developing cities, the overall consumption of global natural resources is very high except for a few African cities.

Due to the increasing population, per capita global hectare (gha; a weighted area used to measure the average productivity of all biologically productive areas in one year) is decreasing every year, resulting in very limited resource availability for the current generation and future generations. Per capita gha in early 1900 was 7.91 hectare, and it reduced to 2.02 hectare in 2005, and it will shrink to 1.63 hectare by 2050 (FAOSTAT, 2006).

Urbanization in developing countries may be the most significant demographic transformation in our century. It is projected that the entire built-up urban area in developing countries will triple between 2000 and 2030 from 200,000 square kilometre (km^2) to 600,000 km^2 (Angel, Sheppard, & Civco, 2005). Cities attract people for the numerous opportunities they offer, and these result in them having higher consumption and carbon footprints. Despite only representing 2% of the world's surface area (UN-MEA, 2006), cities use 75% of the world's energy and are responsible for 80% of energy-related carbon impact (Delorme, Dixon, Huff, & Schierenbeck, 2011).

City centres are the anomalies of hyper-consumption in the context of global natural resource depletion over time in human history. Even though global natural resources are decreasing, the consumption and depletion of natural resources have significantly increased since the mid-eighteenth century. Cities are now becoming the centres of hyper-consumption and generators of huge waste streams. Even though environmental awareness among the mass of people globally has increased because of climate change, sustainable consumption and waste reduction still have a long way to go.

One-third of the planet's natural resources base was consumed from 1965 to 1995 (Hawken, Lovins, & Lovins, 1999, p. 4) and depleted by humans; the rest of the world's natural resources are being extracted in such an unsustainable way that we will soon face the global shortfall of resources. The reality of the global limits to growth was first observed in the 1970s when the great oil crisis affected the raw materials markets (Meadows, Meadows, Randers, & Behrens, 1992). The dependency of the market economy on overexploited natural resources and its direct consequences for our current economy unfolded in 2008 as the Great Global Recession. Despite all odds, the Great Global Recession gave humanity a chance to reflect on the path it is taking and to recognize that this high-consumption way of life is utterly unsustainable, as is the current economic system (Assadourian, 2010).

The purposes of this chapter are to (a) explore global and local consumption of natural resources and (b) better understand the need for sustainable consumption practices in the context of the consumption and sustainability dilemma. This chapter tries to establish links between the concepts of consumption, need, satisfaction, economic growth, human well-being, and the sustainability paradox in relation to waste generation and management.

The rise of modern consumerism

Consumption can be understood as the acquisition and use of resources which lead to the depletion of Earth's finite natural resources (Sagoff, 2001, p. 473). Consumption of resources depletes them and generates unwanted waste. 'Over-consumption' can be linked to three aspects of the issue: waste, sumptuousness, and affluence (T. Jackson, Jager, & Stagl, 2004; Sanne, 2005). Therefore, it is important to understand why people's perceptions have shifted from low consumption to hyper-consumption and the consequences of unsustainable consumption practices.

In the heart of the Brundtland concept of sustainable development is a challenge to meet every day 'needs' and ensure human well-being. According to Maslow, the hierarchy of human needs consists of five categories: physiological, security, affiliation, esteem, and self-accomplishment. A person does not move to the next level until the previous need is fairly well satisfied (Quick, 1991). Economic growth and materialistic consumption can fulfil the first two categories of needs but not the remaining three. For the fulfilment of affiliation, esteem, and self-accomplishment, economic growth is not enough, and it requires effective and efficient functioning of human capabilities to achieve the satisfaction of these needs (A. K. Sen, 1985, 1993). This means that the achievement of satisfaction in the areas of affiliation, esteem, and self-accomplishment cannot be attained through material goods and services alone but require effective human capabilities. Sen defines 'capability' as 'a person's ability to do valuable acts or reach valuable states of being'. The capacity of a person depends on a variety of factors, including personal characteristics and social arrangements (A. Sen, 2008, pp. 270–273). Simply put, human capability is the ability to be happy in a given social structure and avoid suffering or want.

In the pre-modern consumerism era, consumption of luxurious goods and services were only available to affluent people. However, consumerism is not limited to affluent people anymore; it is for everybody in society. Initial signs of consumerism include high demand for sugar in the late Middle Ages (one of the early mass consumer goods), household furnishings (beds instead of straw mattresses) in the early sixteenth century, tea and fashionable clothing in the end of the seventeenth century (Stearns, 2006). According to Stearns (2006), although there was an explosion of shops and new marketing methods in the eighteenth century which played a significant role in consumerism, but it was the shopkeeper and his methods that anchored the first iteration of a consumer society (p. 16).

Shopping became an important cultural activity among the 'elite' people in the eighteenth century, and the Industrial Revolution brought more variety in the clothes and household items not only for the affluent elite but also for ordinary people in America and Europe (Crocker, 2017; White, 2009). After the post-world war era, consumerism was mainly driven by 'economic consumerism' to stimulate economic growth and ensure a good living standard (Crocker, 2017, p. 10).

'Planned obsolescence' – i.e. the design of a product for a limited useful life – was one of the biggest drivers in making products more affordable for the masses and somewhat influenced economic development in 1950s. Along the way, various marketing strategies and approaches, such as 'buy now pay later', 'change it', or 'big is better', were inherent in our modern-consumer culture. Globalization and evolution in information and communication technologies (ICT) are the key influential factors of the modern consumerism.

The key characteristics of the economic growth model are based on a linear material flow – i.e. the 'take-make-disposal' approach where the planned obsolescence is the primary principle for repetitive shopping of 'waste-ready' products. People are obsessed with changing or upgrading their 'almost new' gadgets because a newer and a little more 'fancier' version is available, despite the fact that both perform in a similar way. People find 'pleasure' in consumption and try to establish social identity in a diminished social value system. In addition, economic growth does not always ensure a similar level of human subjective well-being as it 'promised' to deliver.

Clothing is a good example of how consumer culture significantly impacts the environment. Similar to America and Europe, Australia's obsession with new clothes and 'fast fashion' textiles impact the environment significantly. A T-shirt retailed in America often travels over 10,000 miles, and most of the distance (88%) it travels occurs during the production (mainly in Asia) and distribution phases (Xing et al., 2016). As consumers, very few of us truly realize how our consumption choices, even for a single T-shirt, impact people's livelihoods and the environment in the distant part of the world.

Average Australians dispose of 6,000 kilograms of fashion and textile waste every ten minutes, and only 15% of it is actually sold again locally in opportunity shops, and the remaining 85% ends up in landfills (Liu, 2017). The moment we throw our cloths and consumer goods into waste bins, they become somebody else's problem, and the realization of the impacts from waste through GHG and leachate contamination in landfills is not easy to comprehend. Climate change or global warming is a 'heavy' issue for the 'ordinary' consumer and often the impacts of this natural process is a 'slow' process compared to other natural disasters such as earthquake or cyclone. This insists people ignore the consequences of climate change. We are reluctant not to relate climate change to our individual choice that we make in our every consumption activity.

The basic need of human consumption to attain a decent standard of living has shifted in the twenty-first century from desire for access to sufficient goods and services to a desire for 'luxury' goods and services that are not essential to satisfying basic needs (Crocker, 2013, pp. 11–13). Goods and services that were once perceived as luxuries can over time be seen as necessities (Ekins, 1991) due to economic growth, technological innovation, and cultural shift. Modern consumerism that was once accessible to very few people has now become accessible to all.

The greater efficiency of production and spread of consumerism has depended greatly on the 'externalization' of environmental and social costs. For example, the true cost (social and environmental costs) of a consumer good, such as a piece of cloth that we buy from a shop, is often neglected and not considered at the retail price level. In 'the logic of sufficiency', Princen introduced 'sufficiency' as a new economic principle in which external costs are considered and presented as a contrast to 'efficiency', in which external costs are ignored (Princen, 2005). Princen argued that the sense of 'enoughness' should be a primary concern rather than profit maximization and efficiency. The effective decision maker engages the interrelatedness, avoids excess, and considers the long-term impact and external costs, as well as averts irretrievable diminution of ecological integrity (Princen, 2005, p. 18). Jackson (2006, p. 50) also asserts that prosperity is not just about economic growth, and it is possible to ensure prosperity without economic growth through the decoupling of the volume of material throughput and 'wasting' of resources from the volume and profitability of economic activities.

The current trends of consumption have been questioned and criticized by the Oxford Commission on Sustainable Consumption for three basic reasons: (i) increasing material consumption in industrialized countries does not enhance citizens' quality of life, (ii) current consumption patterns are inequitable both within and between countries, and (iii) increasing material consumption is resulting in growing environmental impacts globally, especially associated with energy use and climate change, water consumption and waste, material use and solid waste, and land use. There are three principle interacting actors that control and transform consumer society: business interests (capital), people (consumer), and the political class (Sanne, 2005). However, all these actors are guided and influenced by socio-economic and environmental drivers; for example, business is driven by the need to improve profit margins; people are driven by social norms and values; the political class is driven by a desire to stay in power.

A number of studies suggest that the current trends of over-consumption are mainly directed by technological innovation, fashion, deferral pricing, corporations, branding, and marketing strategies (Crocker, 2013; McKendrick, 1982; Princen, Maniates, & Conca, 2002; Slade, 2006). Over time, these influential factors contribute to product obsolescence and repetitive consumption practices, which are the core cause of generating excessive waste and the depletion of natural resources.

Modern consumerism has a complex history which parallels the history of industrialism (Crocker, 2013). After World War I, the motor industry in North America started mass production of 'luxurious and prestigious' cars and developed a distribution system to make them accessible to the masses (consumers). Soon after introducing the first generation of motor vehicles, they became obsolete due to the technological innovation of an electric starter in a new model (Slade, 2006). Later, style and fashion became the key factors in products' obsolescence instead of waiting for technological improvement (Fine & Leopold, 2003; McKendrick, 1982; Slade, 2006).

Market-driven consumerism has also flourished due to advanced modern production technologies. Due to technological innovation, consumers are now convinced to upgrade and replace their 'yesterday's product' to the latest version. The working life of a mobile phone, for instance, is around 7 years, but, on average, consumers change their mobile phones every 11 months (Sharpe, 2005), despite the latest version being just slightly thinner and faster, with a better battery and camera quality (Crocker, 2012). Most of these 'still-working' outdated mobiles are lying in drawers at home or discarded to landfills (ARP, 2012; Ongondo & Williams, 2009a, 2009b). Profit-maximizing business ethics (where profit maximization is the main business goal instead of social and environmental stewardship) is mainly responsible for this culture of excessive consumption. In addition, existing market conditions and competition for introducing new and innovative products in the market influence excessive consumption. Technological advancements not only bring 'dematerialization' and 'resource productivity' but also create unexpected 'rebound effects' – i.e. the growth of material consumption (Hertwich, 2005). Without effective government regulation and matching economic incentives, this 'race to the bottom', where producers compete on price and style and produce more waste, will continue.

The 'sunk cost' of products is one of the key factors in over-consumption of resources, and it leads to socially irresponsible and environmentally damaging consequences (M. J. Cohen, 2011; Tan & Yates, 1995). Corporate business organizations (producers) reduce the price for end users by not paying the real environmental and social costs (Crocker, 2013; Maniates, 2001; Princen et al., 2002) and mass distributing to consumers to maximize their profits. This has significantly increased social inequity due to the inequitable distribution of profits and global natural resources.

Consumerism is also amplified by the use of personal credit, which has been standardized in developed countries as an inevitable form of modern life. Even if one cannot afford to pay for excessive consumption at that moment, a person can pay later by credit card or loan, which further expands consumerism. Corporate business has evolved as the key promoter of economic growth through mass consumption. Corporations have now become greater than governments and have a superior influence in global policy regimes, also described as 'corporatocracy' (Rivas, Unknown; Shen, 2012). Many corporate businesses (such as those that dominate the energy sector) have now become more powerful than most governments. During 2009–2016, the number of corporations in the world's 100 largest economic entities has increased from 44 to 69, and the number will continue to grow (Keys & Malnight, 2009). Many believe that corporations and their interests are the strongest drivers of the cultural shift towards consumption (L. Cohen, 2003).

The 'planned obsolescence' product design is one of the most environmentally unsustainable production strategies that corporations have ever invented. In the twenty-first century, almost every product is designed with a very short use time to increase consumerism. Around 99% of products that are sold in North America are trashed within six months (Leonard, 2011) and sent to landfills. We are now accustomed to buying 'waste-ready' products and use them for a very short period, and sometimes we even buy discounted products (buy one get one free), which we rarely or never use. People in developed countries are so persuaded to shop that most of them do not even think or ask themselves while shopping whether the products they are buying will be of any use to them or will significantly contribute to their lives.

Media is another technique that corporate businesses use to stimulate consumerism and not just as a vehicle for marketing. Media is a powerful tool for transmitting cultural symbols, norms, customs, myths, and stories through commercials and promotional campaigns. For every additional hour of television people watch each week, they spend an additional $208 a year on 'stuff' (Anderson & Bushman, 2002). Global advertising expenditures hit $643 billion in 2008 (Welsch & Vivanco, 1997), and the average consumer in North America sees or hears about 3,000 advertisements a day (Leonard, 2011) and spends three to four times as many hours shopping than the average European (Cross, 1993).

The silent competition between different corporations has emerged with another clever way to pursue consumerism and encourage social competition among consumers: the 'branding' of products. Branding products (Apple, Sony or Samsung products, for instance) has now become a part of fashion and lifestyle choices. Consumers now express their social status and personal identity through different branded products. Corporate businesses have capitalized on this sense of the consumer's social status and identity being dependent on their product designs and business logos to manipulate consumer choice. Companies now even harness anthropologists (in the toy business) and psychologists (in video game and gambling machine design) to figure out what drives consumers' choices (Clay, 2012; PQ Media, 2009). Therefore, consumers in modern society may not be so keen and willing but are rather locked-in by corporations' deliberately created circumstances (Sanne, 2002).

Since the late 1990s, the sustainability agenda has been used as a trademark of doing well for the environment by corporations. Under the green marketing strategies, different socio-economic and environmental aspects, such as equitable profit distribution through Fairtrade, green-labels, or eco-labels (Christopher, 2005; Nimon & Beghin, 1999; Peter, 2005; Raynolds, 2009), have been integrated to certify corporations' initiatives for sustainable development. However, all of these initiatives have received much criticism due to poor performance and not contributing much to establish equity in society (Hamilton & Zilberman, 2006; Nelson & Robertson, 2008; Nilsson, Tunçer, & Thidell, 2004; Zaman, Sofia, & Veranika, 2010). The annual sustainability report that corporations publish every year may add value to the corporations, and this report has become a specialty within corporate public relations departments (Crocker, 2013; Pearse, 2012; Rogers & Botsman, 2010) in the name of corporate social responsibility (CSR). Many people are starting to believe that CSR, as a business, governance, and ethics system, has failed (Devinney, 2009; Frynas, 2005; Visser, 2011).

In most developed and developing nations, the role of governments is almost invisible when it comes to 'choice editing' by laws, taxes, subsidies, and so on to assist the consumer in making the right decision (Sanne, 2002). An average person in a developed country spends almost all his/her life working to repay credit cards due to the debt-based modern lifestyle. People are encouraged to work more and take pay raises, increasing their disposable income rather than more time off for family or quality time. The motto of modern societies seems to be 'the more you earn, the more you can spend, and the more secure your life will be', which may not be true.

Hence, modern consumerism is one of the direct outcomes of the model of economic growth in which progress or the GDP relies on citizens' higher incomes and spending as a lifestyle. Per capita GDP is often used as a key indicator of economic well-being. However, the GDP measures effective consumption poorly (ignoring the value of leisure and of longer lifespans), and it also ignores the value of accumulation for the benefit of future generations (Osberg & Sharpe, 2002). Research suggests that well-being should be measured by integrating positive and negative emotions, engagement, purpose and meaning, optimism and trust, and the broad concept of life satisfaction (Diener & Seligman, 2004). Unfortunately, very few examples are available that encourage consumers to find an alternative way of discovering meaning in life and well-being rather than following materialistic consumption practices.

What do we really mean by sustainable consumption?

The concept of sustainable consumption is relatively new. However, the principles inherent in sustainable consumption (conservation, health, well-being, social and environmental justice) have been written about for centuries (Bentley, Fien, & Neil, 2004). The term 'sustainable consumption' can be defined based on the dimension of implementation and application of the concepts for a specific outcome or context. For instance, sustainable consumption can be translated in the context of individual satisfaction, family well-being, social, regional, or global sustainable development.

The term 'sustainable consumption' (consumption of products and services) is defined in parallel to the Brundtland definition for sustainable development as

> the use of goods and services that respond to basic needs and bring a better quality of life, while minimising the use of natural resources, toxic materials and emissions of waste and pollutants over the life-cycle, so as not to jeopardise the needs of future generations.
>
> *(Ofstad, 1994)*

Sustainable consumption is not about consuming less but consuming efficiently to improve the individual's quality of life, and the term brings together a number of key sustainable development issues, such as meeting needs, enhancing quality of life, improving efficiency, minimizing waste, and meeting the basic requirements of life for both current and future generations while continuously reducing environmental damage (Tim Jackson, 2005; UNEP, 2001).

The United Nations Rio Declaration in 1992 clearly identified and emphasized the important problems of unsustainable production and consumption. A detailed framework called 'Changing Consumption Patterns' was given at the Earth Summit through Agenda 21 (United Nations, 1992). The framework focused on two broad areas of consumption and national policy and included five key objectives based on sustainable consumption, production, and policies that reduce environmental stress and encourage the development and transfer of environmentally sound technologies around the globe.

Since the Rio Declaration, several studies have been conducted to understand current household consumption and waste generation patterns (Assadourian, 2010; Li, Fu, & Qu, 2011; Otoniel, Liliana, & Francelia, 2008; Patel, Jochem, Radgen, & Worrell, 1998). One such important study was done by the OECD (OECD, 2002). The study identified some key drivers and consumption trends in OECD countries. The study found that, along with economic growth and changes in production and consumption patterns, the generation of waste in OECD countries has steadily increased during the last 20 years. At the same time, higher environmental standards, stricter waste management policies, and cleaner technologies have contributed to reducing the environmental impacts of waste. While waste recovery (e.g. recycling or reuse) has increased considerably, reducing the rate of final disposal or landfills in some OECD countries, it has not been enough to reverse the global trend of increasing volumes of waste destined for final disposal.

Another important case study has been done by Markowitz and Bowerman (2011) on the relevance of consumption beliefs to public policy aimed at reducing GHG emissions. The study showed that a strong majority (74%–88%) of the Oregon public supports reducing consumption and believes doing so would improve societal and individual well-being. The study suggested that the public's attitudes toward consumption are important for reducing GHG emissions; however, the study used only qualitative evidence. But it is clear that a further study is required for understanding which policies, strategies, or principles can be effective in reducing consumption and the amount of household waste. Behavioural change has a major influence on sustainable consumption and on the generation of waste. Thus in-depth study is required to achieve sustainable consumption and generate less waste in our everyday lives.

The economy of our society is based on modern consumer culture. The global economic system runs in a way that makes buying stuff compulsory for the growth of our economy. Consumerism is not simply one of many possible individual lifestyles; it is deliberately inherited within capitalist economies. The 'great promise' of economic growth to ensure 'human well-being' has never been fulfilled by consumerism. Consumption can be viewed as a functional attempt to improve individual and collective well-being by providing the goods and services necessary to meet people's wants and desires. However, the 'insatiability' of consumer desire and the 'sovereignty' of consumer choice may not always satisfy consumer expectations and ensure well-being.

Alternative design and production practices, such as 'C2C design' or 'ZW design', are required to promote economic growth through consumption. The C2C concept was introduced by William McDonough and Michael Braungart in the book *Cradle to Cradle: Remaking the Way We Make Things*. The authors define C2C as 'a framework for designing products and industrial processes that turn materials into nutrients by enabling their perpetual flow' within a biological metabolism or the technical metabolism (McDonough and Braungart, 2002). Various mechanisms, such as extended producer responsibility, should be widely implemented to assist the ZWS, despite the fact that many scholars believe that we need a new form (shifting from a monetary to resources based economy) of global economic system (Fresco, 1995; Tompson, 2005; Zeit Studios, 2011). Within the current monetary-based economy, C2C design can be the optimum solution to promote sustainable consumption and economic growth. However, it is also clear that economic and policy incentives that penalize premature discard, for example, are required to shift current consumer culture towards such a 'closed-loop' system.

Consumption, economic growth, and sustainability paradox

In respect to the expanding consumption of resources, we need an intervention in current consumption trends. One of the important aspects of consumption that we need to understand is whether higher income and consumption really improve human well-being. The answer can be, maybe or maybe not, but if we consider certain levels of consumption, such as fulfilment of basic needs and desires, then the answer would definitely be no. In contrast, the economic growth model claims that 'increasing economic growth (GDP) leads to improve well-being: a higher standard of living and a better quality of life' (Easterlin, 1974; Frey & Stutzer, 2010; Tim Jackson, 2006). Though economic growth delivers affluence, increases spending power, and improves family security, it barely ensures human well-being.

The Easterlin Paradox explains why economic growth does not always ensure similar growth in human subjective well-being. According to Easterlin, subjective well-being is determined by relative circumstance rather than absolute income (Sacks, Stevenson, & Wolfers, 2010). Happiness is not confined, of course, to economic well-being (Easterlin, 1974). Easterlin pointed out that within a given local circumstance, higher income may increase happiness, but on a much wider national and international level, average happiness remains constant over time despite sharp rises in per capita income (A. E. Clark, Frijters, & Shields, 2008). In other words, income can increase well-being for the very poor individual to some extent and eventually reach a satisfaction point. However, after that point, further income has no effect on well-being (Layard, 2005).

A new paradigm called the capability approach, introduced by Amartya Sen, has emerged and explained human well-being with an alternative to standard models of economic and human development (D. A. Clark, 2006). The capability approach suggests that opulence (income, commodities) and utility (happiness, desire fulfilment) do not adequately symbolize human well-being and deprivation. Instead, Sen proposes a direct approach to human functioning and capability to achieve valuable functioning (A. K. Sen, 1985, 1993, 1987). Human functioning refers to the 'use' a person makes of his or her commodities, and capability refers to a person's ability to achieve a given level of functioning. Hence, capability reflects a person's real opportunities or positive freedom of choice between possible lifestyles (D. A. Clark, 2006; A. K. Sen, 1985, 1992, 1999). Thus 'functioning is an achievement (living conditions), whereas capability (notions of freedom) is the ability to achieve' (A. K. Sen, 1987, p. 36).

According to Nussbaum, capability opportunities or freedom of choice are more important than functioning or achievement. She argued that the traditional way of measuring development is flawed and asks if we rely on conventional economic indicators, can we ever grasp how the world's billions of individuals are really managing. She argues that even if the country's GDP increases each year, but due to increasing inequalities a large percentage of its people are deprived of basic education, healthcare, and other opportunities, then the overall GDP growth does not reflect a country's real progress (Nussbaum, 2011). Nussbaum shows that 'by attending to the narratives of individuals and grasping the daily impact of policy it can enable people everywhere to live full and creative lives' (Nussbaum, 2011).

Both Easterlin and Sen's approaches explain that the way we perceive economic growth as a means of human well-being may not be adequate to reflect the development of human well-being. However, there is no doubt that the current consumption-driven lifestyle of the high-consuming world is environmentally damaging (Evans, 2011) and increasing inequity in society due to the disproportionate utilization of ecological systems (Rice, 2007). We need to find alternative development strategies and measurement indicators to assess human progress in regard to individual, family, social, national, and global progress.

The current model of economic growth means improving living standards by consuming more and more resources, resulting in a higher rate of depletion of global natural resources. Economic growth leads to higher consumption, an affluent lifestyle, and, consequently, a greater production of waste, causing irreversible environmental degradation. It is obvious that the $18 trillion global economy cannot replace the valuable global ecosystem services (only 17 ecosystem services worth approximately US$33 trillion) that are being destroyed every day (Costanza et al., 1998; Michaelis, 2003).

The United Nations' Human Development Index (HDI) is one of the key indicators to address human well-being and progress towards sustainable development. The HDI is solely based on life expectancy, literacy and education, and per person GDP to calculate the human well-being and ecological footprint as a measure of demand on the biosphere. Bangladesh, for example, ranked 47 in the global national GDP, 146 in the global HDI, and 11 in the Happy Planet Index (measures the life expectancy adjusted for experienced well-being achieved per unit of resource use) in 2011 (NEF, 2012).

The minimum criteria of sustainable development can be fulfilled by attaining an HDI value of more than 0.8 and by lowering the ecological footprint to 1.8 gha per person (Global Footprint Network, 2005). Even though a higher income per person is assumed to be a key success factor in sustainable development, the opposite scenario seems apparent in developing cities (such as Kerala in India) where human well-being, life expectancy, and literacy rate are higher, and, as a result, the overall HDI is higher compared to many affluent cities (such as cities in the USA) (McKibben, 1996). If Kerala and cities in the US manage to achieve the same physical quality of life, Kerala is vastly more successful than cities in the USA in regard to global resource consumption. In other words, the economic progress meter of GDP does not necessarily reflect the complete picture of happiness and human well-being. We need to find an alternative way to measure human progress in regard to individual, family, social, national, and global progress, along with economic progress.

McKibben (1996) argues that Kerala is an example of such high human functioning capability and low income consumption. In contrast, lower human functioning capability would provide low well-being in higher consumption of natural resources, and most of the cities in developed countries are examples of this group. So the critical question that we need to ask is, how is overall well-being improved by using the least amount of natural resources? The success of sustainable development must rely on the very least depletion of global natural resources. The current trend of resource consumption and depletion is undoubtedly unsustainable. Because of consumption, it not only produces waste but also causes irreversible environmental degradation.

Researchers have suggested that we may need to make drastic cultural shifts in every aspect of life, including social, economic, environmental, technological, and institutional (Buss, Shackelford, Kirkpatrick, & Larsen, 2001; Inglehart & Norris, 2003). The futurist designer and philosopher Jacque Fresco proposed the concept of a resource-based global economy in which national boundaries will be made by realizing the declaration of the world's resources as being the common heritage of all people (TVP, 2011). The development hierarchy should follow as the objectives of eco-centric (perceiving and protecting value in all of nature), anthropocentric (restricting value to humanity alone), and, finally, economy centric (economic progress to all society). However, the system is working in reverse order.

Linking the missing dots

Undoubtedly, current trends of over-consumption to satisfy needs depletes natural resources, contributes to the GHG emissions which enhance global climate change, and, finally, produce an enormous amount of waste. Waste is one of the most visible forms of outcome of our consumption activities and requires an extensive effort to manage it. Thus effective human functioning capabilities could ensure human well-being by consuming and depleting global resources and creating less waste.

Our modern system of consumerism has transformed individual, social, and cultural norms, values, symbols, and priorities by the inappropriate development of the economic system, globalization, corporations, and rapid technological innovation. There is no doubt that, both in low-consuming and high-consuming cities, resources are consumed in significantly greater amounts than are available for them. We need to rationalize our priorities as humans and for our future progress. If we think that we can keep consuming forever at today's rate, it will be the most irresponsible and thoughtless approach to our whole ecosystem, because our life on Earth will not continue for long with today's unsustainable lifestyle. Therefore, we need a combination of ecology-based socio-economic structures, green businesses, empowerment of individual and social values, and, finally, ability to achieve our desired satisfaction within limited global resources through sustainable consumption. As global citizens, we need to be more responsible for our actions and the decisions we make every day, and we need to think beyond the box when it comes to waste management, because waste management is less about managing the end-of-life waste and more about ensuring sustainable design and maintaining responsible consumption practices.

References

Anderson, C. A., & Bushman, B. J. (2002). The effects of media violence in society. *Science*, *2002*(29 March), 2377–2379.

Angel, S., Sheppard, S. C., & Civco, D. L. (2005). *The Dynamics of Global Urban Expansion*. Retrieved from Washington, DC, World Bank: http://siteresources.worldbank.org/INTURBANDEVELOPMENT/Resources/dynamics_urban_expansion.pdf

ARP. (2012). *Why Recycling Mobile Phone*. Retrieved from www.arp.net.au/envwhy.php

Assadourian, E. (2010). Transforming cultures: From consumerism to sustainability. *Journal of Macromarketing, 30*(2), 186–191.

Bentley, M., Fien, J., & Neil, C. (2004). *Sustainable Consumption*. Retrieved from www.facs.gov.au/internet/facsinternet.nsf/aboutfacs/programs/youth-nyars.htm

Buss, D. M., Shackelford, T. K., Kirkpatrick, L. A., & Larsen, R. J. (2001). A half century of mate preferences: The cultural evolution of values. *Journal of Marriage and Family, 63*(2), 491–503.

Christopher, B. (2005). Confronting the coffee crisis: Can fair trade, organic, and specialty coffees reduce small-scale farmer vulnerability in Northern Nicaragua? *World Development, 33*(3), 497–511. doi:10.1016/j.worlddev.2004.10.002

Clark, A. E., Frijters, P., & Shields, M. A. (2008). Relative income, happiness, and utility: An explanation for the Easterlin Paradox and other puzzles. *Journal of Economic Literature, 46*(1), 95–144.

Clark, D. A. (2006). *The Capability Approach: Its Development, Critiques and Recent Advances*. Retrieved from https://pdfs.semanticscholar.org/7a32/9d6403433e47acfa60dd90e929e2b90a2165.pdf, Swindon, UK, ESRC.

Clay, R. A. (2012). *Video Game Design and Development*. Retrieved from www.apa.org/gradpsych/2012/01/hot-careers.aspx

Cohen, L. (2003). *A Consumer's Republic: The Politics of Mass Consumption in Post-War America*. New York: Alfred A. Knopf.

Cohen, M. J. (2011). (Un)sustainable consumption and the new political economy of growth. In K. M. Ekstrom & K. Glans (Eds.), *Beyond the Consumption Bubble* (pp. 174–190). London: Routledge.

Costanza, R., d'Arge, R., De Groot, R., Farber, S., Grasso, M., Hannon, B., . . . Raskin, R. G. (1998). The value of the world's ecosystem services and natural capital. *Nature, 387*(6630), 253

Crocker, R. (2012). Getting to Zero Waste in the new mobile communications paradigm: A social and cultural perspective. In S. Lehmann & R. Crocker (Ed.), *Designing for Zero Waste: Consumption, Technology and Built Environment*. London: Earthscan and Routledge.

Crocker, R. (2013). From access to excess: Consumerism, "compulsory" consumption and behaviour change. In S. L. R. Crocker (Ed.), *Motivating Change: Sustainable Design and Behaviour in the Built Environment*. London: Earthscan.

Crocker, R. (2017). Somebody else's problem: Consumerism, sustainability and design. Routledge.

Cross, G. (1993). *Time and Money: The Making of Consumer Culture*. London: Routledge.

Delorme, P., Dixon, G., Huff, C. A., & Schierenbeck, A. (2011). Energy-entrepreneurship and demand management, investing in cities of the 21st century. *Urbanization, Infrastructure, and Resources*. Retrieved from www.hbs.edu/environment/docs/HBS-Investing-in-Cities-of-the-21st-Century_Energy.pdf

Devinney, T. M. (2009). Is the socially responsible corporation a myth? The good, the bad, and the ugly of corporate social responsibility. *The Academy of Management Perspectives*, *23*(2), 44–56.

Diener, E., & Seligman, M. E. (2004). Beyond money toward an economy of well-being. *Psychological Science in the Public Interest*, *5*(1), 1–31.

Easterlin, R. (1974). *Does Economic Growth Improve the Human Lot? Some Empirical Evidence*. Retrieved from Pennsylvania: http://graphics8.nytimes.com/images/2008/04/16/business/Easterlin1974.pdf

Ekins, P. (1991). The sustainable consumer society: A contradiction in terms? *International Environmental Affairs*, *3*(Fall), 243–258.

Evans, D. (2011). Consuming conventions: Sustainable consumption, ecological citizenship and the worlds of worth. *Journal of Rural Studies*, *27*(2), 109–115. doi:10.1016/j.jrurstud.2011.02.002

FAOSTAT. (2006). *Population Projection, GEO Data Portal Compiled from UNPD 2007-Low Estimate*. Retrieved from www.grida.no/graphicslib/detail/our-shrinking-earth_10aa#

Fine, B., & Leopold, E. (2003). Consumerism and the industrial revolution. In D. B. Clarke, M. A. Doel, & K. M. Housiaux (Eds.), *The Consumption Reader* (pp. 42–47). London: Routledge.

Fresco, J. (1995). *The Redesign of Culture*. Retrieved from www.archive.org/stream/TheVenusProjectTheRedesignOfCulture/1995-TheVenusProject-TheRedesignOfCultureebook#page/n1/mode/2up

Frey, B. S., & Stutzer, A. (2010). *Happiness and Economics: How the Economy and Institutions Affect Human Well-Being*. Princeton, NJ: Princeton University Press.

Frynas, J. G. (2005). The false developmental promise of corporate social responsibility: Evidence from multinational oil companies. *International Affairs*, *81*(3), 581–598.

Global Footprint Network. (2005). *The Africa: Ecological Footprint and Human Well-Being*. Retrieved from www.footprintnetwork.org/download.php?id=502

Hamilton, S. F., & Zilberman, D. (2006). Green markets, eco-certification, and equilibrium fraud. *Journal of Environmental Economics and Management*, *52*(3), 627–644. doi:10.1016/j.jeem.2006.05.002

Hawken, P., Lovins, A., & Lovins, L. H. (1999). *Natural Capitalism: Creating the Next Industrial Revolution*. New York: Little, Brown and Company.

Hertwich, E. (2005). Consumption and the rebound effect: An industrial ecology perspective. *Journal of Industrial Ecology*, *9*(1–2), 85–98.

Inglehart, R., & Norris, P. (2003). *Rising Tide: Gender Equality and Cultural Change Around the World*. Cambridge: Cambridge University Press.

Jackson, T. (2005). *Motivating Sustainable Consumption: A Review of Evidence on Consumer Behaviour and Behavioural Change*. Retrieved from Surrey: www.c2p2online.com/documents/MotivatingSC.pdf

Jackson, T. (2006). *The Earthscan Reader in Sustainable Consumption*. Sterling, VA: Earthscan.

Jackson, T., Jager, W., & Stagl, S. (2004). Beyond insatiability: Needs theory, consumption and sustainability. ESRC Sustainable Technologies Programme Working Paper Series, 2, 1–34.

Keys, T., & Malnight, T. (2009). *Corporate Clout: The Influence of the World's Largest 100 Economic Entities*. Retrieved from www.globaltrends.com/images/stories/corporate%20clout%20the%20worlds%20100%20largest%20economic%20entities.pdf

Layard, R. (2005). *Happiness: Lessons from a New Science.* London: Penguin.

Leonard, A. (2011). *Facts from the Story of Stuff.* Retrieved from www.storyofstuff.org/wp-content/uploads/2011/03/annie_leonard_facts.pdf

Li, Z.-S., Fu, H.-Z., & Qu, X.-Y. (2011). Estimating municipal solid waste generation by different activities and various resident groups: A case study of Beijing. *Science of the Total Environment, 409*(20), 4406–4414. doi:10.1016/j.scitotenv.2011.07.018

Liu, M. (2017) For a true war on waste, the fashion industry must spend more on research. The Conversation, published on 16 August 2017. Retrieved from https://theconversation.com/for-a-true-war-on-waste-the-fashion-industry-must-spend-more-on-research-78673

Maniates, M. F. (2001). Individualization: Plant a tree, buy a bike, save the world? *Global Environmental Policies, 1*(3), 31–52.

Markowitz, E. M., & Bowerman, T. (2011). How much is enough? Examining the public's beliefs about consumption. *Analyses of Social Issues and Public Policy.* doi:10.1111/j.1530-2415.2011.01230.x

McDonough, W., and Braungart, M. (2002). *Cradle to Cradle: Remaking the Way We Make Things* (1st ed.). New York: North Point Press.

McKendrick, N. (1982). The commercialization of fashion. In N. McKendrick, J. Brewer, & J. H. Plumb (Eds.), *The Birth of a Consumer Society: The Commercialization of Eighteenth-Century England* (p. 66). London: Europa Publications.

McKibben, B. (1996). The enigma of Kerala: One state in India is proving development experts wrong. *Utne Reader, 74*(March/April), 102–112.

Meadows, D. H., Meadows, D. L., Randers, J., & Behrens, W. W. (1992). *The Limits to Growth.* New York, USA: Universe Books.

Michaelis, L. (2003). The Oxford commission on sustainable consumption. *Journal of Cleaner Production, 11*(2003), 931–933.

NEF. (2012). *The Happy Planet Index: A Global Index of Sustainable Well-being.* Retrieved from www.happyplanetindex.org/.../happy-planet-index-report.pdf

Nelson, G. C., & Robertson, R. D. (2008). Green gold or green wash: Environmental consequences of biofuels in the developing world. *Applied Economic Perspectives and Policy, 30*(3), 517–529. doi:10.1111/j.1467-9353.2008.00426.x

Nilsson, H., Tunçer, B., & Thidell, Å. (2004). The use of eco-labeling like initiatives on food products to promote quality assurance: Is there enough credibility? *Journal of Cleaner Production, 12*(5), 517–526. doi:10.1016/s0959-6526(03)00114-8

Nimon, W., & Beghin, J. (1999). Are eco-labels valuable? Evidence from the apparel industry. *American Journal of Agricultural Economics, 81*(4), 801–811.

Nussbaum, M. C. (Writer). (2011). Creating capabilities. In H. U. Press (Producer). USA: YouTube.

OECD. (2002). *Towards Sustainable Household Consumption? Trends and Policies in OECD Countries.* Retrieved from https://www.oecd-ilibrary.org/environment/towards-sustainable-household-consumption_9789264175068-en

Ofstad, S. (1994). *Symposium: Sustainable Consumption.* Oslo: Ministry of Environment.

Ongondo, F., & Williams, I. (2009a). *How Are WEEE Doing? Global Trends and Future Perspectives on Electronic Waste.* Retrieved from http://waste-conference.boku.ac.at/downloads/publications/2009/presentations/2-2_Williams.pdf

Ongondo, F., & Williams, I. (2009b). *Mobile Telephone Collection, Reuse, and Recycling in the UK.* Retrieved from http://wasteconference.boku.ac.at/downloads/publications/2009/presentations/2-8_Ongondo.pdf

Osberg, L., & Sharpe, A. (2002). An index of economic well-being for selected OECD countries. *Review of Income and Wealth, 48*(3), 291–316.

Otoniel, B. D., Liliana, M.-B., & Francelia, P. G. (2008). Consumption patterns and household hazardous solid waste generation in an urban settlement in México. *Waste Management, 28*(2008), S2–S6. doi:10.1016/j.wasman.2008.03.019

Patel, M. K., Jochem, E., Radgen, P., & Worrell, E. (1998). Plastics streams in Germany: An analysis of production, consumption and waste generation. *Resources, Conservation and Recycling, 24*(3–4), 191–215. doi:10.1016/s0921-3449(98)00015-9

Pearse, G. (2012). *Green Wash: Big Brands and Carbon Scams*. Melbourne: Black Inc.

Peter, L. T. (2005). A Fair trade approach to community forest certification? A framework for discussion. *Journal of Rural Studies, 21*(4), 433–447.

PQMedia. (2009). *Word-of-Mouth Marketing Forecast 2009–2013: Spending Trend Analysis*. Stanford, CA: PQ Media.

Princen, T., Maniates, M., & Conca, K. (2002). *Confronting Consumption*. Cambridge: MIT Press.

Princen, T. (2005). The logic of sufficiency (Vol. 30). Cambridge, MA: MIT Press.

Quick, T. L. (1991). An HRD refresher: Human resource development. *Training & Development, 45*(2), 74.

Raynolds, L. T. (2009). Fair trade. In Editors-in-Chief: K. Rob & T. Nigel (Eds.), *International Encyclopedia of Human Geography* (pp. 8–13). Oxford: Elsevier.

Rice, J. (2007). Ecological unequal exchange: Consumption, equity, and unsustainable structural relationships within the global economy. *International Journal of Comparative Sociology, 48*(1), 43–72. doi:10.1177/0020715207072159

Rivas, T. (Unknown). *Corporatocracy: A Global Empire*. Retrieved from www3.nd.edu/~druccio/ThomasR.pdf

Rogers, R., & Botsman, R. (2010). *What's Mine Is Yours: The Rise of Collaborative Consumption*. New York: HarperBusiness.

Sacks, D., Stevenson, B., & Wolfers, J. (2010). *Subjective Well-Being, Income, Economic Development and Growth*. Retrieved from www.nber.org/papers/w16441

Sagoff, M. (2001). Consumption. In D. Jamieson (Ed.), *A Companion to Environmental Philosophy*. London: Blackwell Publishers Ltd.

Sanne, C. (2002). Willing consumers or locked-in? Policies for sustainable consumption. *Ecological Economics, 42*(2002), 273–287.

Sanne, C. (2005). The consumption of our discontent. *Business Strategy and the Environment, 14*(2005), 315–323.

Sen, A. (2008). Capability and well-being. In D. M. Hausman (Ed.), *The Philosophy of Economics: An Anthology* (3rd ed.). Cambridge and New York: Cambridge University Press.

Sen, A. K. (1985). *Commodities and Capabilities*. Oxford: Elsevier Science Publishers.

Sen, A. K. (Ed.). (1987). *The Standard of Living: In the Standard of Living*. Cambridge: Cambridge University Press.

Sen, A. K. (1992). *Inequality Re-Examined*. Oxford: Clarendon Press.

Sen, A. K. (1993). Capability and well-being. In M. C. Nussbaun & A. K. Sen (Eds.), *The Quality of Life*. Oxford: Clarendon Press.

Sen, A. K. (1999). *Development as Freedom*. Oxford: Oxford University Press.

Sharpe, M. (2005). Climbing the e-waste mountain. *Journal of Environmental Monitoring, 7*(10), 933–936.

Shen, D. (2012). *Capitalism, Corporatocracy, and Financialization: Imbalances in the American Political Economy*. Retrieved from www.lse.ac.uk/IPA/images/Documents/PublicSphere/2013/2-capitalism-corporatocracy-financialization-20121.pdf

Slade, G. (2006). *Made to Break: Technology and Obsolescence in America*. London, England: Harvard University Press.

Stearns, P. N. (2006). *Consumerism in World History: The Global Transformation of Desire*. London and New York: Routledge.

Tan, H.-T., & Yates, J. F. (1995). Sunk cost effects: The influences of instruction and future return estimates. *Organizational Behavior and Human Decision Processes, 63*(3), 311–319. http://dx.doi.org/10.1006/obhd.1995.1082

Tompson, W. (2005). The political implications of Russia's resource-based economy. *Post-Soviet Affairs, 21*(4), 335–359.

TVP. (2011). *Aims and Proposals of the Venus Project*. Retrieved from www.thevenusproject.com/en/the-venus-project/aims-a-proposals

UNEP. (2001). *Consumption Opportunities: Strategies for Change*. Retrieved from Paris: http://www.unep.fr/shared/publications/pdf/3000-ConsumOpportunities.pdf

UN-HABITAT. (2010). *Solid Waste Management in the World's Cities: Water and Sanitation in the World's Cities* (Earthscan, Ed.). London: Earthscan.

United Nations. (1992). *Agenda 21: Environmentally Sound Management of Solid Wastes and Sewage-Related Issues (Chapter 21)*. Retrieved from www.un-documents.net/a21-21.htm

UN-MEA. (2006). *The UN Millennium Ecosystem Assessment Report*. Retrieved from New York: www.publications.parliament.uk/pa/cm200607/cmselect/cmenvaud/77/77.pdf

Visser, W. (2011). The age of responsibility: CSR 2.0 and the new DNA of business. *Journal of Business Systems, Governance and Ethics, 5*(3), 7–22.

Welsch, R., & Vivanco, L. (1997). *Introduction to Cultural Anthropology*. New York: McGraw Hill.

White, M. 2009. *The Rise of Consumerism*, British Library, London, UK, published on 14 Oct 2009. Retrieved from https://www.bl.uk/georgian-britain/articles/the-rise-of-consumerism

Worldwatch Institute. (2010). *State of the World 2010: Transforming Cultures from Consumerism to Sustainability*. Retrieved from New York: http://www.worldwatch.org/files/pdf/Education.pdf

Xing, K., Qian, W., & Zaman, A. U. (2016). Development of a cloud-based platform for footprint assessment in green supply chain management. *Journal of Cleaner Production, 139*, 191–203.

Zaman, A. U., Sofia, M., & Veranika, N. (2010). Green marketing or green wash? A comparative study of consumers' behavior on selected Eco and Fair trade labeling in Sweden. *Journal of Ecology and the Natural Environment, 2*(6), 104–111.

Zeit Studios. (2011). *ZEITGEIST: Moving Forward, Official Release*. Retrieved from www.youtube.com/user/TZMOfficialChannel

4

ZERO-WASTE IN URBAN SYSTEM

The notion of ZW

The biggest difference between waste and ZW is that waste is an unavoidable by-product that is created at the end of the life phase, and the substance needs to be disposed of or incinerated for proper management, whereas the concept of ZW directly challenges the common assumption of waste as a valueless and unavoidable by-product that is created at the end of the product's life phase. ZW acknowledges that waste is a 'misallocated resource' or 'resource in transition' which is produced during the intermediate phases of production and consumption activities, and thus it should be recirculated to production processes through reuse, recycle, reassemble, resell, redesign, or reprocess (Zaman, 2016). ZW does not see 'waste' as a substance that must be disposed of or incinerated, but considers waste a resource that should be used again (Glavič & Lukman, 2007).

DEFINITIONS: 'ZERO-WASTE'

Designing and managing products and processes systematically to eliminate the waste and materials, conserve and recover all resources and not burn or bury them.

> Zero-waste is a goal that is ethical, economical, efficient and visionary, to guide people in changing their lifestyles and practices to emulate sustainable natural cycles, where all discarded materials are designed to become resources for others to use. Implementing zero-waste will eliminate all discharges to land, water or air that are a threat to planetary, human, animal or plant health.
>
> *(ZWIA, 2018)*

> The conservation of all resources by means of responsible production, consumption, reuse, and recovery of products, packaging, and materials without burning and with no discharges to land, water, or air that threaten the environment or human health.
>
> *(ZWIA, 2018)*
>
> Zero-waste is a design principle for the 21st Century that seeks to redesign the way resources and materials flow through society. Zero-waste requires eliminating subsidies for raw material extraction and waste disposal, and holding producers responsible for their products and packaging 'from the cradle to cradle.' The goal is to promote clean production, prevent pollution, and create communities in which all products are designed to be cycled safely back into the economy or environment.
>
> *(GRRN, 2013)*

From the definitions, it is quite clear that the notion of ZW is a visionary concept, a combination of planning, design, and management ideas that aim for SWM by designing out waste and protecting the environment.

This implies that ZW as a concept is a target for transforming WMSs towards a 'CE', where extraction, production, and consumption become increasingly waste-free. ZW does not mean that we would not create any 'waste' in the transition of resource extraction, production, and consumption; rather, it means no 'waste' would be wasted under the circular economic system which underpins the principles of the ZW philosophy. ZW is a vision, a target, and an aspiration, and it does not refer to the numeric number zero. The difference between traditional waste management and ZW management is given in Table 4.1.

TABLE 4.1 The difference between traditional waste management and ZW management

Traditional waste management	ZW management
Waste considered the end of the resource life cycle	Waste considered a resource in transition or an intermediate phase of a resource life cycle
Perceives waste as mainly a technological problem and thus often relies on engineering solutions	Perceives waste as both a social and technological problem and thus seeks social technology (reuse/recycling) as well as engineering (AD) solutions
Depends highly on landfill and incineration technologies.	Depends highly on waste avoidance and prohibits landfill and incineration technologies
Allows resource depletion for recovering resources from waste – i.e. waste-to-energy	Conservation of resources instead of depletion – i.e. recycle instead of waste-to-energy
Limited job opportunities	Comparatively a higher number of job opportunities

The development of ZWin theory, practice, and research

Paul Palmer first used the term 'ZW' in 1973 for recovering resources from chemicals (Palmer, 2004). During the late 1970s, the idea of ZW failed to attract many people's attention due to their lack of understanding of the links between waste management and design, production, and consumption activities. The term 'ZW' became familiar and applied widely in waste management research and programmes in the late 1990s when the concept of 'C2C' design principles were introduced by McDonough and Braungart (2002) in response to the principles of ecologically sustainable development (Tennant-Wood, 2003). Several organizations worldwide have adopted the concept of ZW, setting a target of ZW disposal to landfills. The radical idea of 'no waste' or 'ZW' took hold in municipalities in Canberra, Australia, where a community consultation process resulted in Canberra becoming the first city in the world to adopt an official target of 'No Waste by 2010' (Snow & Dickinson, 2003, p. 5).

The establishment of the Zero Waste New Zealand Trust in 1997 to support waste minimization initiatives began the ZW movement in New Zealand. The trust's stated goal was to create 'a closed loop materials economy; one where products are made to be reused, repaired and recycled, an economy that minimises and ultimately eliminates waste' (Tennant-Wood, 2003). Since then, ZW programmes have been implemented in different developed countries around the globe. In addition, the concept has been adopted and used with analogous terms in different languages (French, German) in different countries (Krausz, 2012). The key milestones and events pertaining to ZW development are given in Table 4.2.

The ZW concept recognizes recycling as a powerful tool in the critique of excessive consumption waste generation, corporate responsibility, and fundamental causes of environmental destruction (GRRN, 2013). ZW does not see waste as a material that must be disposed of or incinerated but treats waste as a resource that can be used again and so takes full advantage of waste's potential (Glavič & Lukman, 2007). However, the concept is used in conflicting ways in different cities; for example, Zero Waste India claims mass burning technology (incineration) is a ZW solution (ZWI, 2013). Incineration has been considered a solution for developing a ZW society in Borås City, Sweden (Björk, 2012; Rajendran, Björk, & Taherzadeh, 2013), which is contradictory to the core ZW philosophy – i.e. conserve and recover all resources and not burn or bury them (ZWIA, 2004).

Colon and Fawcett (2006) conducted community-based case studies of ZW in two Indian cities. According to Colon and Fawcett, ZW management is a way to clean the neighbourhood by organizing a door-to-door collection service of household waste and sweeping the streets, to alleviate the burden on land from dumping by recycling as much waste as possible locally, and to give recognized social status to local waste pickers by employing them to do the job. Therefore, ZW is not only improving the quality of life and protecting the environment but also creating earning possibilities through recycling and improving the social status of collectors.

TABLE 4.2 The key milestones and events on ZW development

Year	Country	Milestones/events
1970s	USA	The term 'ZW' was coined by Paul Palmer.
1986	USA	The National Coalition against Mass Burn Incineration was formed.
1988	USA	Seattle introduced the pay-as-you-throw (PAYT) system.
1989	USA	The California Integrated Waste Management Act was passed to achieve 25% waste diversion from landfills by 1995 and 50% by 2000.
1990	Sweden	Thomas Lindquist introduced 'Extended Producer Responsibility'.
1995	Australia	Canberra passed the 'No Waste by 2010' bill.
1997	New Zealand, USA	The Zero Waste New Zealand Trust was established. The California Resource Recovery Association (CRRA) organized a conference on ZW.
1998	USA	ZW was included as guiding principles in North Carolina, Seattle, Washington, and Washington, DC.
1999	USA	The CRRA organized ZW conferences in San Francisco.
2000	USA	The Global Alliance for Incinerator Alternatives was formed.
2001	USA	Grassroots Recycling Network published *A Citizen's Agenda for Zero Waste*.
2001	Australia	*Towards Zero Waste Action Plans, WA Vision for Waste 2020*.
2002	New Zealand, USA	The book *Cradle-to-Cradle* was published. ZWIA was established. The First ZW summit was held in New Zealand.
2004	Australia, USA	ZWIA gives a working definition of ZW. The GrassRoots Recycling Network (GRRN) adopts ZW business principles. ZW SA was established in South Australia.
2008	USA	The Sierra Club adopted a ZW producer responsibility policy.
2012	USA	The documentary film *Trashed* premiered at the Cannes Film Festival. The Zero Waste Business Council was established in the USA.
2017	USA	Zero Waste Development and Expansion Act of 2017 passed.
2018	China	From 1 January 2018, China banned importing 24 categories of solid waste. China stopped importing plastic for recycling by setting the acceptable contamination level at 0.05% – compared to the up to 10% it previously accepted.
2018	Global (C40, UK)	Twenty-three global cities and regions advance towards ZW. This commitment will avoid disposal of at least 87 million tonnes of waste by 2030.
2018	Australia	The Australian governments set a 100% packaging target – i.e. all Australian packaging will be recyclable, compostable, or reusable by 2025.
2019	Singapore	Singapore has designated 2019 as the year towards ZW.

Connett (2013, p. 343), in his article, outlines a strategy for ZW: 'The zero waste strategy says no to incinerators, no to mega-landfills, no to the throwaway society and yes to a sustainable society'. Connett also suggests that two 'R's – i.e. 'redesign' and 'responsibility' – are required for ZW in addition to the three 'R' (reduce, reuse, recycle) principles. To achieve the idealistic goal in a realistic time frame, Connett proposed ten steps to ZW. The steps are (i) source separation; (ii) door-to-door collection system; (iii) composting, recycling, reducing; (iv) reuse, repair, and deconstruction of old buildings; (v) waste reduction initiatives; (vi) economic incentives; (vii) residual separation; (viii) ZW research facilities; (ix) industrial responsibility; and (x) interim landfill (Connett, 2013, pp. 347–357). ZW calls for a shift in focus from the 'end-of-pipe' management of waste to the management of resources from extraction to design and use and eventual discard.

According to Curran and William (2012), ZW is a whole-system approach that aims to eliminate rather than manage waste. Waste diversion from landfill and incineration is a design philosophy for eliminating waste at the source and all points down the supply chain. It rejects our current one-way linear resource use and disposal culture in favour of a 'closed-loop' circular system modelled on nature's successful strategies. The whole-system approach includes the ZW of resources, zero emissions, ZW in activities, ZW product life, and zero use of toxics. The study, however, presents very little evidence on how to achieve these goals. The key strategies identified by the study to achieve ZW were eco-design, industrial symbiosis, closed-loop supply chain, use of new technology, product stewardship, life-cycle assessment, and environmental management system.

Lehmann (2010) proposed 'ZW' as one of the 15 principles for green urbanism. For sustainable urban design, resources should be utilized efficiently, and according to Lehmann, 'Sustainable waste management means to turn waste into resource' (Lehmann, 2010, p. 232). The ZW concept directly challenges the common assumptions that waste is unavoidable and has no value, and it redefines waste as misallocated resources that must be recovered (Lehmann, 2011, p. 28).

Braungart, McDonough, and Bollinger (2007) have found divergence between zero emission and eco-effectiveness as ZW encompasses volume minimization, reduced consumption, design for repair and durability, and design for recycling and reduced toxicity. Eco-effectiveness, on the other hand, emphasizes C2C design and celebrates the creative and extravagant application of materials and allows for short product lifespans under the condition that all materials retain their status as productive resources. However, from a holistic point of view, ZW and eco-effectiveness strategies are not contradictory to each other; instead, they can be supportive to each other to promote holistic sustainable development. Therefore, it is important to integrate eco-effectiveness in developing ZWS.

In studies of ZW planning and strategies (Campbell, 2007; Cole, Osmani, Quddus, Wheatley, & Kay, 2014; Fehr, 2012; Phillips, Tudor, Bird, & Bates, 2011; Song, Li, & Zeng), the authors acknowledge that ZWS require short- to long-term action plans to achieve ZW goals. Therefore, identifying indicators and setting priorities and milestones in ZW programmes are important for the motivation and success of ZW initiatives.

ZW initiatives have been considered in many different places over the last decade based on the local contexts. The ZW initiatives have been adopted and implemented from the micro-to-macro-level – i.e. family, communities, organizations, industries, cities, and countries (Alexander, 2002; GAIA, 2012; Johnson, 2013; Phillips et al., 2011). A set of milestones has been identified to promote ZW goals. Measures of success in meeting the goals are outlined in ZWIA's ZW business principles and the global principles for ZW communities. Businesses and communities that achieve over 90% diversion of waste from landfills and incinerators are considered successful in achieving ZW (ZWIA, 2013).

The government in England launched a zero-waste places (ZWP) initiative to develop innovative and exemplary practice to drive behaviour change (Phillips et al., 2011). In the case study of ZWP, it was recommended that the definition of ZW should be broadened to encompass all resources (waste, energy, water, transport) and include carbon reduction. The ZW-certified standard was also developed to assess the performance of selected ZW-identified places.

ZW practices are not only about sustainable behaviour and resource management but also carbon emissions reduction through ZW practices. The main barriers to ZW include the following: short-term thinking of producers and consumers, lack of consistency in legislation across the states, procurement versus sustainability, the attitude that the cheapest offers get commissioned, and lack of community willingness to pay (Sridhar & Shibu, 2004). This economic aspect is critical, since unsustainable systems of production and consumption are perpetuated through the 'externalization' of environmental costs enabled by these evident barriers to ZW. To create a ZW management system will, therefore, also require economic incentives and clear policies to implement ZW objectives.

For an effective implementation of the ZW philosophy, we need to understand the 'urban metabolism' – i.e. the flow of materials and energy within cities (Baccini & Brunner, 2012; Wolman, 1965). The urban metabolism provides a systematic way of analysing resource flow, recycling of waste, and conservation of energy and environment.

Material flow in an urban system

The city is often considered a combination of 'systems' and 'biology' (Marcotullio & Boyle, 2003), and the city can be compared to a cell in the human body. A cell is composed of different elements, such as the cell membrane, nucleolus, mitochondrion, and a nucleus. The nucleus is the core of a cell from which a cell is developed. Similarly, a city has different elements, such as the boundary, infrastructure, and businesses, communities, families, and individuals. The most important core element of the city is the individual inhabitant. Individuals form the families, communities, businesses, and social organizations which give the city shape.

The metabolic requirement of the city is defined as all the materials and commodities needed to sustain the city's inhabitants at home, at work, and at play (Wolman, 1965). Urban systems have formed a complex global network that includes terrestrial and ecological aspects, and this network is called the 'anthroposphere' (Baccini & Brunner, 2012). The anthroposphere combines a complex technical system of energy, material, and information flows. An urban metabolism – i.e. an anthroposphere – functions well when all elements of the city are integrated properly. A city's elements can be divided into two groups, 'soft' and 'hard', which interact (Yusof, Musa, & Rahman, 2012). Soft elements act as a regulatory component for the hard elements. Elements such as infrastructure, policies, regulations, and systems combine to run the city's metabolic systems from the individual level to the largest scale. According to the level of scope, individual, family, community, and business are the different scales on which a city's metabolism operates.

Material flow in the form of products and commodities and end-of-life waste is one of the most complex systems in the built environment. The industry's dependency on ever-increasing demand for natural resources is depleting the environment and threatening the future of human existence. In most technologically advanced countries, such as the USA and UK, only 1%–2% of the total material mass is being used six months after the product sale (Hawken, Lovins, & Lovins, 1999; Watson, 2009). This means around 98% of the resources used in the production of goods becomes waste within six months. This continuous demand for resources which are turned into waste cannot continue forever due to a global limit on finite resources. It is important to better understand the material flow in our cities as a part of the consumption cycle to solve the waste problem. Based on the nature of resource use, there are broadly two types of material flow in our society:

i   Linear material flow
ii Circular material flow

Linear material flow in cities

In a city with a linear metabolism, what is needed is taken from a vast area, with no thought for the consequences, and what remains is thrown away. Input is unrelated to the output (Girardet, 1992). At present, all cities have a linear metabolism (i.e. take-make-use-dispose). Such cities take resources, food, energy, minerals, etc., not only from their territories but also from distant parts of the world as inputs, and after consumption, they produce emissions and waste as outputs. In a linear metabolic city, resources are used once in the production process and then become waste; therefore, resource use in a linear metabolism is very inefficient. Most of the resources used in the manufacture of a product are turned into waste after a very short period of use, resulting in huge daily waste levels.

In a linear metabolism, a major portion of the recoverable waste goes either to landfills or incineration, which is similar to the current practice where globally 85% of the waste goes to landfills. Even though modern technology allows both sanitary landfills and incineration to produce energy, it is the least favourable option in a sustainable WMS. Despite our knowledge of the depletion and scarcity of our natural resources, we produce, consume, and manage our resources in a wasteful

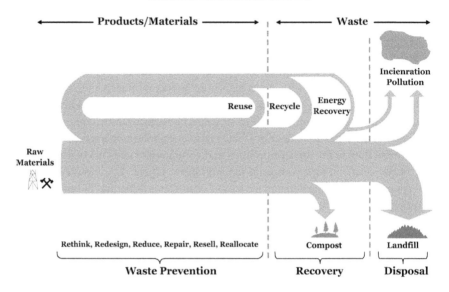

FIGURE 4.1 A schematic diagram of linear material flows in an existing city

Source: Adapted from ZWA (2011) with permission

system without protecting our environment. Since a linear metabolism uses more resources without circulating resources in the production process to meet its inhabitants' needs, the amount of urban ecological space (land area required to provide resources for inhabitants) required is significantly higher in a linear metabolic city. Since the Industrial Revolution, we have imposed an unsustainable linear system: from extraction to production, to consumption, to waste, which mostly ends up in landfills, as shown in Figure 4.1.

Circular material flow and the ZWC

In a circular metabolism, waste is recycled, reused, and recovered in a way which allows resources to be used again and again. Since a circular metabolism uses fewer resources by circulating resources in the production process to meet its inhabitants' needs, the amount of urban ecological space needed in such a city is significantly less than in a linear metabolism (Lehmann, 2011). For example, biomass from organics and food waste can be composted or used to produce gas using AD technology.

Every output can also be used as an input into the production system, thereby affecting a far smaller land area (Girardet, 1992). Circular metabolisms have a closed-loop material flow system, and therefore resources are properly managed over their whole life cycle. Avoidable waste is eliminated from the very beginning of the production system through innovative design practices, so a circular

Circular Material Flows

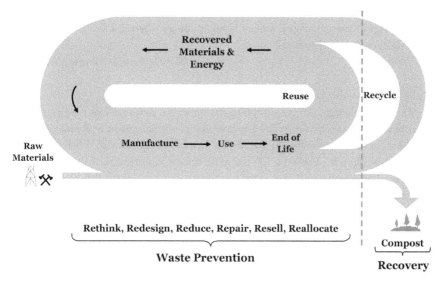

FIGURE 4.2   A schematic diagram of circular (closed-loop) material flows

Source: Adapted from ZWA (2011) with permission

metabolism eventually produces no waste and requires no landfill: it becomes a ZW city. Figure 4.2 shows the schematic material flow in a 'ZW city'.

Having a circular urban metabolism is one of the core principles for developing a ZWC. ZWC means a system where various elements of an urban system maintain the circularity of materials to conserve environment and maximize resource efficiency. In a ZWC, designers and producers apply a C2C design principle with a take-back system so that potentially there would be no waste from the products if they complete the whole material flow (i.e. extraction, production, consumption, return, and re-manufacturing). In ZW cities, citizens consume resources efficiently by maintaining environmental stewardship. 'Waste' in a ZW city is generated in an intermediate phase of the resource consumption process and thus the 'waste' is recirculated in production processes by recovery of all resources from the end-of-life products.

The CE is the core of the ZW philosophy

In the light of various challenges and the underlying limitations of a linear economy – i.e. take-make-use-dispose – the concept of a CE is considered a solution for harmonizing ambitions for economic growth and environmental protection (Lieder & Rashid, 2016).

> By circular, an economy is envisaged as having no net effect on the environment; rather it restores any damage done in resource acquisition, while

ensuring little waste is generated throughout the production process and in the life history of the product. The word circular has a second, inferred, descriptive meaning, which relates to the concept of the cycle. There are two cycles of particular importance here: the biogeochemical cycles and the idea of recycling of products.

(Murray, Skene, & Haynes, 2017, p. 7)

Table 4.3 shows the various definitions of CE.

The CE challenges our consumption-driven linear 'take-make-dispose' economy; it embraces a restorative system by integrating bio-mimicry, industrial ecology, C2C, and blue economy principles in the core of its strategic framework (EMF, 2013).

Certainly, the idea behind a CE has existed for a long time; in fact, the concept of material circularity existed throughout history. For example, before the Industrial Revolution, the concept of waste as unwanted or unusable materials was unknown due to craftsmanship and hard production methods (Strasser, 2000). As early as 1848, August Wilhelm von Hoffman, the first president of the Royal Society of Chemistry, stated 'In an ideal chemical factory there is, strictly speaking, no waste but only products. The better a real factory makes use of its waste, the closer it gets to its ideal, the bigger is the profit'(Cucciniello & Cespi, 2018). According to Turner and Pearce (1990), the term 'CE' was first used in Western literature in the 1980s to describe a closed-system of economy-environment interactions. However, the term was first used to refer to a closed-loop economy by Stahel and Reday-Mulvey (1976).

In the post-World War II era, the principle of planned obsolescence was introduced by producing disposable products with the specific purpose of being discarded after a single use with the intention of creating more jobs through economic growth. Within a short period of time, the world experienced increased economic growth, however, the policy stimulates the throwaway practices and enhances linear consumption behaviour. One of the key consequences of the throwaway lifestyle is

TABLE 4.3 Various definitions of CE

Focus	Definitions of CE
Eco-industrial prosperity	Realization of closed-loop material flow in the whole economic system that follows the principles of reducing resource use, reusing, and recycling.
3R principles	The core of CE is the closed-circular flow of materials and the use of raw materials and energy through multiple phases.
Economic aspects	CE is closed-loop material flow in the whole economic system that minimizes matter, energy flow, and environmental deterioration without restricting economic growth or social and technical progress.
Industrial economy	CE is an industrial economy that is restorative or regenerative by intention and design.

the massive environmental degradation due to pollution from the manufacturing process and disposal of massive amounts of waste to landfills (Subramanian, 2000).

The rapid economic development in China caused a significant environmental degradation. Realizing the consequence in 2002, the government of China adapted a new development strategy based on CE principles and approved the Circular Economy Promotion Law of the People's Republic of China, which went into effect in January 2009 (Faegre & Benson, 2008). Various scholars affirm that the core principle of the eco-initiatives is to eventually establish a so-called CE or 'closed-loop' economy (Mathews & Tan, 2011; Yang & Feng, 2008). The economic opportunities of CE have been outlined in the EU, emphasizing advantages for the industrial sector, such as reduction of material costs or larger profit pools (EMF, 2013).

The principles and a comprehensive framework on CE

The term 'CE' was unfamiliar just a few years ago; now the concept is taking shape as a viable, practical alternative to the current linear economic model. In a recent report on the CE published by the Ellen MacArthur Foundation, the authors asserted that despite increasing eco-efficiency in modern production processes, energy use and resource depletion has been accelerating due to the rebound effect, and thus linear consumption is reaching its limits (EMF, 2014, p. 13). Thus instead of using eco-efficiency to minimize material flows, eco-effectiveness transforms products and related material flows to support ecological systems and economic growth by refurbishing, remanufacturing, and recycling used products. The report claims that the cost of remanufacturing mobile phones could be reduced by 50% per device if the industry made phones easier to take apart, improved the reverse cycle, and offered incentives to return phones (EMF, 2014, p. 17). The CE aims to design out waste and generate employment through this systemic reconfiguration.

Many nations from all over the globe (China, Japan, England, many European countries, etc.) have embraced the CE as a strategic policy for creating a more robust economy (EMF, 2014; House of Commons, 2014; Ji, Zhang, & Hao, 2012) by increasing resource effectiveness through recycling and recovering resources. However, an effective tool is essential to monitor the real progress in a CE which leads to developing ZW cities. As this suggests, policy change and economic drivers are necessary to encourage producers and consumers to move from a linear economy towards a circular one – an economy that will support and integrate the principles and goals of ZW. According to the Ellen MacArthur Foundation (2017), CE is based on three principles:

- Design out waste and pollution
- Keep products and materials in use
- Regenerate natural systems

There are two types of material flows in modern society – i.e. biological materials and technological materials. Most of these biological and technological materials

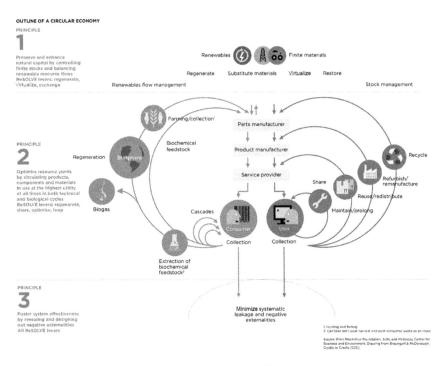

FIGURE 4.3 The key principles of CE – an industrial system that is restorative by design

Source: Ellen MacArthur Foundation (2017) with permission

are currently being lost from the leakage via incineration and landfills (as shown in Figure 4.3). By designing out waste and pollution, we can preserve and enhance natural capital. By recirculating both biological and technical materials within the system, we can optimize resource yield and achieve the highest utility at all times. By minimizing systematic leakage and negative externalities, we can foster system effectiveness.

The needs for an emerging new economy

The ZW philosophy aims to create a CE by increasing eco-effectiveness and economic growth by refurbishing, remanufacturing, and recycling used products and generating employment. The CE-based urban systems integrate industrial ecology, C2C design, cleaner production, and blue economy ideas and phases out waste creation. Therefore, there is an urgency to develop an alternative WMS and an innovative performance assessment tool that can measure the true ZW progress in a circular urban system.

The perceptions and definitions of 'waste' vary from one context to the next. However, the main reason for perceiving anything as waste is that it is 'not valued' anymore. This valuing (or not valuing) can be normative, socio-cultural, and or economic. ZW is an aspirational goal for many cities and countries. Several cities and countries have taken various initiatives to achieve the ZW goals. Despite a number of initiatives in ZW, common ground and understanding of ZW is still missing. There is no definite 'ZW' strategy that cities can apply to become ZW cities, and a consistent model is unavailable. In addition, there is a lack of effective and applicable tools for measuring the performance of cities towards their ZW goals, which makes them especially difficult to achieve.

The ZW philosophy follows the fundamental principles of environmental stewardship in every step of resource extraction, product design, production, consumption, and waste management. ZW does not mean 100% recycling or achieving a 100% diversion rate but rather creating 0% unwanted waste from the production and consumption activities through improved C2C design and sustainable consumption behaviour. Surely, if ZW is a progressive movement towards total diversion and resource recovery, it is important to identify what it is about the case study cities that is particularly helpful in the scaling up of better practices.

In addition, a better understanding of resource and waste flow in cities is important for achieving ZW city goals. ZW cities consist of a closed-loop circular metabolic system, which is a fundamental requirement for environmental stewardship. By achieving ZW goals through their circular metabolism, cities fulfil the goals of the eco-city and sustainable development. It is important to understand that the city metabolism is interlinked with the social and industrial metabolisms (Ayres & Simonis, 1994). Hence a holistic understanding of the urban system metabolism and synergies are essential for achieving the ZW city goals. To better understand the material flow and urban metabolism, a comparative analysis of the WMS in the case study cities is essential.

ZW is as an emerging philosophy; it requires a common understanding of every stage in society (from individual, community, industry, and business) while implementing ZW initiatives. Reliable, effective, and applicable ZWS are required to achieve the visionary ZW goals. From the literature review, it is evident that the concept of ZW is built on the philosophy of long-term sustainable development where products are required to be designed by applying C2C approaches.

References

Alexander, S. (2002). *Green Hotels: Opportunities and Resources for Success*. Retrieved from www.zerowaste.org/publications/GREEN_HO.PDF

Ayres, R. U., & Simonis, U. E. (1994). *Industrial Metabolism: Restructuring for Sustainable Development*. Tokyo: United Nations University Press.

Baccini, P., & Brunner, P. H. (2012). *Metabolism of the Anthroposphere: Analysis, Evaluation, Design* (2nd ed.). Cambridge and London: MIT Press.

Björk, H. (2012). *Zero Waste Society in Borås City, Sweden-Strategies to Action*. Retrieved from www.uncrd.or.jp/content/documents/Hans%20Bjork-Sweden.pdf

Braungart, M., McDonough, W., & Bollinger, A. (2007). Cradle-to-cradle design: Creating healthy emissions: A strategy for eco-effective product and system design. *Journal of Cleaner Production, 15*(13–14), 1337–1348. doi:10.1016/j.jclepro.2006.08.003

Campbell, N. (2007). Setting the standard for zero waste. *Petroleum Review, 61*(731 Supplement), 6–7, 15. Retrieved from www.scopus.com/inward/record.url?eid=2-s2.0-37349107435& partnerID=40&md5=c1587b3681360c58a54705d3eedeaf27

Cole, C., Osmani, M., Quddus, M., Wheatley, A., & Kay, K. (2014). Towards a zero waste strategy for an English local authority. *Resources, Conservation and Recycling, 89* (2014), 64–75

Colon, M., & Fawcett, B. (2006). Community based household waste management: Lessons learnt from EXNORA's waste management scheme in tow South Indian Cities. *Habitat International, 30*, 916–931.

Connett, P. (2013). Zero waste 2020: Sustainability in our hand. In S. L. R. Crocker (Ed.), *Motivating Change: Sustainable Design and Behaviour in the Built Environment*. London: Earthscan.

Cucciniello, R., & Cespi, D. (2018). Recycling within the chemical industry: The circular economy era. *Recycling, 3*(2), 22.

Curran, T., & Williams, I. D. (2012). A zero waste vision for industrial networks in Europe. *Journal of Hazardous Materials, 207–208*(15 March), 3–7. doi:10.1016/j.jhazmat.2011.07.122

EMF. (2013). *The Circular Model: An Overview*. Retrieved from www.ellenmacarthurfoundation.org/circular-economy/circular-economy/the-circular-model-an-overview

EMF. (2014). *Towards the Circular Economy: Accelerating the Scale-Up across Global Supply Chains*. Retrieved from http://www3.weforum.org/docs/WEF_ENV_TowardsCircularEconomy_Report_2014.pdf

EMF. (2017). *What Is a Circular Economy?* Retrieved from www.ellenmacarthurfoundation.org/circular-economy/concept

Faegre and Benson. (2008). *China Law Update*. Retrieved from www.faegrebd.com/en/insights/publications/2008/10/circular-economy-promotion-law-of-the-peoples-republic-of-china

Fehr, M. (2012). Plotting targets for a zero waste strategy on the world summit time scale. In *Municipal Solid Waste* (pp. 1–24). Hauppauge NY: Nova Science Publishers Inc.

GAIA. (2012). *On the Road to Zero Waste: Successes and Lessons from around the World*. Retrieved from Berkley: www.no-burn.org/downloads/On%20the%20Road%20to%20Zero%20Waste.pdf

Girardet, H. (1992). *The Gaia Atlas of Cities: New Directions for Sustainable Urban Living*. London: Gaia Books.

Glavič, P., & Lukman, R. (2007). Review of sustainability terms and their definitions. *Journal of Cleaner Production, 15*(18), 1875–1885.

GRRN. (2013). *Principles of Zero Waste Zero Waste: A New Way to Look at Our Natural Resources*. Retrieved from http://archive.grrn.org/zerowaste/kit/briefing/principles1.pdf

Hawken, P., Lovins, A., & Lovins, L. H. (1999). *Natural Capitalism: Creating the Next Industrial Revolution*. New York: Little, Brown and Company.

House of Commons. (2014). *Growing a Circular Economy: Ending the Throwaway Society* (3). Retrieved from London: www.publications.parliament.uk/pa/cm201415/cmselect/cmenvaud/214/21402.htm

Ji, X., Zhang, Y., & Hao, L. (2012). Analyses of Japanese circular economy mode and its inspiration significance for China. *Advances in Asian Social Science, 3*(4).

Johnson, B. (2013). *Zero Waste Home: The Ultimate Guide to Simplify Your Life by Reducing Your Waste*. New York: Simon and Schuster Inc.

Krausz, R. (2012). *All for naught? A critical study of zero waste to landfill initiatives*. (Doctor of Philosophy), Lincoln University, New Zealand.

Lehmann, S. (2010). *The Principles of Green Urbanism: Transforming the City for Sustainability* (1st ed.). London: Earthscan.

Lieder, M., & Rashid, A. (2016). Towards circular economy implementation: a comprehensive review in context of manufacturing industry. *Journal of Cleaner Production, 115*, 36–51.

Lehmann, S. (2011). Optimizing urban material flows and waste streams through principles of zero waste and sustainable consumption. *MDPI Special Issue: Sustainable Buildings, 3*(1), 155–183. Retrieved from www.mdpi.com/journal/sustainability

Marcotullio, P. J., & Boyle, G. (2003). *Defining an Ecosystem Approach to Urban Management and Policy Development.* Retrieved from Tokyo: http://i.unu.edu/media/unu.edu/publication/28831/UNUIAS_UrbanReport.pdf

Mathews, J. A., & Tan, H. (2011). Progress toward a circular economy in China: The drivers (and inhibitors) of eco-industrial initiative. *Journal of Industrial Ecology, 15*(3), 435–457.

Murray, A., Skene, K., & Haynes, K. (2017). The circular economy: An interdisciplinary exploration of the concept and application in a global context. *Journal of Business Ethics, 140*(3), 369–380.

McDonough, W., and Braungart, M. (2002). *Cradle to Cradle: Remaking the Way We Make Things* (1st ed.). New York: North Point Press.

Palmer, P. (2004). *Getting to Zero Waste.* Sebastopol, CA: Purple Sky Press.

Phillips, P. S., Tudor, T., Bird, H., & Bates, M. (2011). A critical review of a key waste strategy initiative in England: Zero waste places projects 2008–2009. *Resources, Conservation and Recycling, 55*(3), 335–343.

Rajendran, K., Björk, H., & Taherzadeh, M. J. (2013). Borås, a zero waste city in Sweden. *Journal of Development Management, 1*(1), 3–8.

Snow, W., & Dickinson, J. (2003). *The Road to Zero Waste: Strategies for Sustainable Communities.* Retrieved from Auckland: www.zerowaste.co.nz/assets/Reports/roadtozerowaste150dpi.pdf

Song, Q., Li, J., & Zeng, X. Minimizing the increasing solid waste through zero waste strategy. *Journal of Cleaner Production,* (0). http://dx.doi.org/10.1016/j.jclepro.2014.08.027

Sridhar, R., & Shibu K. N. (2004). *Thanal Conservation Action and Information Network, Zero Waste Kovalam and Employment Opportunities.* Retrieved from http://krpcds.org/report/ZEROWASTE.pdf

Stahel, W., & Reday-Mulvey, G. (1976). *Jobs for Tomorrow: The Potential for Substituting Manpower for Energy, Report to the Commission of the European Communities (Now European Commission).* Brussels and New York: Vantage Press. Retrieved from www.product-life.org/en/about

Strasser, S. (2000). *Waste and Want: A Social History of Trash.* New York, USA: Henry Holt and Co.

Subramanian, P. (2000). Plastics recycling and waste management in the US. *Resources, Conservation and Recycling, 28*(3–4), 253–263.

Tennant-Wood, R. (2003). Going for zero: A comparative critical analysis of zero waste events in southern New South Wales. *Australasian Journal of Environmental Management, 10*(1), 46–55. Retrieved from www.scopus.com/inward/record.url?eid=2-s2.0-84893073351&partnerID=40&md5=2c9e73bf1392761292f4ed6b0374adb4

Turner, R. K., & Pearce, D. W. (1990). *The Ethical Foundations of Sustainable Economic Development.* London, UK: International Institute for Environment and Development.

Watson, M. (2009). Waste management. In R. Kitchen & N. Thrift (Eds.), *International Encyclopedia of Human Geography* (pp. 195–200). London: Elsevier Publication.

Wolman, A. (1965). The metabolism of cities. *Scientific American, 213*(3), 179–190. Retrieved from www.irows.ucr.edu/cd/courses/10/wolman.pdf

Yang, S., & Feng, N. (2008). A case study of industrial symbiosis: Nanning Sugar Co., Ltd. in China. *Resources, Conservation and Recycling, 52*(5), 813–820.

Yusof, J. M., Musa, R., & Rahman, S. A. (2012). *The effects of green image of retailers on shopping value and store loyalty*. Paper presented at the ASEAN Conference on Environment-Behaviour Studies, Bangkok, Thailand.

Zaman, A. U. (2016). A comprehensive study of the environmental and economic benefits of resource recovery from global waste management systems. *Journal of Cleaner Production, 124*, 41–50.

ZWA. (2011). Zero waste case. Zero Waste International Alliance. Retrieved from http://zwia.org/affiliates/

ZWI. (2013). *Zero Waste*. Retrieved from www.zerowasteindia.in/#about

ZWIA. (2004). *Zero Waste Definition Adopted by Zero Waste Planning Group*. Retrieved from www.zwia.org/main/index.php?option=com_content&view=article&id=49&Itemid=37

ZWIA. (2013). *Zero Waste Communities*. Retrieved from http://zwia.org/news/zero-waste-communities/

ZWIA. (2018). *Zero Waste Definition*. Retrieved from http://zwia.org/zero-waste-definition/

PART 2

Case studies of zero-waste

5

ZERO-WASTE PRACTICES IN OUR SOCIETY

Zero-waste practices around the world

Since the last decade, there has been an influx of interest among individuals, communities, industries, government institutes, city authorities, policymakers, and many other stakeholders regarding the ZW philosophy. ZW is not always portrayed as a saviour of the planet or an aspiration of an alternative lifestyle, but it has often been used as a tool for green washing. For example, one of the leading carpet companies in Europe claims it will achieve its ZW goals by 2020; however, in reality, the recycling rate is less than 3%, and almost all of the recycled carpets are either landfilled or incinerated (ZW France, 2017).

Despite controversy, debate, and challenges, ZW has been embraced and is being currently implemented in many parts of the world from the micro- (individual/family) to macro-level (city/region). The following sections provide a brief description of ZW practices in the context of family, community, business, and city.

ZW family

There are claims made by a number of people or families of living without producing any waste. Although most of the cases were publicized through social media and blogs, they can be regarded as aspirations that people are trying to achieve after realizing how our way of life is depleting the environment.

Families in California[1] or Phoenix,[2] USA, and Tasmania[3] in Australia and many other places in the world are trying to become ZW families. In all these families, one thing is common: they have embraced the ZW challenge and are working towards the aspirational ZW goals.

Bea Johnson and her family, living in Mill Valley, California, USA, represent one of the most renowned ZW cases on social media. They adopted the ZW lifestyle in 2008. After living the ZW lifestyle for a decade, the outcome is extraordinary in relation to well-being. Bea states, "We not only feel happier, but we also lead more meaningful lives based on experiences instead of stuff" (Zero Waste Home, 2018).

ZW practices in families around the world give mixed messages because the practitioners embrace different levels of enthusiasm, considering the practicality under the current system. ZW requires a transformation of our existing system, which is not 100% equipped to achieve ZW goals, and thus, under the existing situation, ZW practices could mean different things to different families. Whether ZW means to be vegan or using reusable cloth towels instead of single-use paper towels is a different discussion.

The most common practices that ZW families are participating in include the following:

- Focusing on needs instead of desire when it comes to consumption and shopping;
- Avoid shopping single-use goods (bottled water, bags, utensils, etc.);
- Avoid shopping goods with unnecessary packaging and buy bulk with the reusable/refillable bottles/jars from local growers;
- Reuse non-compostable items, such as jars, bottles, and cloths, as much as possible;
- Be mindful about what to buy and how it will contribute to waste generation and seek alternatives;
- Recycle whatever cannot be reused; and
- Compost all organic materials in the household.

Considering only MSW, it would be very difficult and challenging to achieve ZW goals, even though a number of families have shown how they created only a jarful of waste in a year instead of three different bins full of waste every week. However, it is also important to acknowledge that they achieved their goals because of their extreme dedication and desire to change their lifestyles. It is also common that almost all notable ZW families live in stand-alone houses with gardening and composting facilities. It may not be possible to maintain the same level of outcome if one lives in an apartment block without a composting facility.

Families working towards ZW goals make a number of products on their own just to avoid packaging – for example, toothpaste, soap, or shampoo, which could lead to health risks if the mixtures of ingredients are not handled properly. Families that currently maintain the ZW lifestyle surely show a real commitment to the ZW philosophy, and at the same, it is also understandable that to implement ZW in communities, businesses, and cities, we need to transform our existing systems, which are built on consumerism, and we need a dedicated commitment to change our lifestyles.

ZW community: the case of Kamikatsu, Japan

Kamikatsu community

Kamikatsu is a small town in Japan located in Katsuura District. A total of 1,556 people (in 2018) live in 788 households with a higher ratio of females than males (1:1.1) (Kamikatsu, 2018). Over half (50.3) of the population is over 65 years old, and one-quarter of the population is over 85 years old (Suzuki, 2018). Kamikatsu is hilly and dominated by a range of mountains higher than 1,000 meters above sea level with no formal door-to-door waste collection from the local authority; as such, the local community is responsible for collecting and managing their waste.

With the absence of a formal door-to-door waste collection system within the community, waste burning was a common practice in the area as it is in many countryside villages in Japan. However, the local community found it very difficult to cope with the changing characteristic of waste, mainly from the various types of plastic packaging, which creates significant pollution during burning. With the restriction on open burning and the mandate for recycling in the early 1990s, the local community in Kamikatsu started sorting recyclables from non-recyclables. However, the non-recyclables are still managed through incineration or landfills. Due to a high rate of dioxin pollution in Japan, and to meet the new pollution reduction standard, Kamikatsu's incineration plant was closed after operating for three years. As a result, the local community looked for an alternative solution to manage waste more sustainably. They consider ZW a part of their waste management policy and aim to be a 100% ZW town by 2020 (Sakano, 2017).

Kamikatsu Zero Waste Declaration

Kamikatsu is one of the first towns in Japan to declare the ZW goal in 2003, Table 5.1 presents the key waste management milestones at Kamikatsu. The Kamikatsu Zero Waste Declaration manifests the firm commitment to reduce waste to zero by 2020 (ZWA, 2018):

*   Kamikatsu will strive to foster ecologically conscience individuals.
*   Kamikatsu shall promote waste recycling and reusable resources to the best of its ability for eliminating waste incineration and landfills by 2020.
*   Residents of Kamikatsu shall join hands with people around the world to ensure a sustainable global environment.

ZW practices in the Kamikatsu community

Zero Waste Academy (ZWA) is one of the leading organizations working towards achieving ZW goals by changing people's mindsets, actions, and social systems to make waste non-waste in Kamikatsu (Sakano, 2017). Under the ZWSs, 100% of all organic waste is composted at home either with the traditional home composting

TABLE 5.1 The key waste management milestones at Kamikatsu

Year	Options	Brief descriptions
Before 1990s	Informal disposal/open burning	Absence of formal waste collection leads to open burning and informal disposal of household waste
1991–1995	Open incineration with alternative options	Subsidies for household composter, formation of the Kamikatsu Recycle Town Plan, along with open incineration.
1997	Nine segregation categories	Commenced separate collection of wastes under the National Recycling Act (clear, brown, and other coloured glass bottles, aluminum cans, steel cans, spray cans, milk cartons, incineration waste, bulk waste).
1998–2000	Twenty-two segregation categories	Concern regarding dioxin pollution from incineration and increasing the sorting categories from 9 to 22
2001–2015	Thirty-four waste categories	Shut down small incinerators and increased sorting categories from 22 to 34 to improve recycling efficiency. Volunteer group "Recycle Kamikatsu" helped transport waste from households to the collection centre
2016–2017	Forty-five segregation categories	Renewed the *Resource Segregation Guidebook* for residents and established the ZW accreditation system

Source: Adapted from ZWA (2018) with permission

method or an eclectic composting machine. The local government subsidize the cost of the composting devices, as this will help to reduce organic waste volume. Each household and store are responsible for washing, sorting, and delivering their trash to the recycling centre (Hibigaya Waste Station).

Waste at the recycling centre is sorted into 45 different categories (Sturmer, 2018). Each of the main waste types have subcategories, such as cans are subcategorized as aluminium, steel, and spraying cans; glass bottles are subcategorized as clear, brown, other, and returnable, which means a higher level of knowledge and understating of waste sorting and recycling are needed for the local community to recycle waste correctly. Figure 5.1 shows various sorting boxes for different types of waste.

All individuals are responsible for taking their waste to the recycling centre, given that a significant proportion of the community is very elderly, a waste collection system is offered once every two months. The local community not only needs to sort their non-organic waste into 45 different categories, but they also need to meet the recycling requirement, such as properly sorted, cleaned, and dried which is also true for the residents outside of Kamikatsu, and if waste is not properly cleaned and separated, it is not picked up (Sturmer, 2018). After 15 years of implementation of the ZW practices in Kamikatsu, the town currently recycles around 80%

FIGURE 5.1   Sorting options for various resource types at the Waste Station

Source: Courtesy of Akira Sakano, ZWA, Japan

of its waste, and the remaining 20% that can't currently be processed – things like nappies and certain types of plastics – gets sent off to be incinerated (Garfield, 2018; Sturmer, 2018).

At the beginning of the ZW programme, the community found it very difficult, as it was time-consuming and needed extra effort to meet the recycling requirements. For an ageing and declining community like Kamikatsu, correct recycling into a vast number of waste categories is not simple; in fact, a survey in 2008 showed that around 40% of residents were still unhappy about at least one aspect of the ZW policy, which is washing each recyclable item before sending it to the recycling centre (McCurry, 2008). This has become the norm after a decade-long practice. According to Akira Sakano, chair of the board of directors of the ZWA, the sheer inconvenience of the process can act as a deterrent to excess consumption in the first place, and the detailed categorization can make people think about what they should buy, how much, and when – i.e. beginning of the problem (Garfield, 2018).

ZW practices in business

Fuji Xerox: waste-free initiatives

Fuji Xerox ZW strategy

Fuji Xerox is a joint venture company known for its document-related products and services. Under the CSR, Fuji Xerox is committed to contributing to the sustainable development of society by putting its corporate philosophy into practice through sincere and fair business activities (Fuji Xerox, 2017). According to the company's 2017 sustainability report, sustainability is one of the top priorities, and it is supported by the highest authority. The company has adopted a long-term CSR plan 'Sustainable Value Plan 2030' to support its sustainable development goals. In 2000, Fuji Xerox made a ZW commitment not to send their recovered products to landfills, which led to the establishment of recycling systems across the Asia Pacific region. To achieve the waste-free goals, Xerox is aiming to produce waste-free products in waste-free facilities that promote waste-free customer workplaces.

Xerox's ZW programmes

Xerox's ZW aim is to design products, packaging, and supplies that make efficient use of resources, minimize waste, reuse material where feasible, and recycle what cannot be reused (Fuji Xerox, 2017). To meet this commitment, Xerox has put in place several programs:

- Xerox's Green World Alliance initiative provides a collection and reuse/recycling program for spent imaging supplies.
- Xerox's product take-back and recycling program manages equipment at end of life.
- Xerox is investing in technologies that reduce the creation of waste.

Xerox has embraced the product stewardship principle since the early 1990s, and it has pioneered the practice of converting end-of-life electronic equipment into products and parts that contain reused parts while meeting new product specifications for quality and performance. The company developed a comprehensive process for taking back end-of-life products and has established a remanufacture, parts reuse, and recycling program that fully supports the waste-free initiatives (Fuji Xerox, n.d.). While most manufacturers are shortening the lifespan of products, Xerox's manufacturing approach focuses on sustainable strategies to extend the lifespan of equipment, which is the core of the ZW philosophy. Xerox enables reuse according to the following hierarchy:

- Reuse of complete end items as used or new, depending on the condition of the machines (about 6% in 2010 in the USA)
- Remanufacturing or conversion into a newer-generation product or part (nearly 40% in 2010 in the USA sent for remanufacturing)
- Reuse of major modules, subcomponents, and parts for spares or manufacturing (in 2010, around 200,000 parts in the USA were sent to reuse/remanufacturing)
- Material recycling

In 2016, Xerox diverted around 94% of non-hazardous solid waste with a vision to drive the reuse/recycle rate to 100% by 2020. Currently, 99.5% of the end-of-life products either reused, remanufactured, recycled, or produce energy from waste (Fuji Xerox, 2017).

Adidas: ZW sporting project

An estimated 8 million metrics tonnes of plastic trash ends up in our oceans every year, which has formed five gigantic gyres. The prediction shows that if we continue to pollute our oceans, in the future, we will see more plastic waste in oceans than marine species. Adidas, as part of its sustainability initiative, partnered with Parley for the Oceans, an organization that works with the ocean's ecosystem. Adidas launched a ZW sporting project called Sport Infinity in 2015 with a plan for a new breed of sporting goods that will never be thrown away. Sport Infinity products have the potential to be recycled endlessly and combined into new products through a closed-loop supply chain of sport products (Adidas-Group, 2015).

Adidas-Parley's AIR approach is to avoid (A) through reducing and replacing materials with sustainable ones; intercept (I) through retrieving and recycling problematic materials, such as plastic waste from the ocean; and redesign (R) through creating new industry standards (Perley, 2018). In 2016, around 740 tonnes of plastic pollution were collected by the partnership organization Parley for the Oceans from the Maldives Indian Ocean to turn plastic waste into yarn (Figure 5.2; Perley, 2018).

The recycled plastic yarn is used to produce shoes and T-shirts, and the target was to produce one million shoes using ocean plastic (McCarthy, 2018). Each pair of sneakers takes 11 plastic bottles to make, which could mean that Adidas will recycle 55 million plastic bottles in 2018 if they hit their projected sales. In fact, Adidas

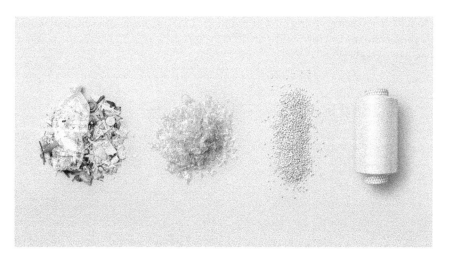

FIGURE 5.2   Converting ocean plastic into yarn

Source: Perley (2018), with permission

wants to make all products from recycled plastic by 2024 (WMC, 2018). As a result of the success of the project, Adidas started producing shoes made from reclaimed and recycled ocean trash (Borchardt, 2017). Even the Fédération Internationale de Football Association-FIFA Ballon d'Or winner Leo Messi praised the initiatives and stated, 'I am proud that Adidas is working to make sure that all their boots, including mine, are being made in a way that protects the environment. For me, this is the future of football' (Adidas-Group, 2015).

The varied notions of ZW

The concept of ZW and its goals are conceptualized differently by its practitioners, and it is understandable that the way an individual or family perceives ZW would be different from the way a company or business entity perceives it. Even the application methods and achievable goals would be significantly different when it comes to various stakeholders and their priorities in relation to waste management. However, one goal is common to all stakeholders practicing ZW: not generating any unnecessary and avoidable waste whether that is through innovative design practice, alternative consumption lifestyle, or consumer's and producer's environmental stewardship. Figure 5.3 conceptualizes the underpinning principle of ZW, which is value retained instead of depleting the value of the resources.

The 'value hill' concept was proposed through a collaboration initiative among Circle Economy, Nuovalente, Sustainable Finance Lab, and TU Delft in 2016 as a business strategy to retain a product's added value for as long as possible, if not forever (Circle Economy et al., 2016). Generally, value is added while the product moves 'uphill', and circular strategies keep the product at its highest value (top of the hill) for as long as possible. Circular design is one of the key principles to apply during the pre-use or the design, production, and distribution phases of a product. 'Tophill' is about the optimal use of resources, and sustainable consumption would be an effective tool. 'Downhill' is about value recovery, which involves the post-use phase of a product.

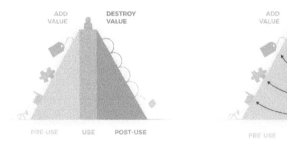

FIGURE 5.3 The value hill as a business strategy tool

Source: Credit: Circle Economy et al., 2016

Notes

1 Zero-waste Home: From a Blog to a Movement. Retrieved from https://zerowastehome.com/
2 Mlynek, Alex, 2018. How we became a zero waste family. Retrieved from www.todaysparent.com/family/activities/how-we-became-a-zero-waste-family/
3 1MW,2016. We Chat To Australia's Zero Waste Family. Retrieved from www.1millionwomen.com.au/blog/we-chat-australias-zero-waste-family/

References

Adidas-Group. (2015). *Messi's Boots Today, Recycled into Yours Tomorrow.* Retrieved from www.adidas-group.com/media/filer_public/51/cd/51cd8d06-a718-4445-a4e7-5fa99d601424/sport_infinity_press_release_en.pdf
Borchardt, D. (2017). *Next Week Adidas Releases A New Running Shoe Made from Ocean Plastic.* 1 May. Retrieved from www.forbes.com/sites/debraborchardt/2017/05/01/next-week-adidas-releases-a-new-running-shoe-made-from-ocean-plastic/#206905e67ebf
Circle Economy, Nuovalente, Sustainable Finance Lab, TU Delft. (2016). *Mastering Circular Business with the Value Hill, Circle Economy.* Retrieved from www.circle-economy.com/wp-content/uploads/2016/09/finance-white-paper-20160923.pdf
Fuji Xerox. (2017). *Sustainability Report 2017.* Retrieved from www.fujixerox.com/eng/company/csr/sr2017/pdf/2017e.pdf
Fuji Xerox. (n.d.). *Product Stewardship.* Retrieved from www.fujixerox.com.au/en/Sustainability/Our-Environment/Product-Stewardship
Garfield, L. (2018). *The Simple Way This Japanese Town Has Become Nearly Zero-Waste.* 31 January. Retrieved from www.independent.co.uk/environment/recycling-zero-waste-town-garbage-plastics-kamikatsu-japan-a8187301.html
Kamikatsu. (2018). *Population and Number of Households.* Retrieved from www.kamikatsu.jp/
McCarthy, J. (2018). *Adidas Is Making Even More Clothes from Recycled Ocean Plastic.* Retrieved from www.globalcitizen.org/en/content/adidas-clothes-from-recycled-ocean-plastic/
McCurry, J. (2008). *Climate Change: How Quest for Zero Waste Community Means Sorting the Rubbish 34 Ways.* Retrieved August 5, 2008, from www.theguardian.com/environment/2008/aug/05/recycling.japan
Perley. (2018). *The Parley Air Strategy.* Retrieved from www.parley.tv/oceanplastic/#the-mission
Sakano, A. (2017). Zero waste: A way to enrich your life & the society. *TEDx Talks.* Retrieved from www.youtube.com/watch?v=pgRnAsK18es
Sturmer, J. (2018). *Kamikatsu: The Japanese Town Working Towards a Zero-Waste Goal by 2020.* Retrieved from www.abc.net.au/news/2018-05-20/kamikatsu-the-japanese-town-with-45-different-recycling-bins/9776560
Suzuki, N. (2018). Creating an age-friendly community in a depopulated town in Japan: A sear for resilient ways to cherish a new commons as local cultural resources. In P. B. Stafford (Ed.), *The Global Age-Friendly Community Movement: A Critical Appraisal* (Vol. 5). Oxford and New York: Berghahn Books.
WMC. (2018). *Adidas Wants to Make All Products from Recycled Plastic by 2024.* Retrieved from https://wellmadeclothes.com.au/articles/AdidasWantsToMakeAllProductsFromRecycledPlasticBy2024/
Zero Waste Home. (2018). *Zero Waste Home.* Retrieved from https://zerowastehome.com/about/bea/

ZWA. (2018). *Zero Waste Kamikatsu: The Zero Waste Measures of Kamikatsu*. Retrieved from http://zwa.jp/wp/wp-content/themes/zwa/assets/pdf/ZeroWaste%20in%20Kami-katsu_infobook_2018.pdf

ZW France. (2017). *Swept under the Carpet: New Reports Reveal the Greenwash of the European Carpet Industry*. Retrieved from www.zerowastefrance.org/swept-under-carpet-report-waste/

6

ZERO-EWASTE

WEEE

Electronic waste or e-waste is the 'waste electrical and electronic equipment that is dependent on electric currents or electromagnetic fields in order to function (including all components, subassemblies and consumables which are part of the original equipment at the time of discarding)', and it includes (ABS, 2013)

- Consumer or entertainment electronics (e.g. televisions, DVD players, and tuners);
- Devices of office, information, and communications technology (e.g. computers, telephones, and mobile phones);
- Household appliances (e.g. fridges, washing machines, and microwaves);
- Lighting devices (e.g. desk lamps);
- Power tools (e.g. power drills) with the exclusion of stationary industrial devices; and
- Devices used for sport and leisure including toys (e.g. fitness machines and remote-control cars).

E-waste is one of the fastest-growing waste streams worldwide with an annual growth rate of 5% since 2005, leading to an overall amount of 44.7 million tonnes in 2016 (Ibanescu, Cailean, Teodosiu, & Fiore, 2018; ITU, 2017). Surprisingly, only 20% (8.9Mt) of the e-waste generated is documented as collected and recycled, and the remaining 80% (35.8 Mt) of e-waste is not documented (Baldé, Forti, Gray, Kuehr, & Stegmann, 2017).

It is predicted that the generation rate will continue to increase due to the rapid development of the ICT, particularly in 'smart technology', and a wider accessibility of smart gadgets with 'smart' functions that have a comparatively low price and product lifespan.

On average, e-waste constitutes 60% by weight of various metals, mostly rare-earth metals, such as lanthanum and cerium, and precious metals, such as gold and silver, and around 15% of its weight constitutes metals with high intrinsic value, such as copper, aluminium or iron, plastic, and glass. The majority of the e-waste was produced in Europe, the US, and Australasia in 2009 (Robinson, 2009). Given the rapid growth rate, complex composition, issues related to improper and unsafe treatment and disposal of e-waste are serious environmental and health concerns.

Emerging challenges of e-waste

There is no doubt that smart gadgets and electronic equipment are beneficial to our society for their innovative solutions. Not only in developed countries but also in developing countries, per capita electronic gadgets have increased significantly. For example, the number of mobile phones in the USA and China increased by 139% and 725% from 2000 to 2009, respectively (United Nations, 2011). Only 1 of 1,000 inhabitants in Bangladesh in 2000 had access to a mobile phone, whereas by 2014, the number increased by 803.

The ICT technologies have been evolving very quickly in recent years due to heavy demand for top-performing gadgets and services. Industries have invested a significant amount of money into new technology. The ICT is the highest research and development spending sector around the world, which received around $204.5 billion in 2016 (IRI, 2016). We have already experienced how fast the computer and mobile phone technologies have changed in just a few decades. This constant varying of technologies also brings new challenges when it comes to managing e-waste. Recycling of televisions is one such example of how fast technology has evolved from CRT (cathode ray tube), LCD (liquid-crystal display), plasma, and LED to OLED (organic light emitting diode). All these different types of TVs need different resource recovery technologies due to their varied physical properties.

Technological innovation, particularly in the electronic motor vehicle and photovoltaic solar panel energy storage technology bring another challenge. The core of the innovation is around battery technology, primarily the lithium-ion battery (LIB). Less than 3% of all LIBs produced globally are recycled, and from recycled LIB, the recovery of lithium is negligible (Vikström, Davidsson, & Höök, 2013; Wang et al., 2014). In Australia, only 2% of its 3,300 tonnes of LIB waste was recycled in 2016, and it is expected that the generation of the LIB will increase to 137,618 tonnes/year by 2036 (King, 2016).

Although LIBs are classified as dangerous goods and not hazardous waste in Australia, unsafe disposal of e-waste could be environmentally polluting and toxic for human health (lead, cadmium, and mercury contamination) (Randell, Pickin, & Grant, 2014). We cannot continue to deplete valuable resources anymore, as most of the precious materials are finite and the price of materials has also been increasing over time. The price of lithium metal increased around eightfold during 2002–2018 (Metalary, 2018).

Although the Basel Convention (Article 11) provides for bilateral, multilateral, and regional agreements regarding the transboundary movement of hazardous wastes or other wastes with parties or non-parties, the shipment of electronic waste from one county to another is a key challenge. A recent study shows that WEEE is transported with or without vehicles from developed countries, such as the USA, China, UK, and many European countries, to developing countries, such as Nigeria. Around 77% of all WEEE imported to Nigeria come from EU member states (Baldé et al., 2017).

The conundrum of innovation and planned obsolescence

On the dawn of the 'Great Depression', planned obsolescence was proposed for 'ending the depression through planned obsolescence' (London, 1932). Planned obsolescence was seen as the inspiring solution to ensure a 'permanent income' to all through systematic production and mass consumerism (London, 1932). London acknowledged that in 30 years' time, some commodities would have been destroyed and replaced around 15 times or less (London, 1932); however, almost a century later, the model has become one of the core challenges to sustainability because we are now replacing commodities and goods more frequently than the products' designed for a lifetime. With many other drivers, such as technological innovation, planned obsolescence has successfully transformed our thoughts and induced our 'desire to own something a little newer, a little better, a little sooner than is necessary' (Stevens, 1960).

Every year, leading mobile companies, such as Apple or Samsung, launch their flagship smartphones, and people all over the world are eager to buy the newest and the most 'modern, feature-rich' smartphone to stay on top of their social domains (Sinha, 2018). This means we are now creating more e-waste faster than ever before. However, the recent smartphone consumer survey data (Deloitte, 2018) shows that the number of people with a phone less than 18 months old has fallen from 61% in 2016 to 58% in 2018. Comparatively, the 18- to 30-month category has moved from 23% to 26% (2016 to 2018).

Planned obsolescence, particularly technological obsolescence, has become the core marketing strategy for most manufacturing companies. There are several occasions in which companies deliberately slowdown electronic products through system updates (Zhou, 2018). We often find that our almost newly bought laptop or computer becomes sluggish only after one to two years, whereas the average lifespan of a laptop is 11.8 years (Statista, 2019).

A new invention is always exciting and often brings new opportunities. The 3D-printing technology is expected to mark the new industrial revolution in the twenty-first century. Three-dimensional printing has already been used by the medical, aerospace, automotive, and many other industries to create product prototypes, product components, or fully functional organs (Gebler, Uiterkamp & Visser, 2014; Ventola, 2014). It is predicted that 3D printing will not only transform the way we design and manufacture things but also the whole supply chain of our existing manufacturing industries (Scott, 2017). Technology experts also believe that 3D printing will have a bigger economic impact than the Internet (Sedghi & Hall, 2015).

However, the biggest challenges we will face in the future when the technology is applied by the masses is managing the waste from 3D-printed products and infrastructure. The integrated and composite manufacturing techniques of 3D-printing technology will be more difficult and challenging for resource recovery and overall waste management.

The current trends of e-waste management: an overview

Already, close to half the world's population uses the Internet, and more and more people in the world will have the access to mobile networks and services soon. According to the global e-waste monitoring report, in 2016, Asia was the region that generated by far the largest amount of e-waste (18.2 Mt), followed by Europe (12.3 Mt), the Americas (11.3 Mt), Africa (2.2 Mt), and Oceania (0.7 Mt) (Baldé et al., 2017). However, Oceania was the highest generator of e-waste per inhabitant (17.3 kg/inh), followed by Europe (16.6 kg/inh) and the Americas (11.6 kg/inh). Table 6.1 presents the e-waste generation and collection in different continents.

Despite being an emerging, complex, and growing challenge, the adoption of e-waste legislation at the global level is still lacking, only 67 countries around the world have e-waste-related legislation (Baldé et al., 2017). The report estimated that approximately 55 billion euros in 2016 were wasted due to the loss of valuable raw materials from e-waste, which is more than the 2016 GDP of most countries in the world.

E-waste management in Australia

Australians are among the highest users of technology, resulting in the highest per capita e-waste generation in the world. Australia generated around 700,000 tonnes of e-waste in 2017, which is equivalent to about 28.68 kg per person (Bedo, 2018).

TABLE 6.1 E-waste generation and collection per continent

Indicator	Africa	Americas	Asia	Europe	Oceania
Country of origin	53	35	49	40	13
Population in region (millions)	1,174	977	4,364	738	39
Waste generation (kg/inh)	1.9	11.6	4.2	16.6	17.3
Total waste generation (Mt)	2.2	11.3	18.2	12.3	0.7
Documented to be collected and recycled (Mt)	0.004	1.9	2.7	4.3	0.04
Collection rate (in region)	0%	17%	15%	35%	6%

Adopted from Baldé et al. (2017)

Around 17 million televisions and 37 million computers have been sent to landfills up to 2008. In the last decade, Australians have hoarded 11 million phones and the total number of unused mobiles now sitting in homes is more than 25 million, which is equivalent to Australia's total population (Bedo, 2018). Only 7.5% of the e-waste generated in Australia is documented as collected and recycled (Baldé et al., 2017).

The National Television and Computer Recycling Scheme is one of the most significant producer responsibility schemes to be implemented in Australia under the Australian government's Product Stewardship Act 2011. The scheme provides Australian households and small businesses with access to industry-funded collection and recycling services for televisions and computers. The television and computer industries are required to fund collection and recycling of a proportion of the televisions and computers disposed of in Australia each year, with the aim to increase the rate of recycling of televisions and computers in Australia from an estimated 17% in 2010–2011 to 80% by 2021–2022 (Australian Government, 2012).

Australia has signed the Basel Convention on the Control of Transboundary Movements of Hazardous Wastes. According to the treaty and under the current national laws, e-waste should be sent to an approved domestic and international recycler which recycles e-waste safely to avoid serious toxic effects on humans and the environment. However, e-waste watchdog Basel Action Network (BAN) reported that Australia has allowed likely illegal export of hazardous e-waste to flow to developing countries (Palmer, Puckett, & Brandt, 2018). As e-waste is categorized as dangerous goods and not as hazardous goods in Australia, this presents a loop-hole in implementing the Basel Convention in Australia and allows local waste management companies to export e-waste to other countries.

The e-waste regulatory policy and strategy needs to be enforced for a better outcome of the e-waste management systems in Australia. There are four key pieces of legislation addressed to manage e-waste in Australia (Morris & Metternicht, 2016):

i   National Waste Policy 2009
ii   Product Stewardship Act 2011
iii Product Stewardship (Televisions and Computers) Regulations 2011
iv   National Television and Computer Recycling Scheme (NTCRS) 2011

The National Waste Policy sets Australia's waste management and resource recovery direction to 2020 and the Product Stewardship Act 2011 aims to reduce the impact of products by avoiding, reducing, and eliminating hazardous waste; to manage waste from products as a resource; and to ensure that waste from products are reused, recycled, recovered, treated, and disposed of in a safe, scientific, and environmentally sound way (Australian Government, 2011). The Product Stewardship regulations and NTCRS are implementing under the Product Stewardship Act 2011.

The Australian government reports that, to date, over 1,800 collection services have been made available to consumers. An estimated total of 122 kilotonnes (kt) of televisions and computers reached end of life in Australia in 2014–2015, out of which around 43 kt were recycled (35%) under this scheme. This a significant improvement from a recycling rate of only 9% in 2008 (Australian Government, 2017).

A new waste recycling industry based on closed-loop ZW philosophy is needed for properly recycling and recovering resources from WEEE. The Commonwealth Scientific and Industrial Research Organisation (CSIRO) study forecasts that the recycling LIB would be a billion-dollar industry (AU$3.09 billion) by 2036 in Australia alone. An alternative business model based on CE would support new opportunities and achieve the ZW vision. A recently published South Australian report estimated that CE would result in an increase of 25,000 jobs and a 27% decrease in GHG emissions by 2030 compared to a business-as-usual scenario in Australia (Lifecycles, 2017).

Urban mining is the pathway towards zero e-waste management

Electronic waste contains up to 60 different elements of the periodic table, and most of them are finite but recoverable. It is the economic limits or benchmarks which hinder the recovery of valuable materials from e-waste. Precious metals, including gold, silver, copper, platinum, and palladium, as well as valuable bulky materials, such as iron and aluminium, along with plastics which can be recycled, make e-waste an opportunity to create a new resource industry. Overall, the United Nation University (UNU) estimates that the resource perspective for secondary raw materials of e-waste is worth EU 55 billion of raw materials (Baldé et al., 2017). However, due to the poor recycling system around the globe, most resources have remained untapped and wasted. Globally, we wasted around 435kt of raw materials from smartphones, which could potential cost around 9.4 billion euros (Baldé et al., 2017).

The concept of 'landfill mining' and 'urban mining' have evolved in recent years as a result of realizing the potentials of the economic benefit of mining resources from waste. In landfill mining, the activities of extraction and process of wastes are limited in particular kinds of landfill deposits i.e. municipal landfills, mine tailings, etc., whereas in urban mining the activities extend to the process of reclaiming compounds and elements from any kind of anthropogenic stock, including buildings, infrastructure, industries, products (in and out of use), environmental media receiving anthropogenic emissions, etc. (Baccini & Brunner, 2012; Lederer, Laner, Fellner, & Recheberger, 2014).

According to Professor Veena Sahajwalla from the University of New South Wales (UNSW), urban mining will be cost-effective within the next decade, and even a living-lab-type 'microfactory' will generate profit in two to three years (Woollacott, 2018). It would not be a surprise to see in the future the focus of mining companies shift from virgin mining to urban mining because the latter is more cost-effective and there is a higher profitability and closed-loop supply of vital materials (Zeng, Mathews, & Li, 2018). The recycling and recovery of resources through urban mining requires a system change in our existing practice and will need government support.

The e-waste recycling supply chain is made up of three major steps: collection, pre-processing, and end-processing. In regard to the end-processing of e-waste based on a CE principle, the concept of an e-waste 'microfactory' has been floating around in recent years in which a small business or community is actively involved in recovering resources from waste using semi-automated mechanical systems. In Australia, the living-lab e-waste microfactory was launched in 2018 at the Centre for Sustainable Materials Research and Technology (SMaRT Centre), University of New South Wales (UNSW). According to SMaRT Centre director Professor Veena Sahajwalla, the e-waste microfactory is primarily focused on e-waste management – i.e. turning computer circuit boards into valuable metal alloys – and it can also turn many types of consumer waste, such as glass, plastic, and timber, into commercial materials and products (UNSW, 2018).

Using artificial intelligence and robotics is a new concept, and the world's leading mobile phone company, Apple, launched Liam in 2016. The robot can 'disassemble' every single part of an iPhone (Rujanavech et al., 2016). In 2018, Apple created a new robot called Daisy, along with its take-back programme called Give-Back in which customers can turn in devices in store or through Apple.com to be recycled (Deahl, 2018). Daisy is capable of taking apart nine different versions of the iPhone, and it can disassemble up to 200 iPhones an hour. Undoubtedly, Apple's Liam or Daisy project will guide the e-waste recycling industry to a better future; however, the initiative needs to be considered by every single producer and manufacturer. With a transformation of the current supply chain (collection, pre-processing, and end-processing) system of e-waste and implementation of the innovative end-processing system, we can manage our e-waste more sustainably than ever before.

Modular design to enable CE

Under the ZW philosophy, designers and producers need smarter and truly innovative solutions for the future. Around 4.3 billion people used mobile phones, half of them were smartphones, in 2016, and around 435 kiloton (kt of wasted mobile phones were generated across the globe (Baldé et al., 2017; Statista, 2018). Often, people change and buy a new phone despite having a fully functional one just to upgrade the product. The modular design which allows us to upgrade different components of a mobile phone, such as storage, camera, and processor, will help the user to upgrade the functionality that he or she wants and not change the 'almost' new smartphone. This will significantly increase resource efficiency and decrease the depletion of resources. This will bring small business opportunities to repair and upgrade smart gadgets based on modular design.

Google's Ara project (Figure 6.1) started in 2015 aimed to design LEGO-style bricks that could be attached, rearranged, and swapped out in seconds. However,

FIGURE 6.1 Project Ara, Google's modular smartphone (Google: creative commons)

Google ultimately shelved the plan, as the device cost would have been very expensive compared to competitors, and it needs to solve a number of technical hurdles (Statt, 2016).

The primary consideration of a closed-loop CE belongs to a product designer and manufacturer. Considering the design solution, producers need to embrace the product stewardship policy so that they can take care of the products they designed and retailed to consumers. The extended producers' responsibility under the product stewardship policy will ensure a closed-loop supply-chain system through a take-back system of the old products and goods. Figure 6.2 shows Apple's next-generation recycling robot 'Daisy' which dissemble different parts of old mobile phones. This will allow the producers to better understand the design and identify the problematic issues in relation to a CE.

The next level of responsibility belongs to the consumer, who can make better decisions about their shopping habits based on a sustainable consumption principle, such as collaborative consumption where the ownership of a product is not required. Instead of buying a product, the consumer can rent the necessary services so that the manufacturers/retailers can take care of the used products. This practice is not new; however, the model has been trailing among the mainstream ICT service providers around the world. In Australia, one can lease the recent model of mobile phone for a certain time (1–2 years), and the mobile operator will provide the necessary services and take care of the used phone after two years.

FIGURE 6.2 'Daisy', Apple's next-generation recycling robot

Source: Patently Apple, 2018

References

ABS. (2013). *4602.0.55.005: Waste Account, Australia, Experimental Estimates, 2013*. Retrieved from www.abs.gov.au/ausstats/abs@.nsf/Products/4602.0.55.005~2013~Main+Features ~Electronic+and+Electrical+Waste?OpenDocument

Australian Government. (2011). *Product Stewardship Act 2011*. Retrieved from www. legislation.gov.au/Details/C2011A00076

Australian Government. (2012). *Product Stewardship (Televisions and Computers) Regulations 2011*. Canberra: Australian Government.

Australian Government. (2017). *National Television and Computer Recycling Scheme*. Retrieved from www.environment.gov.au/protection/national-wastepolicy/television-and-computer-recycling-scheme

Baccini, P., & Brunner, P. H. (2012). *Metabolism of the Anthroposphere: Analysis, Evaluation, Design*. Cambridge and London: MIT Press.

Baldé, C., Forti, V., Gray, V., Kuehr, R., & Stegmann, P. (2017). *The Global E-Waste Monitor: 2017, United Nations University (UNU), International Telecommunication Union (ITU) & International Solid Waste Association (ISWA)*. Bonn, Geneva, and Vienna, United Nations University.

Bedo, S. (2018). *War on Waste Highlights Australia's E-Waste Problem*. 1 August. Retrieved from www.news.com.au/technology/gadgets/mobile-phones/war-on-waste-highlights-australias-ewaste-problem/news-story/24bf6be391f2ce702f32a01b38efb53e

Deahl, D. (2018). *Daisy Is Apple's New iPhone-Recycling Robot*. 19 April. Retrieved from www.theverge.com/2018/4/19/17258180/apple-daisy-iphone-recycling-robot

Deloitte. (2018). *Mobile Consumer Survey 2018: Behaviour Unlimited*. Retrieved from www2.deloitte.com/au/mobile-consumer-survey

Gebler, M., Uiterkamp, A. J. S., & Visser, C. (2014). A global sustainability perspective on 3D printing technologies. *Energy Policy*, *74*, 158–167.

Ibanescu, D., Cailean, D., Teodosiu, C., & Fiore, S. (2018). Assessment of the waste electrical and electronic equipment management systems profile and sustainability in developed and developing European Union countries. *Waste Management*, *73*, 39–53.

IRI. (2016). *Global R&D Funding Forecast*. Retrieved from www.iriweb.org/sites/default/files/2016GlobalR%26DFundingForecast_2.pdf

ITU. (2017). *Global E-Waste Monitor 2017*. Retrieved from www.itu.int/en/ITU-D/Climate-Change/Pages/Global-E-waste-Monitor-2017.aspx

King, S. E. A. (2016). Sustainable regional development through networks the case of ASPIRE (Advisory System for Processing, Innovation and Resource Efficiency) to support industrial symbiosis for SMEs. In UNCRD (Ed.), *Seventh Regional 3R Forum in Asia and the Pacific*. Melbourne: UNCRD.

Lederer, J., Laner, D., Fellner, J., & Recheberger, H. (2014). *A framework for the evaluation of anthropogenic resources based on natural resource evaluation concepts*. Paper presented at the 2nd Symposium on Urban Mining, Bergamo, Italy.

Lifecycles. (2017). The potential benefits of a circular economy in South Australia. Green Industries SA, Adelaide. Retrieved from https://www.greenindustries.sa.gov.au/_literature_172204/Potential_Benefits_of_a_Circular_Economy_in_South_Australia_-_report_(2017)

London, B. (1932). Ending the depression through planned obsolescence. University of Wisconsin, New York. Retrieved from https://babel.hathitrust.org/cgi/pt?id=wu.89097035273&view=1up&seq=6

Metalary. (2018). *Lithium Price*. Retrieved from www.metalary.com/lithium-price/

Morris, A., & Metternicht, G. (2016). Assessing effectiveness of WEEE management policy in Australia. *Journal of Environmental Management*, *181*, 218–230.

Palmer, H., Puckett, J., & Brandt, C. (2018). *Illegal Export of E-Waste from Australia: A Story as Told by GPS Trackers*. 8 August. Retrieved from http://wiki.ban.org/images/7/7c/Australian_e-Waste_Report_-_2018.pdf

Patently Apple. (2018). Today Apple introduces us to Liam's Big Sister 'Daisy', the next-generation Recycling Robot. Retrieved from https://www.patentlyapple.com/patently-apple/2018/04/today-apple-introduces-us-to-liams-big-sister-daisy-the-next-generation-recycling-robot.html

Randell, P., Pickin, J., & Grant, B. (2014). Waste generation and resource recovery in Australia: Reporting period 2010/11. Department of Environment and Energy, Canberra. Retrieved from https://www.environment.gov.au/protection/waste-resource-recovery/national-waste-reports/national-waste-report-2013/data-workbooks

Robinson, B. H. (2009). E-waste: An assessment of global production and environmental impacts. *Science of the Total Environment*, *408*(2), 183–191.

Rujanavech, C., Lessard, J., Chandler, S., Shannon, S., Dahmus, J., & Guzzo, R. (2016). Liam: An Innovation Story. Retrieved from www.apple.com/environment/pdf/Liam_white_paper_Sept2016.pdf

Scott, M. (2017). *3D Printing Will Change the Way We Make Things and Design Them in 2017.* 25 January. Retrieved from www.forbes.com/sites/mikescott/2017/01/25/3d-printing-will-change-the-way-we-make-things-in-2017/#451bdae4310e

Sedghi, S., & Hall, E. (2015). *3D Printing Will Have a Bigger Economic Impact Than the Internet, Technology Specialist Says.* Retrieved from www.abc.net.au/news/2015-04-01/3d-printing-impact-bigger-than-internet-expert-says/6365296

Sinha, M. (2018). *The Electronic Waste Problem: Planned Obsolescence Must Stop!* Retrieved from https://medium.com/@manal.21sinha/the-electronic-waste-problem-planned-obsolescence-must-stop-b680f5b2d220

Statista. (2018). *Mobile Phone Users Worldwide 2015–2020.* Retrieved from www.statista.com/statistics/274774/forecast-of-mobile-phone-users-worldwide/

Statista. (2019). *Average Lifespan of Consumer Electronics and Tech Devices in 2015 (in Years).* Retrieved from www.statista.com/statistics/688455/consumer-electronics-tech-device-average-lifespan/

Statt, N. (2016). *Google Confirms the End of Its Modular Project Ara Smartphone.* 2 September. Retrieved from www.theverge.com/2016/9/2/12775922/google-project-ara-modular-phone-suspended-confirm

Stevens, B. (1960). Planned obsolescence. *The Rotarian, 96*(2), 12.

United Nations. (2011). *Mobile Cellular Subscriptions Per 100 Inhabitants.* Retrieved from http://data.un.org/Data.aspx?d=ITU&f=ind1Code%3AI911#ITU

UNSW. (2018). *World-First E-Waste Microfactory Launched.* Retrieved from https://newsroom.unsw.edu.au/news/science-tech/world-first-e-waste-microfactory-launched-unsw

Ventola, C. L. (2014). Medical applications for 3D printing: Current and projected uses. *Pharmacy and Therapeutics, 39*(10), 704.

Vikström, H., Davidsson, S., & Höök, M. (2013). Lithium availability and future production outlooks. *Applied Energy, 110,* 252–266.

Wang, X., Gaustad, G., Babbitt, C. W., Bailey, C., Ganter, M. J., & Landi, B. J. (2014). Economic and environmental characterization of an evolving Li-ion battery waste stream. *Journal of Environmental Management, 135,* 126–134.

Woollacott, E. (2018). *E-Waste Mining Could Be Big Business: And Good for the Planet.* 6 July. Retrieved from www.bbc.com/news/business-44642176

Zeng, X., Mathews, J. A., & Li, J. (2018). Urban mining of e-waste is becoming more cost-effective than virgin mining. *Environmental Science & Technology, 52*(8), 4835–4841.

Zhou, M. (2018). *Apple and Samsung Fined for Slowing Down Phones with Updates.* Retrieved from www.cnet.com/news/apple-and-samsung-fined-for-slowing-down-phones-with-updates/

7

THE WHOLE HOUSE REUSE PROJECT

Demolition versus deconstruction

The extraction rates of minerals, ores, biomasses, and fossil fuels were tripled globally during 1970–2010 (Schandl, 2016). The circulation of global primary materials though trade has grown at an ever-increasing rate over the past four decades and around 10 billion tonnes of materials were exported globally in 2010 (UNEP, 2016). The UNEP's recent report (2016) suggests that decoupling material use to reduce environmental impacts is the priority of modern environmental policy. Material recovery from waste could ease the stress of high dependency on extraction of primary materials. Even in a very circular system, we need to be highly dependent on our natural system. A study shows that with a very high aluminium collection and pre-processing rates of 97% each (which is very high compared to the current rate of aluminium collection of 49%) and recycling process efficiencies delivering 97% recovery in the smelting process, only 16% of the aluminium remains in the cycle after ten years (EEA, 2016).

It was found that homes and buildings in the developed countries represent 40% of energy consumption, 38% of GHG emissions, and 40% of solid waste generation (UNEP-SBCI, 2012). Although, the contribution of GHG emissions to the atmosphere would be very low from the end-of-life (demolition) waste considering the whole life cycle of a house, recovering resources could be more environmentally beneficial than what would usually offset the burdens of extraction of resources. A study conducted by Blanchard and Reppe (1998) showed that a typical residential house in the USA contributes only 0.2% of the total global warming potential from waste and mostly contributes during the construction phase (7.39%) and the use phase (91.9%). However, housing materials contribute around 63% of carbon emissions during the construction phase, and thus reusing and recycling construction materials would potentially reduce a significant proportion of GHG emissions into the atmosphere.

Demolition generally takes place at the end-of-life phase of a residential building. The traditional demolition process involves knocking down buildings using heaving machinery without caring much about waste materials; as a result, most of the demolition waste is generally sent to landfills. Demolition is an opportunity lost because lots of useable and valuable materials are lost forever due to landfill. Construction material prices are rapidly increasing, resulting in higher housing price (Shiller, 2007). On the contrary, the deconstruction of buildings, which is 'systematic disassembly of buildings in order to maximize recovered materials reuse and recycling', involves carefully taking apart portions of buildings or removing their contents with the primary goal of reuse in mind (CIB, 2005; NAHB, 2000). Due to growing awareness of environmental issues and global climate change, systematic deconstruction is seen as an alternative to demolition. In addition, demolition could positively contribute to housing affordability by reusing and recycling construction materials.

This study aims to conceptualize the key challenges and barriers in applying deconstruction of residential buildings in New Zealand. The study considers a deconstruction project called 'Whole House Reuse' (WHR) in New Zealand as a case study and tries to propose a number of recommendations for the development of comprehensive strategies for deconstruction practices in the Pacific region.

Residential deconstruction practices

Deconstruction is not new; in fact, it is a common practice in many developing countries around the world where the costs of building materials are extremely high, and the labour costs are comparatively low. Due to high labour costs, deconstruction is not widely applied in many developed countries. Only a number of studies have been conducted under the form of pilot project and case study analysis to investigate the key challenges and barriers of the deconstruction process. The study found that deconstruction costs could be 17%–25% higher than demolition costs due to labour costs and disposal costs (tipping fee and transportation); however, it could save approximately 37% for deconstruction over demolition with conservative salvage value (excluding material storage, inventory, and sales personnel costs) (Dantata, Touran, & Wang, 2005; Bradley Guy, 2000; B. Guy & McLendon, 2000).

Denhart (2010) conducted a study on deconstruction programmes in the USA soon after hurricane Katrina hit in 2005. The study reported on the reclaimed materials from four deconstructed houses. A total of 44 tonnes of material was redirected back into the local building material stream (enough to build three new homes out of the four that came down). The study showed that the cost/profit of deconstruction varied from a net cost of $3.80 to a net profit of $1.53 per square foot, compared to an estimated net cost of demolition at a steady $5.50 per square foot.

Housing deconstruction could have significant influences on CE as the fundamental principles of a CE are it preserves and enhances natural capital by controlling finite stocks and balancing renewable resource flows; it optimizes resource yields by circulating products, components, and materials in use at the highest utility at all times in both biological and technical cycles; it fosters system effectiveness by revealing and designing out the negative externalities.

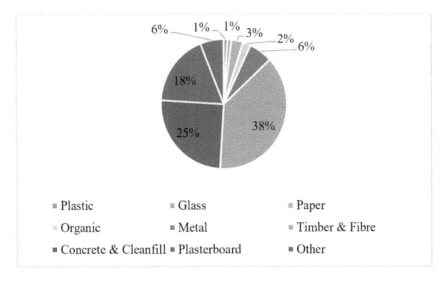

FIGURE 7.1 C&D waste composition in New Zealand

Source: Adapted from Inglis (n.d.); Paterson (1997)

Since the construction industry is one of the main contributors of global resource consumption and environmental pollution with a significantly low rate of resource recovery from waste, deconstruction could potentially be a restorative system that supports CE. Figure 7.1 shows a schematic diagram of a restorative industrial system in which biological and technical materials can be re-circulated within the system for repetitive uses. There is an opportunity to foster CE through deconstruction of housing, as the process creates employment opportunities, conserves materials, recovers resources, and circulates materials within the construction industrial system. It would also be possible to phase out the negative externalities through sustainable design and construction practices so that there is no leakage in the system and no waste for landfills.

C&D waste management in New Zealand

Each year, around 850,000 tonnes of C&D waste is sent to landfills in New Zealand, depending on the level of building activity (Level, 2014). Although, the New Zealand Waste Strategy Towards Zero Waste and a Sustainable New Zealand required a 50% reduction by weight in C&D waste going to landfills by 2008, this has not yet been enforced as a law and offers no strategies for accomplishing this objective (Storey & Pedersen, 2014). Flexible and comparative low clean-up rates compared to MSW rates encourage landfill use (Storey & Pedersen, 2014). Figure 7.1 shows the key composition of C&D waste in New Zealand. The C&D waste in New Zealand mainly consists of timber, metal, concrete, paper, glass, and other construction materials.

TABLE 7.1 Waste strategy and regulations related to C&D in New Zealand

Legislations/policy/strategy	Brief outlines/relevance
The Resource Management Act 1991	The Resource Management Act controls the environmental impacts of waste facilities, such as disposal facilities, recycling plants, and cleanfills.
The Local Government Act 2002	Solid waste collection and disposal are identified as core services to be considered by a local authority.
The Climate Change Response Act 2002	This act also enables the New Zealand Emissions Trading Scheme.
The revised New Zealand Waste Strategy 2002	The revised New Zealand Waste Strategy sets out the government's long-term priorities for waste management and minimization.
The Building Act 2004	The Building Act 2004 contains sustainability principles, including the efficient and sustainable use of materials and the reduction of waste during the construction process.
The Waste Management Act 2008	The Waste Management Act 2008 was introduced to encourage waste minimization and reduce waste disposal by applying a levy on all waste sent to landfills.

There are many regulatory policies available in New Zealand, which regulates waste recycling and disposal activities. Table 7.1 shows the statutory requirement of C&D waste management in New Zealand. Among all relevant regulatory policies, the Resource Management Act (1991), the Climate Change Response Act (2002), the Building Act (2004), and the Waste Management Act (2008) would be very important in promoting deconstruction in New Zealand.

Case study: WHR Project

The earthquakes in 2010 and 2011 in Canterbury, New Zealand, resulted in much devastation and loss, including 10,000 homes being declared fit for demolition, and by 2014, around half of the homes within the Residential Red Zone were demolished. Traditional demolition which crushes and removes materials in a relatively quick and tightly scheduled time frame is the most commonly applied method and homeowners often describe feeling alienated by the demolition process. The WHR project celebrates the careful nature of deconstruction and enables products to be made from salvaged resources. The project was seen as an opportunity for examination, transformation, and reuse of the often over-looked resources that make up one home. Figure 7.2 shows the deconstruction process of the WHR project.

The house was located at 19 Admirals Way, New Brighton, Christchurch, and the project was facilitated by Rekindle with the support of the Sustainable Initiatives Fund Trust, Creative Communities, and Jamon Construction Ltd. A professional

FIGURE 7.2 Deconstruction process of the WHR project

Source: Courtesy of Guy Frederick/Rekindle

team of salvagers from Silvan Salvage and a team of dedicated volunteers undertook the work of carefully dismantling the home, piece by piece. The recovered items were categorized and catalogued.

Assessment of recovered materials

Various construction materials were recovered during the deconstruction process, and all materials were catalogued based on the type and volume of the materials and the number of units available. The physical classification and assessment of the materials and the potential of material recovery were determined using the catalogue based on the criteria presented in Table 7.2. The scores 1–10 were used to rate the materials in the context of reusability, reparability, recyclability, and disposal to landfills. A score of 10 means the item could be reused as is without compromising any material value or aesthetic and a lower score means low efficiency in reusability and recyclability. The study only considers low hanging fruit which requires the lowest level of willingness and effort to recycle. Thus the study only considers the materials that scored 5 or more in the analysis of environmental benefits.

Measuring the environmental benefits of harvested materials

The environmental benefits of harvested materials were calculated based on energy and associated carbon dioxide emission reduction to the atmosphere. The study used the Inventory of Carbon and Energy (ICE) database to calculate the embodied energy and carbon emission reduction from the recovered materials used in Table 7.3. The

TABLE 7.2 The scores used to characterize catalogued materials

Scale (1–10)	Description	Interpretation
01	Disposal/landfill	Not suitable for recycling/composting
02	Composting	Suitable for biodegradation
03	Low recyclability	Recycle requires high effort
04	Medium recyclability	Recycle requires medium effort
05	High recyclability	Recycle requires low effort
06	Repair requires high effort	Substitutes functions with high effort
07	Repair requires low effort	Substitutes functions with low effort
08	Reuse for alternative purposes	Replaces other functionalities
09	Reuse as is	Substitutes similar functions
10	Reuse as is	Substitutes similar functions and aesthetics

TABLE 7.3 The embodied energy and carbon emission reduction from C&D materials (Hammond & Jones, 2011)

Material types	General material		Virgin material	
	Embodied energy (MJ/KG)	CO_2e (Kg/Kg)	Embodied energy (MJ/KG)	CO_2e (Kg/Kg)
Brass	44	2.64	80	4.8
Copper	42	2.71	57	3.81
Aluminium	155	9.16	218	12.79
Lead	25.21	1.67	49	3.37
Stainless Steel	20.1	1.46	35.4	2.89
Bricks	3	0.24	3	0.24
Ceramic	10	0.7	20	1.14
Concrete	0.75	0.107	1	0.15
Glass	11.5	0.59	15	0.91
Masonry	1.1	0.174	1.1	0.174
Melamine	97	4.19	97	4.19
Textile/Fabric	74	3.9	74	3.9
Plastic	80.5	3.31	95.3	3.76
PVC	68.6	3.23	77.2	3.1
Plywood	15	0.45	15	0.45
Timber	10	0.31	16	0.58

calculation used in the ICE database is considered the geographical context of the UK. Since there is no similar database in the context of New Zealand, the study assumed a similar context in New Zealand, and the authors acknowledge that there might be minor errors in the calculation. However, the intention of the article is not to produce a 100% accurate database on environmental benefits of deconstruction of old houses in New Zealand; rather, the paper initiates the dialogue and discussion on the necessity of conducing a wider application and benefits of deconstruction projects similar to the WHR project.

Characterization of recovered materials

The catalogued items were carefully categorized based on the physical assessment of the quality of the harvested materials and level of reusability, reparability, and recyclability. A total of 480 items were catalogued. Figure 7.3 shows the physical rating of various materials. Only 1% of the materials (mainly shelfs) were rated as 10, which means that these items and materials could be reused without compromising the quality, functionality, and aesthetics of the materials. Another 1% of the harvested materials were scored as 9 (mainly timber and hardboard materials), which means that these items can be served to meet the purpose of similar quality and functionality. Around 7% of catalogued materials were scored as 8, and most of the materials were scored between 5 and 7 (around 70%), which indicated that a significant amount of construction materials (around 79%) can be harvested through the deconstruction process and recirculated in the consumption supply chain through reuse, repair, and recycle practices.

A number of studies (Nnorom, Ohakwe, & Osibanjo, 2009; Schultz & Oskamp, 1996) indicate that successful recycling practices require willingness and effort.

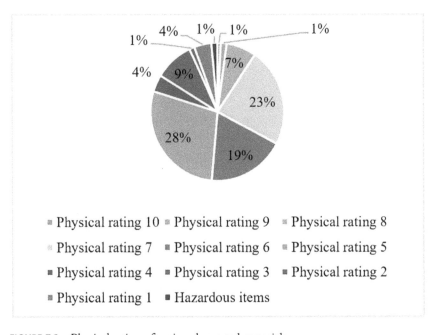

■ Physical rating 10 ■ Physical rating 9   ■ Physical rating 8

■ Physical rating 7   ■ Physical rating 6   ■ Physical rating 5

■ Physical rating 4   ■ Physical rating 3   ■ Physical rating 2

■ Physical rating 1   ■ Hazardous items

FIGURE 7.3 Physical rating of various harvested materials

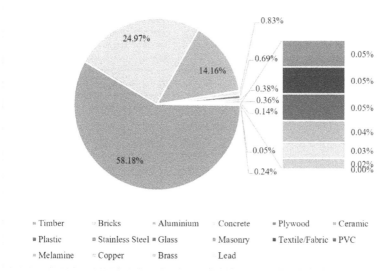

0.83%

24.97%

0.69%   0.05%

14.16%

0.38%   0.05%
0.36%
0.14%   0.05%

0.04%

0.05%   0.03%
58.18%
0.24%   0.02%
0.00%

- Timber   Bricks   Aluminium   Concrete   ▪ Plywood   Ceramic

▪ Plastic   ▪ Stainless Steel ▪ Glass   ▪ Masonry   ▪ Textile/Fabric ▪ PVC

Melamine   Copper   Brass   Lead

FIGURE 7.4   The composition of recovered materials

Thus this study considers all the materials that require low effort, rated 5 or above, based on the assumption that under current recycling practices, these items would be easily recycled instead of disposed in landfills. Figure 7.4 shows the various types of materials recovered through deconstruction, which has high recycling and material value. A total of 12,053.5 kilogram of various materials (scored above 5) were recovered, mainly from timber (58.1%), brick (24.16), and aluminium (14.16%).

Environmental benefits of harvested materials

The environmental benefits of harvesting materials through deconstruction were measured by assessing the embodied energy savings and abatement of carbon emissions (CO_2e) using the values in Table 7.3. 'General' material means the item has a pre-selected recycled content which is usually available in the market, and 'virgin' material means the item has been extracted from primarily virgin material. Table 7.4 shows the embodied energy savings and carbon emissions abatement of harvested materials from the WHR project.

Although timber was the highest contributor (58.2%) compared to general material, followed by brick (25%), and aluminium (14.2%), in regard to embodied energy saving, aluminium contributed the most, around 75.37%, followed by timber (19.98%) and brick (2.57%) and similarly in the abatement of carbon emissions through deconstruction. A total of 350,977MJ of embodied energy was potentially saved, and around 18862 kg (CO_2e) of carbon emissions was potentially reduced by recovering materials compared to general material. Compared to virgin materials,

TABLE 7.4 Embodied energy and carbon emission reduction through harvested materials

Materials	General materials				Virgin materials			
	Embodied energy (MJ)		Carbon reduction (CO₂e)		Embodied energy (MJ)		Carbon reduction (CO₂e)	
	MJ	%	Kg	%	MJ	%	Kg	%
Brass	101.2	0.03%	6.1	0.03%	184.0	0.04%	11.0	0.04%
Copper	142.8	0.04%	9.2	0.05%	193.8	0.04%	13.0	0.05%
Aluminum	264,518.5	75.37%	15,632.2	82.87%	372,032.4	74.09%	21,827.0	80.75%
Lead	12.6	0.00%	0.8	0.00%	24.5	0.00%	1.7	0.01%
Stainless Steel	335.7	0.10%	24.4	0.13%	591.2	0.12%	48.3	0.18%
Brick	9,030.0	2.57%	722.4	3.83%	9,030.0	1.80%	722.4	2.67%
Ceramic	455.0	0.13%	31.9	0.17%	910.0	0.18%	51.9	0.19%
Concrete	75.0	0.02%	10.7	0.06%	100.0	0.02%	15.0	0.06%
Glass	74.8	0.02%	3.8	0.02%	97.5	0.02%	5.9	0.02%
Masonry	6.1	0.00%	1.0	0.01%	6.1	0.00%	1.0	0.00%
Melamine	485.0	0.14%	21.0	0.11%	485.0	0.10%	21.0	0.08%
Textile/Fabric	488.4	0.14%	25.7	0.14%	488.4	0.10%	25.7	0.10%
Plastic	3,445.4	0.98%	141.7	0.75%	4,078.8	0.81%	160.9	0.60%
PVC	432.2	0.12%	20.3	0.11%	486.4	0.10%	19.5	0.07%
Plywood	1,249.4	0.36%	37.5	0.20%	1,249.4	0.25%	37.5	0.14%
Timber	70,125.3	19.98%	2173.9	11.52%	112,200.5	22.34%	4067.3	15.05%
Total	350,977 MJ		18862 Kg CO₂e		502,158 MJ		27,029 Kg CO₂e	

around 502,158 MJ of embodied energy was saved and around 27,029 kg (CO₂e) of carbon emission was reduced.

Potentially, the WHR project could save around 139,488 kWh[1] of energy, which is equivalent to the annual electricity uses of six households in Christchurch, and the amount of carbon emissions prevented could offset the annual emissions of six passenger cars in New Zealand. Now, using the environmental benefits from the context of the 10,000 homes that were declared fit for demolition in 2011 in Christchurch, a similar deconstruction approach could be implemented; then around 5,021,580 gigajoules[2] of energy could be saved and 270,290 tonnes of carbon emission could be potentially prevented.

New Zealand set national emission reduction targets in July 2015 under the United Nations Framework Convention on Climate Change. New Zealand has set an economy-wide target of 30% below 2005 levels by 2030 (which equates to 11% below 1990 levels). New Zealand also has a longer-term target of reducing emissions to 50% below 1990 levels by 2050 (UNFCCC, 2015). Without an alternative and innovative approach, it might not be possible to achieve this emission reduction target. WHR deconstruction project or similar deconstruction projects can potentially prevent a significant amount of national carbon emissions, which will assist in achieving national emission reduction goals.

New products from harvested materials – a restorative industrial system

The WHR project was not only limited to resource recovery from deconstruction but also created innovative products from the recovered materials. The WHR project was mainly sequenced in three different phases, such as deconstruction of the house, creation of innovative products, and a public exhibition of the manufactured products from harvested materials. After the completion of the dismantled process, the deconstructed materials were stored for the next phase of project activities. The project involved 282 people, and around 400 objects were produced from the harvested materials in the WHR project. Figure 7.5 shows the new products created by various designers.

The key challenges and lessons learnt

The project significantly relied on voluntary works of the local community and artists. Around 1,105.5 hours were spent to produce 52 objects – i.e. an average of 21 hours for each object that local artists expended to create new products from the recovered materials. Though around 122 objects were sold worth NZD$43,425, the project may not be 100% economically viable under current market conditions. However, the project indicates that by minimizing labour cost and involving local communities and artists, the products can have the economic value needed to foster a wider application of deconstruction projects.

The landfill tax is an important institutional and policy tool to encourage more recycling and less dumping, as it involves costs. Thus under higher landfill tax,

FIGURE 7.5   New products from recovered materials

Source: Courtesy of Guy Frederick/Rekindle

deconstruction activities would be more viable in the context of cost-benefit analysis. Nevertheless, the WHR project was considerably successful in engaging local communities and to some extent preserving the attachments to the house through the deconstruction process. Deconstruction not only provides resource recovery but also rehabilitates the memories of and attachments to the materials, space, and time. The owners of the case study project have vast memories regarding the house. In a conversation, the owners of the property stated, 'That was the place we brought our two boys back after they were born and we had fantastic birthday parties and different moments there'. Thus by harvesting materials and creating new products from them, their emotional attachment with the property was preserved.

The project has significant potential in regard to CE, as the project involved man power, creative design, and recirculation of resources within the products supply chain. However, the project would have been more successful if the existing economic system supported deconstruction activities by considering external costs, including environmental pollution costs. The key challenges and barriers that can be faced during such projects are listed as follows:

Finding appropriate volunteers. Their available time and ability to commit to deconstruction activities will be crucial for the completion of a similar project.

Temporary storage of harvested materials is also an issue.

- Ensuring resale value of new products will also be an important factor in the deconstruction project
- Commitment and strategic policy from the local authority on deconstruction will make a significant difference

Therefore, institutional and economic supports are essential to promote CE through deconstruction of residential houses. This could be achieved by imposing landfill taxes, supporting local young people and organizations in the deconstruction process, and ensuring a feasible market for the recycling materials as well as the products produced from recovered materials.

This chapter presented the deconstruction of a family house called the WHR project in Christchurch, New Zealand. The project showed both the challenges and opportunities in the deconstruction process. Although the deconstruction process has considerable potential for material recovery and environmental benefits, the associated labour costs and resale value of the harvested items would significantly influence the viability of a deconstruction project. Deconstruction may not be completely economically viable under current market conditions, but considering the greater socio-economic aspects and overall environmental benefits in regard to energy savings and abatement of carbon emissions aligned with the national emission reduction targets, the deconstruction process could be an alternative and innovative approach to dismantling old house in New Zealand instead of demolition. It is expected that an alternative business approach involving local community and commitments from local authorities to ensuring viable economic conditions could promote deconstruction activities. Since the housing and building industries significantly contribute to energy consumption, GHG emission, and waste generation, a systematic deconstruction process would reduce a massive environmental burden and promote greater sustainability worldwide.

Notes

1 1 megajoule = 0.277 kilowatt hour.
2 1 megajoule = 0.001 gigajoule.

References

Blanchard, S., & Reppe, P. (1998). *Life Cycle Analysis of a Residential Home in Michigan: Center for Sustainable Systems.* Michigan: University of Michigan.

CIB. (2005). *Deconstruction and Materials Reuse: An International Overview, Final Report of Task Group 39 on Deconstruction.* Retrieved from www.irbnet.de/daten/iconda/CIB1287.pdf

Dantata, N., Touran, A., & Wang, J. (2005). An analysis of cost and duration for deconstruction and demolition of residential buildings in Massachusetts. *Resources, Conservation and Recycling, 44*(1), 1–15.

Denhart, H. (2010). Deconstructing disaster: Economic and environmental impacts of deconstruction in post-Katrina New Orleans. *Resources, Conservation and Recycling, 54*(3), 194–204.

EEA. (2016). *Circular Economy in Europe-Developing the Knowledge Base.* Retrieved from www.eea.europa.eu/publications/circular-economy-in-europe

Guy, B. (2000). *Building Deconstruction: Reuse and Recycling of Building Materials.* Retrieved from www.lifecyclebuilding.org/docs/Six%20House%20Building%20Deconstruction.pdf

Guy, B., & McLendon, S. (2000). *Building Deconstruction: Reuse and Recycling of Building Materials.* Gainesville, FL: Center for Construction and Environment, Florida. Retrieved from http://www.lifecyclebuilding.org/docs/Six%20House%20Building%20Deconstruction.pdf

Hammond, G., & Jones, C. (2011). Inventory of Carbon and Energy (ICE) version 2.0. *Sustainable Energy Research Team.* Retrieved from www.carbonsolutions.com/Resources/ICE%20V2.0%20-%20Jan%202011.xls

Inglis. (n.d.). *Construction and Demolition Waste: Best Practice and Cost Saving, Ministry of Environment.* Retrieved from www.cmnzl.co.nz/assets/sm/2260/61/057-INGLISMahara.pdf

Level. (2014). *Material Use: The Authority on Sustainable Building.* Retrieved from www.level.org.nz/material-use/minimising-waste/

NAHB. (2000). *A Guide to Deconstruction, National Association of Home Builders.* Retrieved from Washington, DC: www.huduser.gov/portal//Publications/PDF/decon.pdf

Nnorom, I., Ohakwe, J., & Osibanjo, O. (2009). Survey of willingness of residents to participate in electronic waste recycling in Nigeria: A case study of mobile phone recycling. *Journal of Cleaner Production, 17*(18), 1629–1637.

Paterson, C. J. (1997). *Report on a Sorting Trial of Construction Bin Waste as Part of Stage 2 of Project C&D.* Auckland, New Zealand: Auckland Regional Council (ARC) Environment.

Schandl, H. (2016). *How Do We Uncouple Global Development from Resource Use?* Retrieved from https://theconversation.com/how-do-we-uncouple-global-development-from-resource-use-62730

Schultz, P. W., & Oskamp, S. (1996). Effort as a moderator of the attitude-behavior relationship: General environmental concern and recycling. *Social Psychology Quarterly, 59*(4), 375–383.

Shiller, R. J. (2007). *Understanding Recent Trends in House Prices and Home Ownership*. The National Bureau of Economic Research, Cambridge, MA. Retrieved from https://www.nber.org/papers/w13553

Storey, J. B., & Pedersen, M. (2014). Overcoming the barriers to deconstruction and materials reuse in New Zealand. In S. Nakajima (Ed.), *Barriers for Deconstruction and Reuse/Recycling of Construction Materials* (p. 397). Delft, The Netherlands: CIB Publication.

UNEP. (2016). *Global Material Flows and Resource Productivity*. Retrieved from New York: http://unep.org/documents/irp/16-00169_LW_GlobalMaterialFlowsUNEReport_FINAL_160701.pdf

UNEP-SBCI. (2012). *Building Design and Construction: Forging Resource Efficiency and Sustainable Development*. Retrieved from New York: http://ec.europa.eu/environment/eussd/pdf/Resource%20efficiency%20in%20the%20building%20sector.pdf

UNFCCC. (2015). *New Zealand's Intended Nationally Determined Contribution*. Retrieved from www4.unfccc.int/submissions/INDC/Published%20Documents/New%20Zealand/1/New%20Zealand%20INDC%202015.pdf

8

ZERO-WASTE IN
THE GLOBAL CITIES

Implementation of the 'zero-waste' urban setting

Solid waste management in Adelaide, South Australia

Adelaide is the capital city of South Australia and the fifth largest populated city in Australia. A total of 1,089,728 inhabitants live in an area of 841.5 km², with a population density of about 1,295/km² (UN-HABITAT, 2010). South Australia is often called the driest state on the driest continent (Gargett & Marden, 1996). Geographically, Adelaide is surrounded by the Adelaide Hills (Mount Lofty Ranges) in the east and the coast of Gulf St Vincent on the west, one of the planned capitals of what was originally an independent colony founded in 1836 under the British Empire. It was originally inhabited by the Kaurna Aboriginal people more than 40,000 years ago (McDougall & Sumerling, 2006). Adelaide was established as a 'commercial centre' for a region dominated by farming and mining (Gargett & Marden, 1996). Soon after the establishment of new settlements, the city of Adelaide became the capital of South Australia, and its economic and industrial centre (Forster, 1999).

Adelaide is one of the typical high-income cities of Australia, and the per capita GDP was US$41,300 in 2010 (CIA, 2011). Almost 85% of the population of South Australia lives within the Adelaide metropolitan area. The Adelaide metropolitan area comprises 19 city councils. The remaining 15% of people live outside the metropolitan area and are not covered by the traditional waste management services provided by the metropolitan waste authority. Zero Waste SA (ZWSA) is a South Australian state government agency established by legislation called the Zero Waste SA Act (2004) to develop an integrated resource recovery and recycling strategy and to eliminate waste and its consignment to landfills (ZWSA, 2007b).

Municipal waste management and treatment

The composition of MSW varies widely, both within and between countries and between different seasons of the year (UN-HABITAT, 2010). A reliable waste database is important for any waste management planning and effective waste decision making. The Australian Waste Database was created in 1993 to provide a monitoring mechanism for waste minimization policies and to address future waste management (AWD, 2004). The national waste database is categorized into organic, paper, glass, plastic, metal, hazardous, and miscellaneous waste. An inconsistency was found on the way waste composition is reported in Adelaide's municipal WMS despite having a proposed waste database. C&D waste is considered a fraction of MSW in Adelaide, which indicates an inconsistent waste performance, especially in measuring the waste diversion rate.

Adelaide is one of the world's relatively developed cities. The consumption of natural resources is high, and, consequently the generation of waste in Adelaide is also high, compared to other cities. In 2009, 742,807 tonnes of MSW (a significant amount of which is C&D waste) was generated, and the average person generated around 681 kg of MSW. However, South Australia possesses the best waste recycling and resource recovery records in Australia. Waste recycling and composting are considered the key waste management techniques in Adelaide. Around 46% of all MSW was recycled, and 8% was composted. Landfill, another main municipal waste method, accounts for 46% of municipal waste disposal. Table 8.1 shows the composition of MSW and the WMS in Adelaide.

Local governments – namely, city councils – are responsible for collecting household waste and taking it to recycling and disposal sites in Adelaide. In general, local councils provide two types of waste bins: a general waste bin that goes to landfills and a recycling bin that goes to transfer stations and recovery centres. Recently, a number of councils in Adelaide have started to provide three bins to their residents;

TABLE 8.1 Waste composition and management in Adelaide

Waste composition	Waste streams	Per cent (%)
	Organic	26
	Paper	7
	Plastic	5
	Glass	5
	Metal	5
	Others	52
Waste management	Waste management options	Per cent (%)
	Compost	8
	Recycle	46
	Landfill	46

Source: Adapted from UN-HABITAT (2010)

however, the service has not yet covered the whole metropolitan Adelaide area (currently available in 9 city councils out of 19 metropolitan city councils). Waste bins are collected and transported by waste collection vehicles. There are 14 medium- to large-scale transfer stations operating in metropolitan areas of Adelaide (SA-EPA, 1999). Currently, it is mandatory to collect and return waste to the transfer stations before being deposited to landfills to maximize resource recovery and recycling. After sorting and processing in the transfer stations, waste is sent to landfills.

South Australia's long and successful history of implementing CDL goes back to 1977. A total of 124 approved collection depots are operated statewide, 40 in the Adelaide metropolitan region and 84 in regional South Australia, to return and refund the deposit of packaging containers. In 2008, the refund increased from 5c to 10c per deposit. In 2011–2012, over 609 million containers, representing 47,510 tonnes, were returned for recycling and diverted from landfills, resulting in a record return of 81.4% for the full year (EPA-SA, 2012a).

The collected recycling materials are transferred to recycling industries in Australia and abroad. Glass, concrete, brick, soil and rubble, asphalt, timber, food, and garden organics are reprocessed in South Australia. Other recovered materials, such as paper, plastic, steel, non-ferrous metal, textile, and rubber, are largely reprocessed interstate or overseas (ZWSA, 2007b). According to state legislation, city councils are obliged to empty the general waste bins weekly and recycling waste bins on a fortnightly basis. Figure 8.1 shows a schematic flow diagram of municipal SWM in Adelaide.

Despite the availability of formal waste collection services in Adelaide, there are also informal waste collectors, especially packaging container collectors who gather containers and deposit them to get a refund for extra income. The rise of this informal collection within formal WMSs reflects economic drivers in waste policy. Informal collectors primarily recycle from public bins. Even though this collection is informal and voluntary, the system is integrated with the formal WMSs, because informal waste collectors return containers to the formal waste recycling depot. Most of the transfer stations in South Australia accept almost all types of waste,

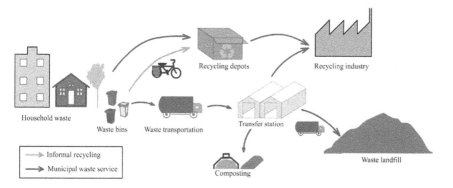

FIGURE 8.1   A schematic flow diagram of municipal SWM in Adelaide

including hazardous waste. However, none of them accept deposits except for free electronic waste. Organic waste drop-off fees range from AU$8 to 150, depending on the volume of waste. Recycling depots do not accept hazardous waste, and it can cost between AU$80 and 330 to drop off materials such as asbestos and wet paint (IWS, 2013; NAWMA, 2013).

The composting of organic waste has been increasing in Adelaide in the past decade. Household garden waste is collected in metropolitan areas primarily through a small proportion of sign-up fees for residents. Ten city councils out of 19 in the metropolitan areas offer some form of free garden waste collection system. Around 35% (157,000 households) of all households in the metropolitan area in Adelaide enjoy a garden waste collection service (EPA-SA, 2013). There are nine landfill sites currently operating in the metropolitan area (EPA & LGA, 2003). The total capacity of landfill is around 43 million tonnes of putrescible waste disposal, and the lifespan is approximately until 2030 (DEWHA, 2009).

The waste levy has increased from AU$21/tonne in 2007 to AU$42/tonne in 2010 for metropolitan areas. For non-metropolitan areas, the waste levy is AU$21/tonne. A further increase to AU$50/tonne was proposed in metropolitan Adelaide to meet the target of a 35% reduction of waste to landfill by 2020 (ZWSA, 2013). The local recycling industries have been promoted by the state government's ZWSs, and, hence, a significant amount of around 2 million tonnes (82%) of waste is treated locally in South Australia, 5% (123,250 tonnes) is treated interstate, while 13% (325,177 tonnes) is shipped overseas (ZWSA, 2011a). The diversion rate of waste from landfill has increased noticeably since 2003 and continues to increase, resulting in less per capita waste disposal to landfills. There was a significant increase in waste generation in year 2010–2011, and this could be treated as a data anomaly. One of the key reasons for the sudden increase of waste generation in Adelaide in this period was several redevelopment projects, which led to a rapid increase of waste generation due to C&D waste.

Regulatory policies and ZWSs

Regulatory policy defines the process of whether to adopt and use regulation as a policy instrument through evidence-based decision-making. Regulatory policy is about achieving the government's objectives through the use of regulations, laws, and other instruments to deliver better economic and social outcomes (OECD, 2012). Regulatory policy is thus important for regulating and guiding WMSs. Adelaide has a higher percentage of waste recycling compared to the other capital cities in Australia because of South Australian's CDL. The CDL has a significant influence on WMSs in South Australia. The CDL is supported by the local community in Adelaide, as it offers refunds from waste. Recycling activities in South Australia increased significantly when the refund for containers increased from 5c to 10c in 2010.

The Zero Waste SA Act (2004) was one of the most significant waste management initiatives, which formed the organization ZWSA to promote ZW activities in Adelaide. ZWSA has been working in many different aspects of waste management, such as promoting public awareness of and knowledge about waste, waste avoidance, recycling, SWM and diversion of waste from landfill. The generation of waste has increased significantly in Adelaide despite the waste reduction target in the ZW strategy.

In 2009, the South Australian government enforced a ban on lightweight single-use plastic shopping bags and expected to produce almost 400 million fewer plastic bags in South Australia (EPA-SA, 2012b). The plastic bag ban also reserves the right to fine any retailers who do not follow the rule. Food or organic waste recycling is one of the major areas of waste management in Adelaide. Around 670,000 tonnes of organic waste were recovered in 2011 for recycling, including food, garden material, timber, and by-products from food processing industries.

Since 2004, ZWSA has reinvested AU$20.25 million of levy funds into recycling and waste reduction projects, integrating local government, the recycling industry, business organizations, academic institutes, community groups, and other stakeholders in waste management sectors (Government of SA, 2011). The targets of ZWSs in South Australia in 2011–2015 were (i) to reduce waste to landfill by 35% by 2020 (from 2002–2003 levels) and (ii) reach a milestone of 25% reduction by 2014. MSW targets are 60% diversion by 2012 and an increase of the diversion rate to 70% by 2015 (ZWSA, 2011b). Table 8.2 shows the key milestones of municipal waste management in Adelaide.

Waste management development drivers

Different socio-economic and environmental drivers have been promoting WMSs in metropolitan Adelaide. Environmental awareness and climate change are global drivers, and people in Adelaide are very environmentally conscious (UN-HABITAT, 2010). The CDL is one of the main drivers in packaging recycling in Adelaide. The CDL has been operating successfully for more than 30 years. The recycling market in Adelaide has been influencing waste strategies, and, hence, business is always in favour of recycling activities. A rise in the price paid for returned packaging from 5c to 10c encouraged consumers to store and recycle their packaging more. However, despite South Australia's successful implementation of CDL for recycling activities, CDL has not been implemented in other states in Australia due to corporate lobbing against this refund system. In the case of the Northern Territory, Coca-Cola won a legal battle to dismantle the Northern Territory recycling scheme, which is similar to CDL (Sharwood, 2013). An independent review of CDL in New South Wales (NSW) was commissioned, and the CDL review found that 'stakeholder attitudes to CDL are highly heterogeneous, with strong support from local government and environment groups, majority support from the community, limited support from the recycling industry, and opposition from the beverage, packaging, and retail industries' (White & Aisbett, 2002). Compared to other waste management businesses, the recycling business is a growing sector in Adelaide and has created a large number of jobs for local people. Recycling activities create over three times more

TABLE 8.2 Key milestones of municipal WMSs in Adelaide

Year	Milestones in WMS	Goal and focus
1977	CDL	CDL is an important piece of waste recycling legislation for packaging waste
1993	Environmental Protection Act	Under the national Environmental Protection Act, environmental pollution, emissions from waste, and waste depot levies are regulated
1993	Waste minimization policies	A monitoring mechanism for commonwealth and state waste minimization policies and for addressing next-generation waste management
1994	Environmental protection (fees and levies) regulations	Landfill fees and waste levies are regulated
1999	Wingfield Waste Depot Closure Act	Restricted on waste landfill to Wingfield Waste Depot
2004	Zero Waste SA Act	Establishment of the ZWSA organization
2008	10c refund system	The deposit on beverage containers is 10c
2009	Plastic bag ban	Single-use shopping bag ban in South Australia
2011	ZW strategy 2011–2015	Thirty-five per cent reduction of waste to landfill by 2020 and the goal of reaching a milestone of 25% reduced by 2014 and achieving a diversion rate of 70% by 2015
2010	Used packaging materials legislation	Reducing the volume of packaging sent to landfills
2010	Movement of controlled waste between states and territories	National Environment Protection Measures ensure that controlled wastes that are to be moved between states and territories are properly identified, transported, and handled in ways that are consistent with environmentally sound practices
2010	Environmental protection (waste to resources) policy	Aims to achieve SWM by applying the waste management hierarchy consistently with the principles of ecologically sustainable development
2012	Product stewardship regulation	Manufacturing activity related to products or waste, including reuse, recycling, recovery, and disposal during the supply and use phases
2017	Zero Waste SA Revocation Regulations 2017	Reform of Zero Waste SA as Green Industries SA to promote innovation and business activity in the waste management, resource recovery, and green industry sectors in the state and for other purposes

jobs than landfill (9.2 jobs/10,000 tonnes of waste recycling and 2.8 jobs/10,000 tonnes of waste landfill (ZWSA, 2007b)).

ZWSA is the main government body that drives waste reduction, recycling, and reuse practices in Adelaide, and the South Australian government's commitment to ZW goals is not limited to the establishment of ZWSA; it also supports the organization with strong financial inducements. Fifty cents out of every dollar is made available to ZWSA for initiatives which divert waste from landfills (UN-HABITAT, 2010). Adelaide has been aiming to achieve zero landfills, and to reach that goal, the waste landfill levy has been increased several times to reduce the volume of waste sent to landfills as well as increasing funds for promoting waste diversion from landfills.

Community engagement, particularly in food waste recycling, is one of the major drivers of WMSs in Adelaide. It is predicted that by 2020, the amount of organic waste composting in Adelaide will be greater than the amount of waste disposed of in landfills. Local government (city councils) has been promoting organic waste recycling by providing separate bins for food waste collection to households. Different non-profit organizations have been working in Adelaide to promote food donation from processing industries, groceries, and restaurants to feed homeless people. The provisions of second-hand shops (Finding Workable Solutions) and online-based swap options are also increasing to promote the reuse and reselling of used products in order to avoid the creation of unexpected waste.

Solid waste management in San Francisco

San Francisco is the financial and administrative capital of Western USA. San Francisco was established in 1776 as an urban area (O'Day, 1926) where the Yelamu (Native American) people had lived since 3000 BC (Stewart, 2003). During the California Gold Rush, San Francisco experienced very rapid urban growth and became a consolidated city-county in 1856 (Coy, 1919). San Francisco is now the 14th-most populous city (population of 835,364) in the USA, covering 122 km², with a population density of 6,847/ km²(UN-HABITAT, 2010).

Even though the administrative boundary of San Francisco is subdivided into 14 different zones, the waste management authority acts centrally under the Environment Department of San Francisco. The city is located on a hilly peninsula separating San Francisco Bay from the Pacific Ocean. The climate in San Francisco is a mild Mediterranean one, with wet winters and dry summers. The city of San Francisco is typical of developed cities. The average San Franciscan has relatively high spending power and living standards. The USA has the world's highest GDP of US$15.29 trillion and the third-highest HDI of 0.958 (UN-HABITAT, 2010).

Municipal waste management and treatment

In the UN-HABITAT (2010) study of SWM in the world's cities, San Francisco has been identified as one of the most resourceful cities in waste management services. San Francisco has a long history in waste collection systems from informal waste recycling in the early twentieth century to the modern collection systems of today. During the Great Depression in the 1930s, many poor people in California collected and sold other people's trash as a means of survival. This was also seen in the last global economic crisis in 2008–2010. Mostly homeless people and jobless immigrants in San Francisco are actively involved in the informal recycling industry (Gowan, 1997). Informal recycling worked as a 'captive' economy for the homeless and jobless recyclers in San Francisco (which is also true for most of the other informal recyclers around the world). San Francisco has successfully implemented its current WMSs by integrating informal waste recycling activities with the formal WMSs. Recycling activities in San Francisco are now a community activity, combining different groups of people, communities, and stakeholders.

San Francisco is one of the leading cities that have considered ZW as the core of its waste management manifesto. The ZW challenge in San Francisco is reflected in the solid waste systems' support for reducing consumption, maximizing diversion, and encouraging reuse, repair, and green purchasing. Banning troublesome goods, such as plastic bags and superfluous packaging, and promoting alternatives, such as recyclable or compostable takeout food packaging and reusable transport packaging, are the most prominent initiatives for achieving ZW goals in San Francisco (UN-HABITAT, 2010).

The composition of MSW waste in San Francisco includes organic (34%), paper (24%), plastic (11%), glass (3%), metal (4%), and miscellaneous (24%). Household hazardous waste is included in municipal waste, and, therefore, hazardous waste is also managed by the local waste management authority. A total of 508,323 tonnes of MSW (609 kg per person per year) was generated in 2008, which makes San Francisco one of the highest waste-generating cities in the world. MSW is primarily managed by recycling (52%) and composting (20%), and the remainder of the waste (28%) is managed by landfill. Table 8.3 shows the composition of MSW and management systems in San Francisco.

Waste management services in San Francisco are operated by both centralized and decentralized WMSs. Decentralized waste recycling systems encourage local people and recyclers to collect recyclables from the community and return them to the local recycling depots. The three bins collection system successfully operates throughout the city to maximize sorting and recycling efficiency. Waste service

TABLE 8.3 Waste composition and waste management in San Francisco

Waste composition	Waste streams	Per cent (%)
	Organic	34
	Paper	24
	Plastic	11
	Glass	3
	Metal	4
	Others	24
Waste management	Waste management options	Per cent (%)
	Compost	20
	Recycle	52
	Landfill	28

Source: Adapted from UN-HABITAT (2010)

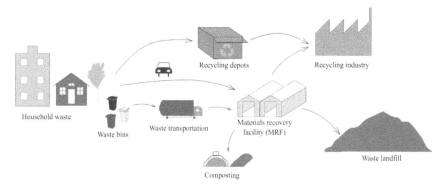

FIGURE 8.2   Material flow of WMSs in San Francisco

providers, such as Recology, collect waste from households and public waste bins and transport it to the central material recovery facility, which has a sorting and baling capacity of up to 2,100 tonne of recyclables per day (Dutko, 2004). Recology accepts all sorts of household and commercial waste, including plastic, metal, fibre, etc. Individuals are also allowed to drop off recyclables at Recology by paying extra fees. Figure 8.2 shows the schematic WMSs in San Francisco.

In the last decade, San Francisco has adopted a pilot program called 'Fantastic Three', a three bins collection system (Cal-recycle, 2012). After its successful operation and effective outcomes in terms of resource recycling efficiency, the three bins program was widely implemented all over the city. San Francisco enforced a mandatory recycling and composting ordinance in 2009 to promote separation and recycling activities, and under this ordinance, 'everyone in San Francisco is required to separate and put their recycling, composting, and trash in the right place' (SF-Environment, 2010). As a result, higher composting and recycling of waste occurs in the WMSs. A higher diversion rate (80% in 2010) in San Francisco results in less waste to landfills. Currently, waste travels 90 km from San Francisco to the Altamont landfill for final disposal; after 2015, waste will be transported to the Ostrom Road landfill by rail in sealed custom-designed containers (SF-Environment, 2011).

Regulatory policies and ZWSs

San Francisco is one of the national and international leaders in waste management policy development and successful implementation. In waste management, its history can be outlined back to the formation of the Scavengers Protective Union in 1879 (Perry, 1978, p. 19), which later evolved into the Golden Gate Disposal and Sunset Scavenger. In 1970, the first community recycling centre operated under a buy-back system, accepting paper, glass, and metals. In 1981, San Francisco first started kerbside waste collection systems under the San Francisco recycling programme. The proposed incinerator for MSW was suspended in 1987 due to public concern over air pollution, ash disposal, and negative impact on recycling (US-EPA,

1993). The local waste management authority in San Francisco has always been visionary and, therefore, in the year 1988, San Francisco set a goal of 32% reduction in the city's waste stream by 1992 and 43% by 2002 (US-EPA, 1993).

The SWM strategy in San Francisco started in 2005, when the city initiated the UN Urban Environmental Accords, which include ZW, manufacturer responsibility, and consumer responsibility under the Waste Reduction Accord (City of Berkley, 2005). San Francisco has adopted a range of regulatory policies to ensure maximum resource recovery from waste by integrating many stakeholders' involvement. The policies include aspects such as producer to consumers responsibility, waste storage in building planning, and restricted waste disposal. Table 8.4 shows the key milestones of municipal waste management policies and strategies in San Francisco.

Waste management development drivers

San Francisco's unique socio-cultural structure has always played a significant role in its waste management development. The old informal waste recycling activities have shaped the current advanced WMSs. Recycling had once appeared as a captive economic incentive to jobless illegal immigrants and homeless people. Currently, recycling is a new business and management industry. San Francisco's success in waste management is deeply implanted in the city's strong commitment to the precautionary principle and visionary strategies. One of the main reasons for a higher diversion rate (about 80% in 2010) in San Francisco is due to its motivation for recycling. If San Francisco had established an incineration plant in 1987, then its WMSs would not have achieved its current ZW goals.

San Francisco has always been supportive of the development of local recycling industries. Market instruments are always key drivers in WMSs. Higher landfill costs and subsidized waste recycling activities lead to greater recycling rates in San Francisco. Combined decentralized and centralized waste processing systems also contribute significantly in improving the effectiveness of WMSs.

Solid waste management in Stockholm

Stockholm, the capital city of Sweden, is one of the largest Scandinavian cities in Europe. It is believed that the City Council of Stockholm was first established between 1296 and 1478. Stockholm consists of 14 islands, located on Sweden's south-central east coast, connecting Lake Mälaren to the Baltic Sea. The administrative boundary of the city of Stockholm consists of three major parts, Stockholm City Centre, Southern Stockholm, and Western Stockholm, with six subdivision wards that accommodate around 22% of Sweden's population. There were 847,073 inhabitants in Stockholm city in 2010, living in an area of 188 km^2 with a population density of 4,503 persons/km^2 (Statistics Sweden, 2010; USK, 2011). As a high-income country, Sweden's per capita GDP was US$39,000 in 2010, and Stockholm accounts for about 28% of the GDP (Index Mundi, 2011) and the HDI was 0.916 in 2012.

TABLE 8.4 Key milestones of municipal WMSs in San Francisco

Year	Milestones in WMS	Goal and focus
1879	Scavengers Protective Union	The union protects scavengers' right and promotes recycling
1932	Refuse Collection and Disposal Initiative Ordinance	Waste collected only by license holder: waste service provider (Recology)
1970	Community Recycling Centre	Community recycling centres promote recycling activities within the city and involve local people
1981	Kerbside Waste Collection	Collect recyclables from the community by the systematic kerbside collection system
1987	Suspension of Incineration Plant	Incinerator for waste management deferred due to environmental pollution
1988	Waste Diversion Targets	Visionary diversion targets for higher recycling and less landfill
2003	Extended Producer Responsibility Resolution	Ensure producers' responsibility on the end-of-life product
2004	Fantastic Three Program	Promote higher sorting efficiency and recycling rate
2004	Green Building Ordinance	Requires city construction to manage waste and provide adequate recycling storage space in buildings
2005	Urban Environmental Accords	Visionary ZW strategy, producer and consumer responsibility
2006	C&D Debris Recovery Ordinance	Requires C&D projects to use city-registered transporters and processing facilities to increase debris recovery
2006	Food Waste Reduction Ordinance	Requires restaurants and food vendors to not use Styrofoam food service ware and instead use food ware that is recyclable or compostable
2007	Plastic Bag Reduction Ordinance	Requires the use of compostable plastic, recyclable paper, and/or reusable checkout bags by supermarkets and drugstores
2010	Mandatory Recycling and Composting Ordinance	Everyone is required to separate and put their recycling, composting, and trash in the right place
2010	The Alameda County Landfill Ban	Alameda does not receive any contaminated recyclables to promote recycling and ZW
2012	Extended Bag Reduction Ordinance	Reduction of single-use plastic bags and promotion of reusable shopping bags
2014	Bottled Water Legislation	Restricted sale or distribution of drinking water in plastic bottles of 21 ounces or less on city property

Municipal waste management and treatment

Stockholm has high environmental standards and ambitious goals for environmental improvement. The Municipality of Stockholm is responsible for the WMS in the capital. Avfall Sverige is an organization that supports all municipalities in Sweden. In 2007, the Stockholm municipality started a project called 'Vision Stockholm

2030' for Stockholm's sustainable development in the future. Stockholm has established the goal to be fossil fuel free by 2050 (City of Stockholm, 2009). One of the key objectives of the 2030 vision is transforming Stockholm into a resource-efficient region (RUFS, 2010).

The composition of MSW in Stockholm includes organic waste (31%), paper (29%), plastic (7%), metal (3%), glass (8%), textile and rubber (2%), and others (20%). Electronic and hazardous waste are collected separately in Stockholm. A total of 406,596 tonnes of waste was generated in Stockholm in 2008–2009, which was around 480 kg per person per year (Avfall Sverige, 2011; Stypka, 2007). Sweden has a very long history of waste management by thermal waste treatment technology – i.e. by incineration. A significant amount of MSW (59%) is managed by incineration. Residents in Stockholm recycled 31% of MSW in 2009 and composted about 1%. The remaining 9% of waste was disposed of in landfills. Table 8.5 shows the composition of MSW and WMSs in Stockholm.

Stockholm has been developing and improving its waste collection and management infrastructure in an advanced way. Three stages of waste sorting and collection systems have been implemented in Stockholm. The first stage is building-based separation at the source (combustible, organic, and recyclables), the second one is block-based recycling room (separate recycling bins for metal, glass, paper, plastic, electronic waste, and bulk waste), and the final stage is area-based hazardous waste (paint, varnish, glue, solvents, battery, etc.) collection points (Hammarby Sjöstad, 2007). Stockholm has also developed an advanced mobile automated waste disposal system in which waste is collected by the vehicle with a vacuum suction system from docking points located in apartment buildings.

An underground vacuum suction waste collection network is the most advanced waste collection technology at this moment. In highly dense urban areas where

TABLE 8.5 Composition and waste management in Stockholm

Waste composition	Waste streams	Per cent (%)
	Organic	31
	Paper	29
	Plastic	7
	Glass	8
	Metal	3
	Textiles and rubber	2
	Others	20
Waste management	Waste management options	Per cent (%)
	Compost	1
	Recycle	31
	Incineration	59
	Landfill	9

Source: Adapted from Avfall Sverige (2011) and Stypka (2007)

the surface area is very limited and very costly, underground service networks for energy, water, sewage, and waste are highly viable and effective as solutions. Despite very high investment costs, many new development areas, such as Hammarby Sjös-tad (in Stockholm for 100,000 households), are implementing the most advanced underground automated vacuum collection systems (AVAC) with operation costs two to three times lower than conventional waste collection systems (ISWA, 2013).

Stockholm also offers a range of waste collection systems, including household door-to-door waste collection, roadside waste collection, community recycling, and decentralized recycling depots. Hence the operating cost of the traditional waste collection system would be much higher compared to the underground AVAC system. However, a feasibility study of a similar project, 'Green Square Town Centre' in Sydney, shows that the underground AVAC system, planned for a period of 30 years, is more costly than the conventional truck collection systems (City of Sydney, 2011) because Sydney offers only a door-to-door waste collection and centralized waste depot system. Hence, based on socio-economic and environmental priorities, AVAC systems can either be highly or less feasible for WMSs. However, a single vacuum collection system for organic waste can be applied to make the system economically viable. This approach can significantly improve organic waste sorting, recycling, collection, and recovery rates, and there will be less contamination and greater resource recovery rates from organic waste. Figure 8.3 shows the AVAC and roadside waste collection systems in Stockholm.

Organic waste is collected in Stockholm on a weekly basis from households, communities, and area-based collection points. Organic waste bins and chute collection systems are used, respectively, in single households and multiunit apartments in Stockholm. Out of the total 3,925 tonnes of food waste collected from households, in 2010, around 1,440 tonnes were treated by digestion, 1,485 tonnes were treated by central composting, and the remaining 1,000 tonnes were treated by home composting. On average, every community or block has either

FIGURE 8.3   AVAC (left) and roadside (right) waste collection systems in Stockholm

a block-based recycling room or street-side recycling facilities. For specific types and volumes of waste, individuals can drop off the waste at nearby recycling depots without any fees.

Recycling centres then further process the recyclables. The total waste collected from the recycling centre is 73,200 tonnes, and the total waste collected by recycling contractors is 59,518 tonnes. Figure 8.4 shows the waste collection and management systems in Stockholm. Advanced automated vending machines are used at retail centres for collecting bottles and cans for refund systems. Hence most households sort their bottles and cans and return them to a retail shop during their shopping. This ensures mass participation in recycling bottles and cans under the extended producer responsibility scheme in Stockholm.

Under the municipal (Kommun) waste collection systems, waste is collected and transported to the incineration plants, AD plants, and disposal facilities. Personal recycling activities in Stockholm are common and play key roles in waste recycling systems. People bring their bottles and cans for recycling to the shopping malls and return them at the automated 'take-back' centres for refunds. For other types of waste, people travel to the local recycling centres to deposit the waste without any additional costs. Even though the major waste fraction was organic, only 1% of organic waste in Stockholm was managed by AD systems. Incineration was predominantly used in WMSs to produce heat and electricity from waste. Landfills were also one of the key waste management methods in Stockholm. MSWs, as well as commercial and industrial wastes, are managed by 13 waste recycling and treatment facilities in Stockholm. Of the treatment facilities in Stockholm, five

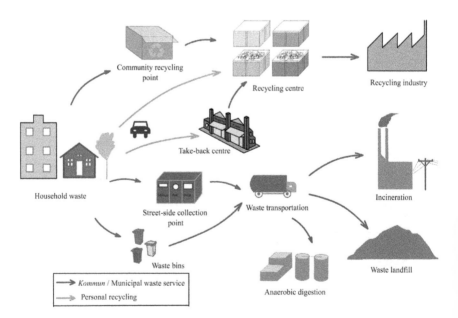

FIGURE 8.4 A schematic diagram of waste collection and management in Stockholm

are government-owned facilities, which treated 746,742 tonnes of solid waste in 2006. Nine private waste recycling and treatment facilities treated 985,877 tonnes of waste in 2006.

Regulatory policies and ZWSs

Sweden, being a member state of the EU, has amended its national WMSs to meet regional and international regulations. Stockholm is very prominent in its regulations and policies in waste management. The history of incineration in Stockholm started at the beginning of the twentieth century. In the 1960s, large-scale waste disposal to landfills started in the Stockholm region. The regulation on aluminium can recycling was enforced in 1982. Under extended producer responsibility legislation, paper and plastic waste are also recycled and recovered in Stockholm.

Stockholm recognizes the environmental pollution from hazardous waste, particularly batteries, and hence regulations on hazardous waste were strictly developed and implemented in Stockholm. Landfill taxes and fees promote less waste going to landfills and encourage a higher rate of recycling and incineration. Bans on combustible and organic waste to landfills are key diversion strategies in Stockholm. Table 8.6 shows the key milestones of MSW management in Stockholm.

Waste management development drivers

Historically, waste handling regulations were first introduced in 1869 as a result of the fears for cholera epidemic (Björklund, 2000). Sweden's geo-climatic condition is one of the key drivers in the development of incineration of waste in Sweden. Due to the need for heat and energy, incineration has become the main waste treatment technology in Sweden. The three stages – i.e. building, block/community, and area-based collection systems – drive maximum sorting and recycling efficiency in Stockholm.

Environmental regulations and policies are also the key drivers in WMSs in Stockholm. Regulations on packaging recycling under extended producer responsibility influenced local people to sort and return these wastes to the recycling depots for refunds. Currently, many products operate under the extended producer responsibility (EPR) scheme in Stockholm. The integration of advanced waste sorting and collection systems, such as chute systems in high-rise buildings and mobile-vacuumed systems, are also playing innovative roles in waste management.

Economic instruments, such as landfill taxes and incentives for community recycling systems, are increasing recycling rates in Stockholm. However, its higher recycling rates have also forced Sweden to import waste from other EU countries to generate heat and energy from waste. This trans-boundary movement of municipal waste may have a significant economic benefit for waste recycling and management in Europe.

TABLE 8.6 Key milestones of municipal WMSs in Stockholm

Year	Milestones in WMS	Goal and focus
1901	The first waste incineration plant in Sweden in Lövsta	Heat and energy recovered from waste
1960s	Landfills started for MSW disposal	Disposal of waste to landfills on a large scale
1969	Miljöskyddslag – Environmental Protection Act	Environmental pollution control and conservation of resources
1982	The act on recycling of aluminum drinking containers	Recycling of aluminum cans
1991	The act (1991:336) on certain beverage containers (PET)	Recycling of plastic bottles
1997	Packaging: producer responsibility for packaging	Extended producer responsibility for paper and plastic waste
1997	Regulation for batteries	Hazardous battery recycling regulation
1998	The Swedish Environmental Code (16 EQOs)	A series of legal targets and deadlines for implementing 15 overarching environmental quality objectives
2000	Introduction of landfill tax	Landfill tax to reduce disposal to landfills
2002	Ban on putting combustible waste to landfill	To maximize combustibles to incineration rather than landfills
2003	Regulation on incineration of waste	Control of combustible waste
2005	Ordinance on producer responsibility for electronic products	To expand the extended producer responsibility for various wastes
2005	Ban on organic waste to landfill	To promote AD and composting
2009	Incorporating the EU Battery Directive to the Swedish legislation	To protect the environment from hazardous lead pollution
2010	Stockholm vision	Declaration of Stockholm vision for 2030
2018	Swedish Environmental Protection Agency sets out the milestone targets in five broad areas, including waste	The milestone targets indicate steps along the way to the environmental quality objectives and the generational goal

Solid waste management in Dhaka

Dhaka, the capital city of Bangladesh, is located in Southeast Asia. Under Mughal rule in 1576, Dhaka was known as Jahangir Nagar, and Dhaka became the capital city of the new province of Eastern Bengal and Assam in 1905 (Bahl & Syed, 2003, p. 55). After the liberation war in 1971, Dhaka became the capital city of independent Bangladesh. The climate in Dhaka is subtropical monsoon with an annual rainfall from 1,429 mm to 4,338 mm. Dhaka is one of the most densely populated cities in the world. Over seven million people live in 360 km² of land area. The population growth rate of Dhaka is 3%, and the population density is 19,178 people/km². Around 42% of the people in Dhaka live in slums, and more than 55% of the population lives below the poverty level (UN-HABITAT, 2010). The average resident in Dhaka has a low income, with GDP US$1,700/capita, and the HDI was 0.567 in 2012.

The Dhaka City Corporation (DCC) is responsible for the daily collection and disposal of 3,000–4,000 tonnes of MSW from the city's 90 wards. The DCC area is divided into ten zones for the management of solid waste generated in the domestic, commercial, industrial, and medical sectors. However, the DCC can collect and dispose of only 40%–50% of the total waste generated every day due to a lack of funds and infrastructure (DCC, 2013). Only 14%–17% of the total municipal budget is used for SWM, which is approximately US$0.5 per capita per year (Matter, Dietschi, & Zurbrügg, 2013). As a result, uncollected waste is primarily dumped illegally in the streets, wastewater drains, ponds, lakes, etc., or managed informally. A significant number of health and environmental problems are created as a result of the inefficient management of waste.

Municipal waste management and treatment

Waste collection in Dhaka is officially conducted through 1,030 roadside containers and 41 private containers (DCC, 2005). Due to a lack of waste infrastructure and narrow road networks, DCC does not provide door-to-door collection systems. Community-based private micro-organizations collect waste from households instead and transfer it to the DCC's designated waste collection and transfer points. Only 22% of the urban poor have access to municipal waste collection bins (World Bank, 1998). From its roadside collection points, DCC collects waste and transfers it to the landfill sites.

The composition of MSW predominantly consists of paper (10%), food (66%), glass (1.4%), metals (0.9%), plastic (2.3%), yard (2.1%), and others (17.3%) (DCC, 2005). Metals are usually pre-sorted and informally collected from the households prior to the disposal of waste due to the high economic value of metal. DCC collects 44% of the waste from 43% of the city corporation's area. Informal recycling deals with 18%. Private organizations compost about 0.02% of MSW, and the remaining 38% remains uncollected and illegally dumped at nearby water bodies and lowland areas (UN-HABITAT, 2010). Table 8.7 shows the waste composition of MSW and WMSs in Dhaka.

The informal recycling sector mainly recycles waste and diverts it from landfills in Dhaka. About 120,000 people are involved in the informal recycling trade chain in Dhaka City, without any government funding or support. Any valuable materials are either reused or sold by their owners or informal waste pickers. There are four stages of informal waste recycling in Dhaka city. More valuable recyclables (metals, paper, glass, or old items) are sorted at the household level, and the sorted recyclables are sold to the door-to-door recyclables buyer (*Feriwalla*). Community-based door-to-door waste collectors (*Vangariwalla*) sort recyclables from waste during

TABLE 8.7 Waste composition and management in Dhaka

Waste composition	Waste streams	Per cent (%)
	Organic	66
	Paper	10
	Plastic	2
	Glass	1
	Metal	2
	Yard	2
	Others	17
Waste management	Waste management options	Per cent (%)
	Compost	0.5
	Informal recycle	17.5
	Uncollected waste	38
	Landfill	44

Source: Adapted from UN-HABITAT (2010)

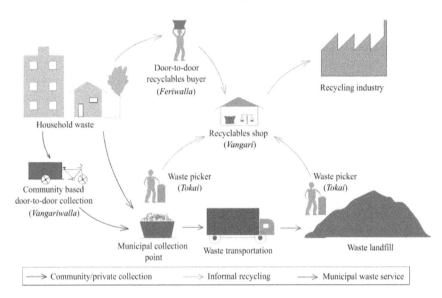

FIGURE 8.5 A schematic flow diagram of municipal waste management in Dhaka

collection. Relatively fewer valuable recyclables (plastic, newspaper) are collected by waste pickers from designated waste bins, landfills, and illegal dumping sites. All recyclables are traded at the local small recyclables shops (*Vangari*), and, finally, these items are sold to the recycling industry for resource recovery. Figure 8.5 shows the formal and informal WMSs in Dhaka city.

As a recent report (Prothom-alo, 2014) on WMSs in Dhaka in 2014 shows, there are 511 garbage containers in different areas of Dhaka city, which is equivalent to one bin for 32,093 people. Informal collectors (mainly deprived people) collect waste from each household due to a lack of government waste collection facilities. Locally made rickshaw vans are used to collect household waste. It is estimated that each van covers around 100 flats or households, and about 20 vans unload their garbage in each container. So, it can be calculated that at least 10,220 vans carry the whole city's waste and put it in the containers provided by the city corporation. For this informal waste collection system, each household pays about 50–70 TK (US$0.75–1) each month, which is equivalent to TK 613,200000 per month (equivalent to US$786,153/month or 9.44 million dollar/year). However, the informal garbage business in Dhaka is controlled by politically influential persons or organizations (Prothom-alo, 2014).

Around 83% of plastic, 65% of paper, and 52% of glass were informally recycled from waste and returned to the recycling industries. Metals are not usually wasted because they would lose their high economic value. Despite risky market conditions for composting of waste, Waste Concern, a local non-profit organization, has initiated community-based decentralized composting in 2008 by adopting low-cost technology, community participation, and partnerships among various local and international actors (Yedla, 2010). The project is registered and approved by the executive board of the Clean Development Mechanism (CDM) under the Kyoto Protocol to the United Nations Framework Convention on Climate Change and is gradually scaling up (UN-HABITAT, 2010).

The key income of DCC comes from a 2% tax based on a property's annual rental value. The only income from waste in Dhaka comes from the informal recycling sector. A study shows that every year, TK 10,706 million (US$137 million) is being saved through recycling. Around 120,000 urban poor are involved in the informal sector of the recycling trade chain of Dhaka city. The per capita expenditure for SWM in Dhaka is very low (TK 53.00) compared to other Asian cities, such as Mumbai (TK 304.00) (Enayetullah, 1994). DCC spent only 15.42% of the total annual expenditure for municipal waste management. The SWM cost of DCC is TK 313.12/cubic metre, of which collection cost is TK 120.54 (32.75%), transportation cost is TK 150.09 (47.90%) and disposal cost are TK 60.60 (19.37%) per cubic metre (Salam, 2001).

Existing formal waste collection systems only cover the transfer of waste from the collection points to the landfill sites. Currently, DCC disposes of 3,340 tonnes/day at three landfill sites located in Matuail (20 ha), Beri Band (2 ha), and Uttara (1 ha). The Matuail landfill site receives 65% of the total volume disposed; Beri Band and Uttara receive 30% and 5%, respectively (RCC-AP, 2005). Despite a 100% waste collection capacity, the generation of waste is mounting every year due to the rising migration of the rural population into Dhaka city.

Regulatory policies and ZWSs

As a developing nation, Dhaka is facing a huge challenge to manage its solid waste sustainably, as Dhaka does not have a ZW strategy. On one hand, urbanization is growing faster and resulting in increased generation of waste. On the other hand, a lack of funds and infrastructure limit current WMSs. The first waste management objective of Dhaka city is to provide 100% waste services to its citizens and collect all waste from the generation points. Informal waste recycling is playing a vital role in WMSs. Considering the socio-economic and environmental contributions of informal waste recycling, a formalized and integrated WMS is required to incorporate informal recycling activities into the formal WMSs.

With the financial and technical assistance of the Japan International Cooperation Agency, Dhaka city designed a solid waste master plan in 2005 with a target year of 2015. By improving the current waste infrastructure through using more than 250 trucks and 440 containers, the project aimed to improve the collection rate to approximately 70% by 2015. The total investment cost of the master plan was estimated at US$61,982,760 for activities during the following 11 years, with the expectation of eventually creating 7,600 new jobs in waste management (DCC, 2005).

Several waste management regulations and strategies have been developed by incorporating national and international stakeholders. A National 3R (reduce, reuse, recycle) Law was developed and went into effect in 2009 (DoE, 2009). The government has banned production, distribution, marketing, and use of polythene bags for any purpose from 2002 in Dhaka city. The study found that 90% of the total 5.5 million polythene bags flow into the sewerage system every day in Dhaka city. Banning polythene bags might reduce water clogging (Ahmed, Nahiduzzaman, & Rahaman, 2002). The government of Bangladesh recently contracted with an Italian company to install the first ever WTE (WtERT, 2013) plants in Bangladesh to generate around 50 MW of electricity for Dhaka. Table 8.8 shows the key milestones of waste management regulations and strategies in Dhaka city.

Waste management development drivers

Even though environmental awareness has increased sound WMSs, public health issues are still the key drivers in waste management in Dhaka. Inefficient waste management leads to various health impacts. Informal waste management is the only recycling and waste diversion option in Dhaka city. Most of the recyclable items in the waste have economic value due to scarcity of resources and fewer income opportunities in Dhaka. Low labour costs and marginal socio-economic conditions are favourable for informal recycling. Institutionalization of informal recycling system is important to improve current WMSs in Dhaka. Because of low labour costs, waste picking and recycling is incentivized in much of the developing world. A formalized process of integrating informal recycling into formal WMSs is also required.

Lack of waste infrastructure and services has led local people to develop community-based, door-to-door waste collection systems. The local authority promotes composting by using the CDM through a technical cooperation initiative with the government of Japan. The development intervention consists of assessing the existing SWM situation, formulation of a master plan, and follow-up implementation of some of the priority issues in waste management.

TABLE 8.8 Key milestones of municipal WMSs in Dhaka

Year	Milestones in WMS	Goal and focus
1995	Environment conservation act	To improve the waste disposal system for the industry
1995	National environmental management action plan	Community-based SWM
1998	Urban management policy statement, 1998	Solid waste disposal for slum areas
1998	National policy for water supply and sanitation 1998	Local government may transfer collection, removal, and management of solid waste to the private sector
2002	Plastic bag ban in Dhaka city	The government has banned production, distribution, marketing, and use of polythene bags in Dhaka city
2004	National CDM strategy	Methane reduction through composting
2004	Urban SWM is handling the rules of Bangladesh	Safe handling of informal recycling with proper personal protective equipment
2009	National 3R strategy	Promote the principle of reducing waste, reusing, and recycling resources and products
2013	Agreement on WTE plant in Dhaka	Advanced WTE technology for waste management
2019	Sanitary landfill and land development	Several sanitary landfill expansion and land development projects are underway to accommodate the ever-growing disposal waste in Dhaka

Comparison of SWM systems in case study cities

Each case study city has its own unique circumstances and strategies for WMSs. Adelaide, San Francisco, and Stockholm represent typical high-consuming cities with high per capita generation of MSW. WMSs in these cities are more systematic and advanced. Dhaka, on the other hand, represents developing and low per capita waste generating cities. WMSs in Dhaka rely significantly on informal WMSs. Both high-consuming and developing cities are experiencing numerous SWM challenges.

Comparison of geo-administrative issues

The study of waste management in Adelaide considered the metropolitan Adelaide area. Since the population density of Adelaide is low to medium, only 1,295 people live per km² of land. Adelaide has the lowest population density of the other case study cities. San Francisco and Stockholm are medium- to high-density cities with similar land area. In contrast, Dhaka has the highest density population

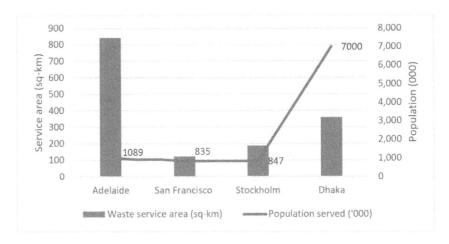

FIGURE 8.6   Comparative waste service area and population

(14.8 times greater than Adelaide); around 19,178 people live per km² of land area. Despite the per capita low-generation rate of waste compared to the developed cities, the population of Dhaka produces an enormous amount of waste every day. Figure 8.6 shows the comparative waste service area and the number of populations served by the local waste management services. Good governance is always an important factor for a city to provide effective waste services to its citizens. Adelaide, San Francisco, and Stockholm have higher governmental and institutional coherence than Dhaka.

The population density and per capita waste generation influence the total amount of waste that needs to be managed by the local authority. Due to its large population, Dhaka produces a significant amount of waste every day, despite a lower per capita waste generation rate. Owing to the lack of infrastructure and funds, most of the waste remains uncollected in Dhaka. In the case of Adelaide, the operational cost of waste collection and recycling is higher than the other cities due to the large land area that needs to be covered under the waste service area. Hence, for effective waste management service, the geo-administrative boundary is important.

Comparison of socio-cultural issues

The development of waste management and recycling depends largely on socio-cultural factors. People's income, consumption behaviour, participation in recycling activities, knowledge, awareness, and willingness are a few examples of socio-cultural drivers in WMSs. Cities from developed counties, such as Adelaide, San Francisco, and Stockholm, have higher per capita incomes and HDI, as well as higher economic footprints. Dhaka has the lowest ecological footprint among the four case study cities. The HDI consists of life expectancy, education, and income indexes

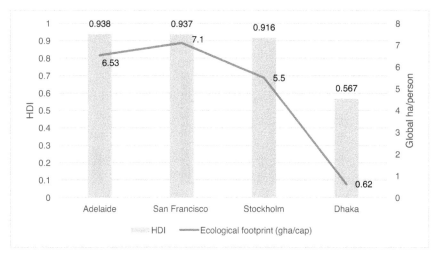

FIGURE 8.7   Comparative HDI and ecological footprint

to measure the overall human development in any country. HDI is one of many indicators used as a benchmark of human development. In this study, the country's HDI is assumed to be the city's HDI, as only country data are available. The ecological footprint measures the human share of bio-capacity: simply, the environmental pressure associated with the consumption of resources. Due to the lack of available data on the ecological footprints of the case study cities, the countries' data on HDI were assumed to be similar to their cities. Figure 8.7 shows the comparative HDI and ecological footprints in the case study cities.

On one hand, Adelaide, San Francisco, and Stockholm represent high-income cities with higher literacy rates, greater environmental consciousness, and higher consuming individuals. Despite these advantages, per capita waste generation is higher in these cities. Dhaka, on the other hand, represents low-income cities with the least literacy and a majority of poor citizens. The people of Dhaka are also less informed about proper recycling and waste avoidance practices. However, due to their different socio-cultural contexts, the residents of Dhaka rely on informal community-based collection and recycling systems.

Comparison of waste management scenarios

San Francisco has the highest generation rate of MSW 609 kg/person/year compared to the other developed cities in this study – namely, Adelaide (490 kg/person/ year) and Stockholm (480 kg/person/year). Adelaide has considered C&D waste within the MSW fraction; therefore, according to the study in UN-HABITAT 2010, the average generation rate of solid waste in Adelaide showed a higher per capita and a higher recycling and diversion rate than the actual scenario. San Francisco has the highest diversion rate (72% in 2009) among the four cities. Adelaide

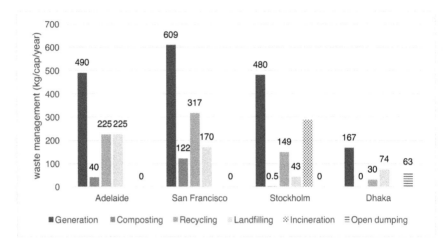

FIGURE 8.8 Comparative waste management in case study cities

and Stockholm have a diversion rate of 54% and 32%, respectively. Waste diversion from landfills in Dhaka only occurs through its informal recyclers, at around 18%.

According to Figure 8.8, WMSs in Adelaide, San Francisco, and Stockholm represent the most advanced waste collection, recycling, treatment, and disposal systems. Stockholm has implanted AVAC systems in parallel with the conventional waste collection from households. San Francisco has recovered biogas from landfills, and Adelaide has implemented on effective CDL policy to maximize waste recycling. All three developed cities generate high amounts of waste per capita and almost half of the waste produced is recycled. WMSs in Dhaka represent a low-cost WMS, dependent on community-based informal and formal WMSs. Community initiatives in waste collection systems in Dhaka are very effective and strong compared to those in the developed cities. Informal waste recycling is the backbone of waste diversion from landfills in Dhaka.

Comparison of the cost-benefits of landfills

Adelaide, San Francisco, and Stockholm depend on advanced waste management technologies, which require a significant amount of public funds. Environmental management standards are also higher in these cities. As a result, the operational and management costs of waste are higher than the WMSs in Dhaka or other developing cities. Landfill taxes and levies are financial instruments used to encourage more resource recovery and to cover waste disposal costs from tax revenue based on a polluter-pays principle, which is not common in low-income cities, such as Dhaka. Figure 8.9 shows the comparative revenue and cost of landfill disposal. As economic and financial aspects were not the main priorities of this study, the comparative cost-benefits of landfills rely on very brief and basic landfill revenue and cost data.

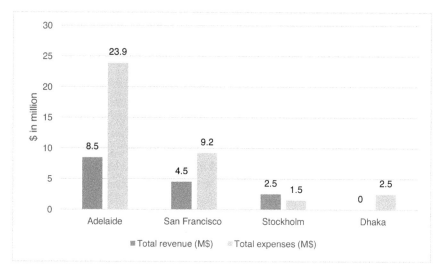

FIGURE 8.9   Comparative landfill revenue and cost in case study cities

Most of the developed cities have a waste landfill tax and levy policy to encourage low landfill and higher diversion rates. Landfill cost is higher compared to the landfill levy in Adelaide and San Francisco, almost two times higher than the disposal cost. Interestingly, Stockholm's landfill tax is higher than the process cost, and, hence, Stockholm earned around US$1 million from landfill revenue in 2009. There is no levy system for waste disposal in Dhaka; therefore, a significant amount of the taxpayer's money is allocated to provide waste services to citizens.

Comparison of regulatory policy and ZW strategy

There are different issues that emerge from the case studies of each city's WMSs, and they provide some important insights into the development of strategies towards becoming a ZW city. At the moment, the ZW goal is being targeted in Adelaide, San Francisco, and Stockholm by achieving zero landfills through diverting waste from landfills. However, the study acknowledges that achieving a 100% diversion rate is not possible in the current production, consumption, and WMSs in our society. It requires a global transformation of existing extraction, production, marketing, consumption, management, and treatment systems.

Adelaide has implemented CDL, and this regulation is considered a success in waste recycling in Adelaide. San Francisco has a long history of informal waste recycling. The strategy of integrating the informal sector with the formal WMS has been a success in WMSs in San Francisco. Both Adelaide and San Francisco have visionary ZW targets and are progressing towards those targets. Stockholm has a cold climate, and, hence, WTE technology, such as incineration, has been in practice from the early history of waste management in Sweden. However, one study shows that more energy can be saved from the recycling of combustible materials, such as paper (2.4–7.1 GJ saving/tonne) and plastic (10.2–26.4 GJ saving/tonne) instead of generating electricity in an incineration process (ICF Consulting, 2005).

In general, recycling of waste is more beneficial than energy recovery, and that is why recycling is on the top of the waste hierarchy compared to energy recovery. A European Court of Justice judge ruled that an operation should only be regarded as recovery if the use of waste meant replacing other materials, the decision makes the incineration of waste a disposal operation rather than recovery, and energy recovery is only incidental (Hansen, Christopher, & Verbuecheln, 2002, p. 4).

Despite effective government efforts and the lack of waste management services in Dhaka, community-based waste collection systems have already been recognized as a potential waste management policy. Informal waste recyclers play a significant role in the diversion rates of WMSs in Dhaka. Community-based decentralized composting is another potential way of developing more sustainable WMSs in Dhaka. Dhaka could apply San Francisco's lessons and adapt the formalization process developed there to integrate the informal sector within its own formal WMS.

Strategic ZW management aims to develop an effective WMS through citizens' pro-environmental recycling behaviour and an optimum resource recovery system from waste. The ZW policies promote recycling activities by creating waste recycling jobs and, hence, contribute to circular economic growth. The case of Dhaka is an example of informal WMS; there are about 120,000 people involved in the waste recycling trade chain in Dhaka city, which contributes significantly to both a circular economic and a resource recovery system. The WMS in Dhaka can benefit from the institutionalization of the current informal waste recycling system into a formal WMS.

Comparison of techno-environmental issues

Proper waste management is essential to ensure minimum resource depletion and optimum resource recovery. As an effective social technology, recycling has been implemented in each city and protects the city from potential environmental degradation. Uncollected waste in Dhaka has introduced various social problems, including illegal dumping, water clogging, drainage blocking, higher mosquito breeding, etc., as well as other serious environmental problems, such as water pollution, emissions, and health issues.

Appropriate social and environmental technologies are required to overcome these problems. Consumers' responsible activities and producers' product stewardship can be effective tools for recycling and recovering consumer products. Consumers' responsible activities can be ensured through empowering awareness about the socio-economic and environmental benefits of waste recycling and by providing sufficient waste management services. Extended producer responsibility has been implemented in many developed countries, and the aluminium cans recycling mandate in Sweden is an example of product stewardship for reclaiming cans (Franklin, 1997).

Proper waste management not only reduces pollution and emissions but also recirculates resources into the production process. For example, resources that are recovered from organic waste and combustible waste (such as paper and plastic) reduce landfill costs and emit fewer emissions into the atmosphere. When resources are used in the production process, they also substitute virgin materials. Adelaide, San Francisco, and Stockholm have been identified as highly motivated and technologically advanced cities trying to solve waste problems. Incineration plants with combined power and heat in Stockholm contribute heat and energy to local households. WTE technology refers to incineration because only Stockholm uses incineration technology among the four case study cities. Other WTE technologies (such as gasification, pyrolysis, and plasma) are not considered. Poor governance and lack of funds may delay the progress of success in waste management in Dhaka. Dhaka's recent WTE plant agreement may lessen its waste problem considerably, but it will not definitely solve all its waste problems.

An integrated ZW management system is essential for all cities, in which producers and consumers play their vital roles in waste recycling and resource recovery activities. Cities can benefit from expanding current recycling practices and promoting circular economic growth through social technologies, such as recycling and collaborative consumption and product stewardship practices under extended producer responsibility schemes. Table 8.9 shows the comparative snapshot of WMSs in the four case study cities. In all cities, the role of economic levers can be seen in the success (and failure) of strategies to reduce waste. These might include a landfill levy, a tax to encourage recycling, or a container deposit scheme in which recycling directly rewards the recyclers.

Conclusion

WMSs in the case study cities are different from one another. It is evident from the case studies of WMSs in Adelaide, San Francisco, Stockholm, and Dhaka that WMSs have been developed and implemented based on their local socio-economic and environmental priorities. Despite various waste management strategies in the different cities, a number of common problems that all four cities have been facing include the devaluation of resources, an increasing generation of waste, the complex composition of waste streams, and challenges around waste avoidance and minimization, optimum resource recovery, and zero landfills.

A strong waste recycling policy (CDL) in Adelaide has significantly influenced the future WMSs in the region. There are several initiatives that have been deployed to make the CDL successful in South Australia. For instance, establishment of recycling depots, awareness programmes regarding the CDL, and increase in the refund from 5c to 10 c act as success factors in Adelaide. A study (EPA-SA, 2012a) shows that around 98% of the respondents (n = 803) were aware of and strongly supportive of (93%) the CDL in Adelaide. Despite Adelaide's success in applying the CDL for recycling activities, a similar policy has not been implemented in other states in Australia due to the resistance and power of corporate packaging businesses.

TABLE 8.9 A comparative snapshot of WMSs in the selected four cities

Key sectors	Indicators	Adelaide	San Francisco	Stockholm	Dhaka
Geo-administrative	City area (km²)	841.5	122	188	360
	Population	1,089,728	835,364	847,073	7,000,000
	Population density (no/km²)	1,295	6,847	4,505	19,178
Socio-cultural	HDI	0.938	0.937	0.916	0.567
	Purchasing power parity★ (US$)	$889.6 billion	$15.29 trillion	$354 billion	$285.8 billion
	GDP per capita★ (US$)	$41,300	$49,000	$39,000	$1,700
	Consumption of meat (kg/year)	128	123	79	4
	Ecological footprint (gha/cap)	6.53	7.1	5.5	0.62
Waste management	Waste generated (tonne/year)	742,807	508,323	406,596	1,168,000
	Generation of waste (kg/cap/yr)	490	609	480	167
	Waste composted	7.68%	20	1%	0.19%
	Waste recycle	46%	52%	31%	18% informal recycling
	Waste incinerated	0%	0.01%	59%	0%
	Waste diverted	54%	72%	32%	18% informal recycling
	Waste landfilled	46%	28%	9%	44%
Cost-benefit	Waste collection frequency	Weekly, fortnightly	Weekly, fortnightly	Daily, weekly, fortnightly	Daily
	Landfill tax/ton (US$)	$25 (2007)	$32.12–$140.76	$67.5 (2007)	NA
	Landfill disposal cost (US$)	$70	$64.49	$40.5	$4.8
	Landfill revenue (US$/year)	$8.5 million	$4.5 million	$2.5 million	$0
	Landfill cost (US$/year)	$23.9 million	$9.2 million	$1.5 million	$2.5 million

Category		Column 1	Column 2	Column 3	Column 4
Regulatory policy	Waste regulations	CDL Zero Waste SA Act Plastic bag ban	Plastic bag ban Climate Action Plan Mandatory composting and recycling	Landfill tax in 2000 Ban combustible waste to landfill Ban organic waste to landfill	Plastic bag ban – Composting under CDM
	Key strategies	ZWSs	ZWSs	ZW Sweden	3R national strategy
Technical	Waste technologies used	Composting, recycling and landfill	Composting, recycling and landfill	Composting, recycling, incineration, AD, and landfill	Composting, informal recycling, and landfill
	Priority areas	Optimum recycling, EPR and ZW	Optimum recycling, EPR and ZW	Optimum recycling and EPR	100% collection and proper landfill
Environmental	GHG emissions from waste*	3%	<1%	2.92%	3.2%
	Environmental targets	60% diversion by 2012 75% diversion by 2015	20% reduction of GHG emissions by 2012 ZW by 2020	ZW by 2020 Vision Stockholm 2030	70% waste collection by 2015 WTEplant by 2016

Sources: Ahmed, Islam, & Reazuddin (1996); APH (2008); Avfall Sverige (2011); Bartelings, Beukering, Kuik, & Oosterhuis (2005); CIA (2011); DCC (2009); EPA-SA (2011); Fager & Davidson (2008); Index Mundi (2013); Stypka (2007); Swedish EPA (2008); UN-HABITAT (2010); UNDP (2013); ZWSA (2007a);

*national average

Informal recycling in Adelaide exists partly due to the direct economic benefits from refund systems.

San Francisco has a unique history in the institutionalization of informal waste recycling systems into formal WMSs. However, a small part of the container (glass, can, plastic) is still recycled through informal homeless recyclers in San Francisco due to their direct economic benefits. Stockholm is strategically forward-thinking in implementing the most advanced waste collection and recycling systems compared to the other developed cities. The number of recycling options (household, community, roadside, and area-based recycling depot) in Stockholm are also significantly greater than the recycling options in the other case study cities. People in Stockholm also receive tokens from bottles and containers by returning them through vending machines. All these findings indicate that people's proactive behaviour (an intended action/direction for the better) in waste recycling activities is influenced by economic incentives.

The case of Dhaka represents WMSs in developing countries, where 100% waste collection is a key challenge for the city authority. Due to the lack of services and formal WMSs, the residents of Dhaka have adapted informal waste collection and recycling systems. Due to its socio-economic situation and lack of waste management services, the community-based informal waste collection systems in Dhaka play a significant role in waste management. It is debatable whether we should emphasize individual recycling activities, similar to those in developed cities, or community-based collection efforts, similar to those in developing cities. However, many believe that individual actions are often derived from the collective intention. For a ZW management system, a balance between individual actions and collective community participation seems essential.

From the case studies, it is evident that every city has its best management practices and key challenges for future development. The CDL is one of the best management practices in Adelaide. Hazardous waste collection systems in Adelaide have failed to be effective. The three bins system is one of the main best management practices in San Francisco. Despite the three bins system and ZW targets, waste generation is significantly higher in San Francisco compared to the other cities. Stockholm has the highest recycling and collection facilities for all sorts of wastes, including hazardous waste. As a result, a comparatively higher number of waste types and waste volume are recycled in Stockholm. Despite their higher percentage of waste collection and recycling, a significant amount of waste is incinerated in Stockholm, which is unsustainable in the context of resource recovery and zero depletion. As mentioned in Chapter 1, ZW supports waste prevention policies (reduce/reuse) instead of treatment and disposal policies. The proposed waste policy in Sweden, importing waste from neighbouring countries, shows a high dependence on incineration plants, which can act as a barrier for reducing waste volume in the long run.

Despite a lack of proper waste services in Dhaka, community-based waste collection is one of the best practices of waste management. Recent initiatives in community-based decentralized composting are also another best management practice in Dhaka. Waste is seen as a source of income for informal recyclers in Dhaka due to a lack of access to basic necessities, income, and resource scarcity. Informal recycling activities also exist in developed cities, such as Adelaide and San Francisco among the very poor and homeless people because waste generates a source of income.

This chapter explored the WMSs in four cities with different socio-economic and environmental contexts. The study concludes that while each city has its own waste management strategy, lessons can be learnt from each city, and, hence, based on the knowledge acquired more, advanced and effective waste management strategies can be developed by considering local conditions. However, it is not simple or logical to propose a single solution for WMSs for all four cities. Based on their waste management priorities, cities need to adapt their own local strategies to tackle global waste problems.

References

Ahmed, A. U., Islam, K., & Reazuddin, M. (1996). An inventory of greenhouse gas emissions in Bangladesh: Initial results. *Greenhouse Gas Emissions: Mitigation Strategies in Asia and the Pacific, 25*(4), 300–303.

Ahmed, S. A., Nahiduzzaman, K. M., & Rahaman, K. R. (2002). *Public Environmental Awareness Regarding the Use of Polythene Bags: Before and After Effects of the Ban Over Their Use and Production*, Dhaka. Retrieved from https://www.researchgate.net/publication/233742253_Plotting_targets_for_a_zero_waste_strategy_on_the_world_summit_time_scale

APH. (2008). *Domestic Jurisdictional Comparison of Waste Levies*. Parliament of Australia Retrieved from www.aph.gov.au/senate/committee/eca_ctte/aust_waste_streams/qon/qon_envnsw.pdf

Avfall Sverige. (2011). Vision för 2020 "Det finns inget avfall". Retrieved from www.avfalls-verige.se/topmenu/om-avfall-sverige/aarsmoete-2011/

AWD. (2004). *The Australian Waste Database*. Retrieved March 19, 2013, from Australian Waste Database: http://awd.csiro.au/

Bahl, T., & Syed, M. H. (2003). *Encyclopaedia of the Muslim World*. New Delhi: Anmol Publications.

Bartelings, H., van Beukering, P., Kuik, O., & Oosterhuis, V. (2005). *Effectiveness of Landfill Taxation*. Retrieved from Amsterdam: www.ivm.vu.nl/en/Images/Effective%20land-fill%20R05-05_tcm53-102678_tcm53-103947.pdf

Björklund, A. (2000). *Environmental Systems Analysis of Waste Management: Experiences from Applications of the ORWARE Model*. (Doctor of Philosophy), Royal Institute of Technology (KTH), Stockholm.

Cal-recycle. (2012). *Curb-Side Recycling, the Next Generation, Case Study: San Francisco Fantastic Three Program*. Retrieved from www.calrecycle.ca.gov/LGCentral/Library/innovations/curbside/CaseStudy.htm

CIA. (2011). *The World Fact Book*. Retrieved from www.cia.gov/library/publications/the-world-factbook/geos/us.html

City of Berkley. (2005). *UN Urban Environmental Accords*. Retrieved from www.ci.berkeley.ca.us/Planning_and_Development/Energy_and_Sustainable_Development/UN_Environmental_Accords.aspx

City of Stockholm. (2009). *Stockholm City Plan: Summary*. Retrieved from http://international.stockholm.se/Future-Stockholm/Stockholm-City-Plan/

City of Sydney. (2011). *Green Square Town Centre: High Level Feasibility Assessment for an Automated Waste Collection System*. Retrieved from http://meetings.cityofsydney.nsw.gov. au/council/about-council/meetings/documents/meetings/2011/Committee/Environment/281111/111128_EHC_ITEM13_ATTACHMENTA.PDF

Coy, O. C. (1919). *Guide to the County Archives of California Sacramento, California*. Sacramento, California State Printing Office. Retrieved from https://archive.org/details/guidetocountyar00davigoog

DCC. (2005). *The Study on the Solid Waste Management in Dhaka City*. (Mail Report). Dhaka.

DCC. (2009). *Australia's National Greenhouse Accounts, National Greenhouse Gas Inventory (Accounting for the Kyoto target)*. VIC: Department of Climate Change.

DCC. (2013). *Solid Waste Management Dhaka, Bangladesh*. Dhaka: Dhaka City Corporation. Retrieved from www.dhakacity.org/Page/Hotlinks/Department/Category/hotlink/Id/12/Solid_Waste_Management

DEWHA. (2009). *The Full Cost of Landfill Disposal in Australia*. Retrieved from www.environment.gov.au/settlements/waste/publications/landfill-cost.html

DoE, B. (2009). *National 3R Strategy for Waste Management*. Dhaka: Ministry of Environment and Forests, Government of the People's Republic of Bangladesh. Retrieved from www.wasteconcern.org/Publication/draft_national_3R_strategy.pdf

Dutko, A. S. (2004). *Recycle Central Debuts on San Francisco Pier*. Retrieved from San Francisco: www.recologymedia.com/press_room/articles/pdf/recyclecentraldebuts.pdf

Enayetullah, I. (1994). *A Study of Solid Waste Management for Environmental Improvement of Dhaka City*. (Master), Bangladesh University of Engineering and Technology, Dhaka.

EPA-SA. (2011). *Container Deposit Refunds*. Retrieved from www.epa.sa.gov.au/environmental_info/waste/container_deposit_legislation

EPA-SA. (2012a). *CDL Awareness and Support Research Report*. Adelaide EPA, South Australia. Retrieved from www.epa.sa.gov.au/environmental_info/waste/container_deposit_legislation

EPA-SA. (2012b). *Plastic Bag Ban*. Adelaide Environmental Protection Agency. Retrieved from www.epa.sa.gov.au/councils/resources_for_councils/plastic_bag_ban

EPA-SA. (2013). *Review of Recycled Organic Wastes in South Australia*. Adelaide: EPA. Retrieved from www.epa.sa.gov.au/xstd_files/Waste/Report/organicwaste.pdf

EPA, & LGA. (2003). *Draft Metropolitan Adelaide Waste to Resources Plan: Infrastructure and Kerbside Services*. Adelaide EPA and LGA. Retrieved from www.lga.sa.gov.au/webdata/resources/files/Draft_Waste_to_Resources_Plan_for_Metro_Adelaide___2003_pdf1.pdf

Fager, C., & Davidson, C. (2008). *Greenhouse Gas Emissions Inventory 1990–2006*. Retrieved from https://sustain.sfsu.edu/sites/default/files/assets/doc/SF_State_Greenhouse_Gas_Emissions_Inventory.pdf

Forster, C. (1999). *Australian Cities: Continuity and Change* (2nd ed.). Melbourne: Oxford University Press.

Franklin, P. (1997). *Extended Producer Responsibility: A Primer*. Retrieved from www.container-recycling.org/index.php/issues/extended-producer-responsibility

Gargett, K., & Marden, S. (1996). *Adelaide: A Brief History*. Adelaide: National Library of Australia.

Government of SA. (2011). *South Australia's Strategic Plan 2011*. Retrieved from Adelaide: www.saplan.org.au/

Gowan, T. (1997). American Untouchables: Homeless Scavengers in San Francisco's Underground Economy. *International Journal of Sociology and Social Policy, 17*(3–4), 159.

Hammarby Sjöstad. (2007). *Hammarby Sjöstad: A Unique Environmental Project in Stockholm*. Retrieved from www.hammarbysjostad.se/inenglish/pdf/HS_miljo_bok_eng_ny.pdf

Hansen, W., Christopher, M., & Verbuecheln, M. (2002). *EU Waste Policy and Challenges for Regional and Local Authorities*. Retrieved from www.arctic-transform.eu/files/projects/2013/1921-1922_background_paper_waste_en.PDF

ICF Consulting. (2005). *Determination of the Impact of Waste Management Activities on Greenhouse Gas Emissions*. Retrieved from Canada: www.recycle.ab.ca/uploads/File/pdf/GHG_Impacts_Summary.pdf

Index Mundi. (2011). Sweden GDP: Per capita (PPP). Retrieved from www.indexmundi.com/sweden/gdp_per_capita_(ppp).html

Index Mundi. (2013). *County Profile and Data Base*. Retrieved from www.indexmundi.com/factbook/countries

ISWA. (2013). *Underground Solutions for Urban Waste Management: Status and Perspectives*. Retrieved from http://www.iswa.org/index.php?eID=tx_iswaknowledgebase_download&documentUid=3157

IWS. (2013). *Wingfield Price List*. Retrieved from http://iwsgroup.com.au/index.php?/about/wingfield

Matter, A., Dietschi, M., & Zurbrügg, C. (2013). Improving the informal recycling sector through segregation of waste in the household: The case of Dhaka Bangladesh. *Habitat International, 38*(April), 150–156.

McDougall, K., & Sumerling, P. (2006). *The City of Adelaide a Thematic History*. Retrieved from www.adelaidecitycouncil.com/assets/acc/Council/docs/city_of_adelaide_thematic_history.pdf

NAWMA. (2013). *NAWMA's Waste Management Services*. Retrieved from http://nawma.sa.gov.au/about/

O'Day, E. F. (1926). *The Founding of San Francisco: Water*. Retrieved from www.sfmuseum.org/hist6/founding.html

OECD. (2012). *Recommendation of the Council on Regulatory Policy and Governance*. Retrieved from Australia: www.oecd.org/gov/regulatory-policy/49990817.pdf

Perry, S. (1978). *San Francisco Scavengers: Dirty Work and Pride of Ownership*. Berkeley: University of California Press..

Prothom-alo. (2014). Brisk business thru' waste collection. *The Daily Prothom-alo*. Retrieved June 3, 2014, from http://en.prothom-alo.com/bangladesh/article/48447/Brisk_business_thru_waste_collection

RCC-AP. (2005). *Dhaka City State of Environment: Solid Waste Management*. Final report. Retrieved from www.rrcap.ait.asia/reports/soe/dhakasoe05.cfm

RUFS. (2010). *Office of Regional Planning, Stockholm County Council*. Retrieved from www.tmr.sll.se/english/RUFS-2010/

SA-EPA. (1999). *Integrated Waste Strategy for Metropolitan Adelaide*. Retrieved from www.epa.sa.gov.au/xstd_files/Waste/Report/iwsp.pdf

Salam, M. A. (2001). *Analysis and Design of Solid Waste Management System for A Residential Zone of Dhaka City*. (M.Sc. Engineering), Bangladesh University of Engineering and Technology, Dhaka.

SF-Environment. (2010). *San Francisco Mandatory Recycling and Composting Ordinance*. Retrieved from www.sfenvironment.org/sites/default/files/editor-uploads/zero_waste/pdf/sfe_zw_mandatory_fact_sheet.pdf

SF-Environment. (2011). *Landfill Contract Set for Hearing at Board*. Retrieved from www.sfenvironment.org/news/press-release/city-introduces-measure-to-approve-new-landfill-contract

Sharwood, A. (2013). Coca-Cola wins Federal Court case, cash for containers recycling found illegal. Retrieved from www.news.com.au/finance/business/coca-cola-wins-federal-court-case-cash-for-containers-recycling-found-illegal/story-fnda1bsz-1226590179763

Statistics Sweden. (2010). *Statistic Centralbyrån: RegionalatjänsterochIndelningar.* Retrieved from www.scb.se/Statistik/MI/MI0802/2010A01/mi0802tab3_2010.xls

Stewart, S. B. (2003). *Archaeological Research Issues for the Point Reyes National Seashore: Golden Gate National Recreation Area.* Retrieved from www.sonoma.edu/asc/projects/pointreyes/overview2.pdf

Stypka, T. (2007). *Integrated Solid Waste Management Model as a Tool of Sustainable Development* (12). Retrieved from Stockholm: www2.lwr.kth.se/forskningsprojekt/Polishproject/rep12/StypkaSt.pdf

Swedish EPA. (2008). *Swedish Greenhouse Gas Emissions at Record Low in 2008.* Retrieved from http://swedishepa.com/en/In-English/Menu/GlobalMenu/News/Swedish-greenhouse-gas-emissions-at-record-low-in-2008/

UNDP. (2013). The rise of the South: Human progress in a diverse world. *Human Development Report 2013.* Retrieved from New York: http://hdr.undp.org/en/media/HDR_2013_EN_complete.pdf

UN-HABITAT. (2010). *Solid waste management in the world's cities: Water and sanitation in the world's cities* (Earthscan Ed.). London: Earthscan.

US-EPA. (1993). *In-Depth Studies of Recycling and Composting Programs: Designs, Costs, Results.* Retrieved from US-EPA, Washington, DC: https://nepis.epa.gov/Exe/ZyPDF.cgi/40001087.PDF?Dockey=40001087.PDF

USK. (2011). Folkmängd den 31 Dec 1995–2019. Stockholm. Retrieved from www.usk.stockholm.se/tabellverktyg/tv.aspx?t=a1&sprak=eng

White, S., & Aisbett, E. (2002). *Container Deposit Legislation: An Independent Assessment of the Introduction of CDL in NSW.* Retrieved from Mackay, Queensland: www.uts.edu.au/research-and-teaching/our-research/institute-sustainable-futures/our-research/resource-futures-0

World Bank. (1998). *Sectoral Analysis: Solid Waste Management.* Washington, DC: The World Bank.

WtERT. (2013). Waste-to-Energy Plants for Dhaka. Retrieved from www.wtert.eu/Default.asp?Menue=18&NewsPPV=11978

Yedla, S. (2010). Replication of urban innovations: Prioritization of strategies for the replication of Dhaka's community-based decentralized composting model. *Waste Management & Research.* doi:10.1177/0734242X10380116

ZWSA. (2007a). *Review of Solid Waste Levy.* Retrieved from www.zerowaste.sa.gov.au/upload/resources/publications/reuse-recovery-and-recycling/levy_review_final_report_5_feb_8.pdf

ZWSA. (2007b). *South Australia's Waste Strategy 2005–2010 Benefit Cost Assessment, Volume 1: Summary Report.* Retrieved from www.zerowaste.sa.gov.au/upload/resources/publications/cost-benefit-analysis/2188/BenefitCostAnalysisVolume_summary.pdf

ZWSA. (2011a). Free e-waste drop off depot in Adelaide. Retrieved from www.facebook.com/events/188879897868049/#!/photo.php?fbid=248408835223805&set=a.162491863815503.42194.118692401528783&type=1&theater

ZWSA. (2011b). *Zero Waste SA: About Us.* Retrieved from www.zerowaste.sa.gov.au/about-us

ZWSA. (2013). *Waste Levy.* Retrieved from www.zerowaste.sa.gov.au/About-Us/waste-levy

PART 3

Zero-waste strategy and tool

9

ZERO-WASTE STRATEGY

Introduction

'ZW' is one of the most studied, yet most debatable, topics in waste management research in the last decades (Seltenrich, 2013; Zaman, 2015). ZW is defined by the ZWIA as 'designing and managing products and processes systematically to eliminate the waste and materials, conserve and recover all resources and not burn or bury them' (ZWIA, 2004). Thus, ZW is about waste prevention through sustainable design and consumption practices, as well as optimum resource recovery from waste and not about managing waste by incineration or landfills. It is understandable that ZW strongly supports waste avoidance and prevention approaches rather than waste treatment and disposal. However, it may not be feasible to achieve zero incineration and zero landfill goals under the existing resource consumption and WMSs.

Strategic waste management plans are commonly used by local governments and business organizations for managing waste problems (ZWSA, 2013). A strategic waste management framework is essential for the successful implementation of a waste management plan, as it is the foundation of an effective planning process (King, 2004). The aim of this study is to develop a ZWS. The purpose of the development of ZWSs is to articulate principles that underpin all activities relating to policy formulation. The term 'waste' refers to MSW that the holder discards or intends to discard or is required to be discarded. The parameters and issues identified are relevant to the MSW.

A number of studies have been conducted on the development of waste management frameworks (Gillwald, Anyango Tocho, & Mwololo Waema, 2013; Lu & Yuan, 2011), including decision frameworks (Ramesh & Kodali, 2012), legislative frameworks (Sentime, 2013), and hierarchical frameworks (Liao & Chiu, 2011). A framework helps decision makers understand, improve, evaluate, and guide WMSs. The purpose of the strategic ZWF is to guide waste management policy and decision makers while developing and proposing waste management strategies and policies.

The key aspects for the development of a ZWS

Many local councils set their ZW goals to 'diversion of waste from landfills'; however, diversion of waste may not be sufficient, as it requires innovative design and sustainable consumption to achieve the long-term goals. The 3R principles (reduction, reuse, and recycling) are among the top three in the waste hierarchy, and they are considered the founding principles of sustainable WMS (Hansen, Christopher, & Verbuecheln, 2002). In the EU Waste Framework Directive 2008, the '3R' principles have been extended to five steps of the waste hierarchy: prevention (avoidance), reuse, recycling, recovery (including energy recovery), and disposal (European Commission, 2012). The ZW primarily focuses on the top of the waste management hierarchy (avoidance and reduction of waste creation, reuse, and recycle of wasted product), and the secondary focus of the ZW concept is resource recovery from waste using environmentally friendly technologies (Zaman, 2015; Zotos et al., 2009).

A number of approaches have been identified in various studies, such as eco-design and responsible shopping behaviour, in relation to waste prevention and avoidance (Braungart, McDonough, & Bollinger, 2007; Schmidt, 2012). Waste prevention is one of the most important issues in ZW, and it requires collective social awareness and knowledge of waste and innovative manufacture and business models (Cox et al., 2010). Awareness and transformative knowledge are often believed to motivate behaviour change in relation to pro-environmental lifestyle choices (Jackson, 2005).

Responsible and sustainable consumer behaviour is another important issue in waste prevention. Collaborative consumption increases efficiency in resource consumption and enhances social collaboration (Rogers & Botsman, 2010). The collaborative ownership or collaborative consumption model promotes service-based business and waste prevention (DEFRA, 2013). Therefore, recirculation of post-consumer products through reuse and resell is important; it boosts the CE and enhances social capital.

Waste management and treatment technologies have been used for solving waste problems for centuries (UNEP/GRID-Arendal, 2006). ZW takes the position that technology alone cannot solve waste problems sustainably, as it requires community participation, service infrastructure, regulatory policy, and environmentally friendly treatment technology. A number of studies have identified that effective collection systems; decentralized waste recycling centres; social technology, such as recycling; composting; regulatory policies, such as PAYT; and environmentally friendly advanced waste treatment technologies are the key issues in waste management and treatment (Dahlén & Lagerkvist, 2010; Seyfang, 2005). The fundamental differences between traditional waste management and ZW management is that ZW management restricts the application of WTE, which burns waste to generate energy (heat and electricity) and landfills in an 'ideal' ZW environment. Therefore, this study is also intended to investigate the waste experts' opinion on restricting certain technologies to promote ZW activities.

Performance evaluation is an integral part of a strategic framework to determine the future direction of WMSs. Moreover, accurate and reliable data on WMSs is utterly important to assess and monitor the overall performance of the waste management strategies and programmes. ZW research in relation to data analysis, forecasting waste generation and management trends, and continuous improvement in waste prevention and avoidance techniques are also main issues in ZW management (Connett, 2013). Hence waste categories which are related to MSW are relevant to this study. Table 9.1 summarizes the key issues of ZW management based on the literature review completed for this study.

A study conducted by Zaman (2017) identified the key elements of a ZWS based on a survey of waste experts around the globe. Experts involved in WMSs in different professions, such as academic institutes, businesses, government agencies, community organizations, and environmental organizations were invited to participate in the survey to identify the key aspects of WMSs.

The survey consisted of a number of questions associated with waste prevention and avoidance, waste management and treatment, and monitoring and assessment. As the expert survey required a specific group of people – i.e. waste management experts – the expert survey was done by applying expert sampling methods. In expert sampling

TABLE 9.1 The key selected issues of ZW management

Phases	Key aspects of ZW
Waste prevention and avoidance	Awareness and education of waste
	Transformative knowledge and willingness to behaviour change
	Innovative product design (C2C)
	Producer responsibility (take-back scheme)
	Responsible shopping and consumption practices (sustainable consumption)
	Collaborative consumption practices
	Extended product lifespan through repair/reuse
	Market creation for post-consumer products recirculation
Waste management and treatment	New infrastructures (bins, collection vehicles, etc.)
	Effective waste collection services (kerbside waste collection)
	Decentralized recycling and resource recovery centres
	Enabling social technology through community participation (recycling, composting, etc.)
	Improve source reduction through PAYT principle
	Waste incentives (levy, taxes, token, etc.)
	Environmentally friendly waste treatment solutions
	Regulations on restricted mass use of landfill and WTE
Monitoring and assessment	Available and reliable waste data
	Performance evaluation through ZW research

method (Mack, Woodsong, Macqueen, Guest, & Namey, 2005), the sample is chosen based on known and demonstrable experience and expertise in some specific area (in this case waste management). Waste management experts were selected based on available information about their expertise on WMSs. The study applied purposive sampling and non-random sampling techniques, as the survey was mainly conducted on the waste experts (a specific expert group). Experts were identified and selected based on their (i) contributions to peer- reviewed academic publications identified using Scopus Database, (ii) involvement with waste management organizations and institutions, and (iii) affiliation with waste management policy and decision-making processes. The expert group was contacted by e-mail and invited to participate in the survey.

The survey questions used a five-point Likert scale for agreeing or disagreeing with any statement, rating the effectiveness (not effective to very effective) of any technique, and identifying levels of priorities or importance (low to very high). There are number of advantages and disadvantages in using a Likert scale because the outcome of the survey depends on how the ratings are made and the level of understanding of the respondents (Ogden & Lo, 2012). The study showed that there are benefits from using continuous rating scales in online survey research (Treiblmaier & Filzmoser, 2011). The questionnaire was validated and tested by applying a pilot survey.

The survey results were analysed with statistical data analysis software statistical package for the social sciences (SPSS). Cross-tabulation was used to (with a chi-square test for independence) explore the relationship between two independent categorical variables. The chi-square test compares frequency or proportion of cases in each category (Pallant, 2013). As the study investigates the importance of various key priorities given by various waste expert groups, the chi-square test was applied.

A total of 68 experts from 23 countries participated in the expert survey. The questionnaire was sent to about 450 waste experts around the globe and the response rate was 15.1%. Most of the participants were from Asia-Pacific, Europe, or America. A total of 15 waste experts were from Asia, 20 from Europe, 16 from America, and 16 from Oceania. Despite a similar number of the targeted experts from different regions, the survey poorly attracted responses from Africa, as only one expert from Africa participated in the survey. The average year of expertise of the participants was 15.4 years. The survey covered experts from various sectors in WMSs. Figure 9.1 shows the affiliation of the participants. The affiliations of the experts are categorized according to four types: (i) government organizations, including local and central government and policymaker; (ii) business organizations, including recycling, transporting, and landfill business organizations and service providers; (iii) academic institutes, including research institutes, teaching, and training; and (iv) environmental organizations, including non-government environmental, community, national, and international waste management organizations.

Issues and factors relevant to WMS

A number of issues and factors of WMS, including waste prevention and avoidance, waste management and treatment, and monitoring and assessment, were considered

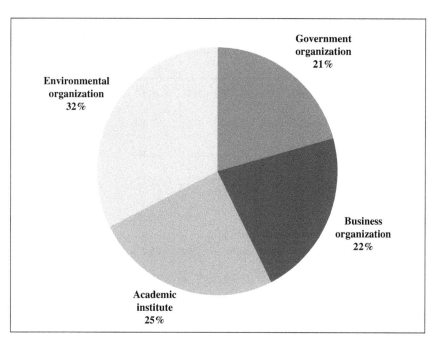

FIGURE 9.1 Participants' affiliations

in the survey to identify the relevance, important, and priorities of different waste management approaches. Table 9.2 summarizes the focus group survey findings.

Over 80% of the all respondents agree or strongly agree on a number of issues, such as the importance of awareness and education on waste and it influences in behaviour change and C2C design, along with extended producer responsibility and collaborative consumption through a shared ownership of products. Statistically insignificant differences were observed in the responses, which means there is no statistically significant difference in the experts' opinions, whereas statistically significant differences were observed in the responses (p=0.05 = 0.05) on waste incentives (refunds) and penalties (taxes, fees).

Waste incentives have significant influence in waste prevention, recycling, and management practices (Cossu & Masi, 2013; Yang & Innes, 2007). Around 60.3% were of the view (agreed and strongly agreed) that a higher incentive (refund/financial benefit) will increase the performance of the CDL. About 33.8% of the experts were undecided, and only 5.9% of the experts opposed more incentives for CDL.

Similar responses were also provided on the issue of the PAYT system. Statistically, an insignificant difference (p=0.07 > 0.05) is observed in the cross-tabulation between the different groups of professionals and their responses to the PAYT system. A total of 4.4% experts ranked PAYT as not effective, 13.2% ranked it as slightly effective, 20.6% ranked it as moderately effective, 32.4% ranked it as very effective, and 29.4% ranked it as extremely effective for waste recycling systems.

TABLE 9.2 Issues and factors relevant to existing WMS

Issues and factors of waste management	Likert scales				
	Strongly disagree	Disagree	Neither disagree nor agree	Agree	Strongly agree
Importance of awareness and education about waste	2.9%	0%	4.4%	35.3%	57.4%
Proper education and environment for behaviour change	1.5%	0%	7.4%	47.1%	44.1%
Importance of innovative C2C product design	1.5%	0%	4.4%	35.3%	58.8%
Extended producer responsibility (take-back scheme)	1.5%	4.4%	7.4%	48.5%	38.2%
Effective policy on responsible shopping and consumption practices	0%	2.9%	22.1%	42.6%	32.4%
Collaborative consumption or shared ownership of products	0%	2.9%	13.2%	48.5%	35.3%
Importance of market creation for post-consumer products recirculation	1.5%	7.4%	13.2%	33.8%	44.1%
Higher incentives for CDL	1.5%	4.4%	33.8%	41.2%	19.1%
Restriction on incineration	14.7%	13.2%	25.0%	25.0%	22.1%
High landfill tax and ban on waste to landfills	4.4%	5.9%	26.5%	27.9%	35.3%
Effectiveness of waste management programmes	Not effective	Slightly effective	Moderately effective	Very effective	Extremely effective
Training on correct recycling	0%	4.4%	25.0%	48.5%	22.1%
Individual bins system (organic, recycling, hazardous, etc.)	0%	2.9%	22.1%	48.5%	26.5%
Kerbside or door-to-door waste collection	0%	2.9%	14.7%	44.1%	38.2%
Community recycling centre	0%	4.4%	27.9%	47.1%	20.6%
Priority of issues	No priority	Low priority	Moderate priority	High priority	Extreme priority
Enabling social technology through community participation	0%	0%	8.8%	33.8%	57.4%
Effectiveness of improving efficiency through PAYT systems	4.4%	13.2%	20.6%	32.4%	29.4%
Environmentally friendly treatment technology	26.5%	42.6%	14.7%	10.3%	5.9%
Research on material flows and waste performance	0%	2.9%	11.8%	44.1%	41.2%
Priority of data availability and reliability	1.5%	0%	4.4%	26.5%	67.6%
Priority of composting	0%	5.9%	16.2%	38.2%	39.7%
Priority of AD	0%	5.9%	17.6%	60.3%	16.2%
Priority of WTE technology	8.8%	20.6%	17.6%	36.8%	16.2%
Priority of landfills	26.5%	42.6%	14.7%	10.3%	5.9%

In recent years, a number of studies have been conducted on how to achieve ZW through zero landfills (IWMB, 2005; Lang, 2005; Usapein & Chavalparit, 2014). Bans on waste going to landfills and high landfill taxes are necessary for sustainable WMSs. Statistically insignificant differences were observed in the responses (p=0.708 > 0.05). Table 9.2 shows that around 63.2% of the experts supported (agreed and strongly agreed) landfill waste bans and high landfill taxes. Around 26.5% of the experts were undecided, and only 10.3% were unsupportive of landfill bans and high landfill taxes.

Availability and reliability of waste data are important for measuring progress and developing waste management strategies (Hoornweg & Bhada-Tata, 2012). Statistically insignificant differences were observed in the responses (p=0.753 > 0.05). Table 9.2 shows overall around 67.6% of the experts ranked data availability and reliability for waste management as extremely important, 26.5% ranked it as very important, and only 4.4% and 1.5% ranked it as moderately important and not important, respectively.

A study identified that research on ZW is essential to achieve overall ZW goals (Connett, 2013). Statistically insignificant differences were observed in the responses (p=0.775 > 0.05). Table 9.2 shows that most of the waste experts agreed and strongly agreed (around 85.3%), and only 2.9% disagreed with the need for research on material flow. Around 86.3% experts from academic institutes and about 85.7% government institutes, support such research.

Four selected technologies, such as composting, AD, WTE, and landfills, were rated according to their environmentally friendly waste treatment technology. Composting and AD were rated (around 78% and 76%, respectively) as the higher priority environmentally friendly technologies compared to WTE and landfills (around 53% and 16%, respectively).

Thermal waste treatment technologies are very popular in the European region due to energy provision, despite their various environmentally damaging consequences. Waste experts were asked whether city councils should restrict the mass implication of WTE technologies, as they pollute and deplete natural resources. Statistically insignificant differences were observed in the responses (p=0.664 > 0.05). A mixed response to restricting incineration by the experts is shown in Table 9.2. A total of 47.1% of the experts supported (agreed and strongly agreed) restriction on thermal waste treatment technologies, 25% remain undecided, and the remaining 27.9% of the experts opposed the restriction on mass burning of waste, which indicates restriction of WTE technologies is not a feasible option under current circumstance.

Around 63.2% of the respondents agreed or strongly agreed on high landfill taxes and bans on landfills; however, a significant proportion of the respondents (26.5%) were undecided, and the remaining 10.3% disagreed or strongly disagreed with the statement. It is also important to consider that inert materials need to be disposed in landfills, as it is not possible to recycle them. Unfortunately, no question was asked in the survey about what would happen if the ban and restrictions on landfills were truly impose. Therefore, restrictions on certain materials, such as paper and organic items, could be possible, but a complete ban on landfills may not be feasible and practical under current management systems.

Key issues for ZWS

The identified key issues for the development of a ZWS were rated by experts' from less important to extremely important. The mean value of the survey responses (least important to extremely important) are presented in Table 9.3 and the standard deviation shows the variation of ratings from the mean. The key ZW issues were ranked according to the 'minimum mean', which is the value of the mean minus the standard deviation.

The survey findings of the waste experts show that the innovative product design using C2C principle was ranked as the top-most important issue in ZW, followed

TABLE 9.3 The key ZW issues

Key Issues	Mean	Std. dev.	Mean-std. dev.	Rank
Innovative product design (C2C)	4.5294	0.63412	3.895	1
Transformative knowledge and willingness to behaviour change	4.5441	0.74180	3.802	2
Producer responsibility (take-back scheme)	4.5147	0.76280	3.752	3
Enabling social technology through community participation (recycling, composting, etc.)	4.4030	0.75998	3.643	4
Regulation and restriction on the mass implication of landfills and WTE	4.4179	0.781398	3.636	5
Available and reliable waste data	4.3382	0.74534	3.593	6
Market creation for post-consumer products recirculation	4.3382	0.765103	3.573	7
Responsible shopping and consumption practices	4.3824	0.81092	3.517	8
Awareness and education of waste	4.3134	0.82036	3.493	9
Decentralized recycling and resource recovery centres	4.3182	0.82572	3.492	10
Performance evaluation through ZW research	4.2206	0.807531	3.413	11
Extends product life cycle through repair/reuse/resell	4.2059	0.92331	3.282	12
Improve source reduction through PAYT principle	4.1765	0.89678	3.279	13
Effective waste collection services (kerbside waste collection)	4.0294	0.809839	3.219	14
Environmentally friendly waste treatment solutions	4.0147	0.872339	3.142	15
New infrastructures (bins, vehicles, etc.)	4.0149	0.895993	3.118	16
Collaborative consumption practices	3.9403	0.919166	3.021	17
Waste incentives (levy, taxes, token, etc.)	3.9688	0.991532	2.997	18

by transformative knowledge motivating behaviour change (Gilg, Barr, & Ford, 2005), producer responsibility, enabling social technology through community participation, and so on. Even though a mixed response was received in response to the question on the restricted use of mass implication of WTE and landfill technology, experts ranked higher on the regulation and restrictions on mass implication of WTE and landfills for achieving ZW goal.

Participants associated with environmental organizations had a higher percentage of agreement on the fact that a lack of awareness is the key cause of waste problems and that creating a positive environment for behaviour change will allow the waste problem to be addressed more effectively.

Experts from government organizations mostly supported various waste policies and strategic issues compared to experts from academic or environmental organizations. For waste collection systems, kerbside door-to-door waste collection systems were supported by most of the waste experts. Most of the experts agreed that there is a need to promote social technologies, such as recycling, collaborative consumption, shared ownership, and so on, to reduce waste generation.

The experts provided a mixed response to thermal waste treatment technology. Mostly, experts from business and government organizations supported WTE technology, and experts from academic and environmental organizations were supportive of promoting recycling. In this survey, waste incentive received a mixed opinion regarding its effectiveness in waste management. However, various studies suggest that waste incentives (financial or moral) can be beneficial for motivating people to recycle waste.

Interestingly enough, experts gave high importance to key ZW issues regarding available and reliable waste data and ZW research, which indicates that waste management performance evaluation is important to measure existing WMSs and improve and guide future direction. It is important to acknowledge that the survey captured a simplistic view of very complex WMSs, and the number of responses is also an important factor in generalizing the survey findings. A comprehensive qualitative (such as a survey) and quantitative (life-cycle assessment) analysis are required to identify most important issues in the development of an environmentally friendly ZW strategy.

Development of a strategic ZWF

The study considered all identified ZW issues as the guiding principles for the development of a strategic ZWF. It is essential to acknowledge that the importance and application of each guiding principle would be dependent on the local conditions. Some of the guiding principles are equally important for any geographical location while consigning the ZW goals – for instance, C2C design, education and awareness of waste. However, priority of the other guiding principles, such as ZW research, environmentally friendly treatment technology, and waste incentives, would be different in developed and developing countries. The ZW strategic framework is based on 18 key aspects for achieving ZW goals in cities. This study proposed 18 strategies under each aspect for achieving the ZW goals and the ZWS:

Strategy 01: Effective public awareness programme on the WMS should be provided by the governing body (educational institutes, city councils, etc.) through education.

Strategy 02: Both short-term and long-term programmes should be designed and applied to improve the fundamental understanding of the ZW concept.

Strategy 03: Research on ZW should be conducted to provide a better industrial design solution for manufacturers and to improve resource recovery efficiency from waste.

Strategy 04: Consumption of resources should be improved through a shared ownership of product service systems (collaborative consumption).

Strategy 05: ZW programmes should provide proactive support strategies to motivate behaviour change towards responsible and sustainable resource consumption practices.

Strategy 06: Sustainable and responsible living should be embraced and practiced by both producers and consumers by focusing on the principle of environmental conservation and stewardship.

Strategy 07: Appropriate waste infrastructure, such as waste bins, collection systems, resource recovery, and treatment and disposal systems, should be provided and insured for conscious improvements of waste management practices.

Strategy 08: Alternative and innovative technologies should be developed and incorporated to ensure continuous improvement to achieve ZW goals.

Strategy 09: A robust ZW governance system should be in place to enable and adapt appropriate regulatory policies for today and the future.

Strategy 10: Products should be designed by following a C2C design principle so that resources can be recovered at the end-of-life phase.

Strategy 11: Manufacturing of products must ensure an optimum level of resource use with a minimum level of socio-economic and environmental burden by following eco-efficiency and cleaner production practices.

Strategy 12: Manufacturers are responsible for managing their end-of-life products, and thus waste products should be managed and recycled under the extended producer responsibility schemes.

Strategy 13: Waste reduction programs should be developed and promoted in every resource consumption and utilization phase under a comprehensive national waste reduction policy.

Strategy 14: Facilitate community-based repair shops to extend the product's lifetime and to promote reuse techniques by involving the local community.

Strategy 15: Recyclable items should be segregated, collected, and processed under a comprehensive waste recycling and resource recovery scheme.

Strategy 16: Regulatory policy must be developed and implemented to achieve a zero-landfill goal, and the sanitary landfills should be used only as a temporary and least preferred solution when alternative solutions are not feasible.

Strategy 17: Thermal technology depletes materials while recovering heat and energy, and thus thermal technology should be restricted to mass-burn application when alternative solutions are not available or feasible.

Strategy 18: Incentive (both financial and motivational) mechanisms should be integrated into the local WMSs to enable and promote local recycling and resource recovery activities.

Table 9.4 summarizes the important guiding principles of the elements of the ZWF (in no particular order). The key waste prevention strategies for achieving the ZW goals are as follows:

TABLE 9.4 The key strategic elements and action plan for the ZW

Phases	Strategic elements	Action plan
Waste prevention and reduction	Effective public awareness programme on the WMS should be provided by the governing body (educational institutes, city councils, etc.) through formal and informal education system	Inclusion of waste education programmes at the school curriculum and organize awareness promotional programmes on waste avoidance and reduction
	ZW programmes (transformative knowledge) should provide proactive support strategies to motivate behaviour change towards responsible and sustainable resource consumption practices	Hands-on training and knowledge sharing programmes (short-term and long-term) that motivate behaviour change should be organized
	Sustainable and responsible living should be embraced and practiced by consumers by focusing on the principle of environmental conservation and stewardship	Global citizenship initiatives through responsible shopping and consumption behaviour should be enabled
	Consumption of resource should be improved through a shared ownership of product service systems	Collaborative consumption (shared ownership) activities and services should be promoted
	Products should be designed by following a C2C design principle so that resources can be recovered at the end-of-life phase	Designing for disassembly practices at the design and manufacturing phases of products should be promoted
	As manufacturers are responsible for managing their end-of-life products, waste products should be managed and recycled under the extended producer responsibility principle	Mandatory take-back scheme for producers, especially for hazardous and non-disassembly products, should be introduced
	The use-life of post-consumer products should be expanded by up-cycling (repairing/reusing) and contributing to CE	Revitalize social capital in reuse and repair activities to expand the use-life of post-consumer products should be revitalized.
	A favourable market condition for post-consumer goods and recycling materials should be ensured and considered economically viable commodities	Regulatory and economic policy to promote completive market conditions for post-consumer recycling products should be introduced

(Continued)

TABLE 9.4 (Continued)

Phases	Strategic elements	Action plan
Waste management and treatment	Appropriate waste infrastructure, such as separate bins and kerbside collection system systems, should be provided for continuous improvement of waste management practices	Three bin and kerbside collection systems should be introduced to improve waste sorting, recycling, and collection efficiency
	Local government should provide decentralized recycling and resource recovery facilities within the close proximity of the community	Both community-based and remote recycling facilities in urban precincts should be established
	Empower social technologies, such as reuse, repair, and recycle, through community participation	Activities that promote social technology and enhance social capital should be promoted
	Source reduction through enabling and introducing regulatory policies and programs should be improved	PAYT scheme to promote source reduction should be introduced
	Application of environmentally friendly waste treatment technology to ensure a maximum resource recovery with a minimum environmental pollution should be encouraged	Environmentally friendly technology, such as composting and AD, instead of landfills should be ensured
	WTE technology should not be applied as a mass-burn solution of waste treatment unless a feasible alternative solution is available	The mass application of WTE should be regulated and restricted unless a feasible alternative solution is available
	Landfills should be banned and applied as an interim disposal option	Waste diversion from landfill targets should be introduced
	Economic incentive mechanisms should be facilitated to motivate and promote effective management practices	Various economic incentives policies, such as refunds and landfill levies, should be introduced
Monitoring and assessment	Annual waste management data should be collected by maintaining standardized data collection and reporting systems	Implementation of waste data collection and monitoring systems is necessary at the city/ municipality level for building a national waste database
	Research on ZW should be conducted to provide a better industrial design solution for manufacturers and to improve resource recovery efficiency from waste	National and international collaborative ZW research activities should be promoted

Applications and limitations of the ZWF

The strategic elements should be implemented by following both short-term (i.e. 1–4 years) and long-term (i.e. 5–10 years) action plans. It is important to acknowledge that the proposed strategic elements and action plans are contextual and may not be applicable to all countries, especially in developed and developing countries, because there would be a significant difference in the priorities in implementing the strategic elements for these countries. However, it is anticipated that each strategic element with a consideration of local circumstances would guide countries to achieving the overall ZW goals.

The steps in ZW action plans start with the preliminary assessments (clockwise in Figure 9.2) of existing WMSs. The preliminary assessment and evaluations are important for measuring existing waste management performance. Waste characterization and key problems in achieving ZW goals need to be identified at this pre-evaluation stage. After a comprehensive pre-assessment of the existing waste

FIGURE 9.2   Steps in the ZW action plan

scenario, the elements of the ZWF should be implemented in an integrated manner. It is essential to have ZW goals and targeted milestones when applying a ZWF for progressing towards ZW. As explained, local authorities should prioritize and implement the strategic elements according to their requirements under a comprehensive action plan. After implementing ZW action plans, a post-evaluation of the ZW management performance needs to be carried out.

The strategic ZWF aims to guide existing cities towards a state of ZW by ensuring and empowering a CE. An effective CE integrates all cities' stakeholders, including designers, producers, retailers, consumers, policymakers, planners, and individuals, to maximize the value of resources and thus recycle, recover, and conserve natural resources. The performance of these strategies should be measured continuously to evaluate the progress towards the ZW goals.

ZW needs a new generation of people with clear concepts regarding what is waste and what is not waste. Without having a better understanding of waste by the majority of people, it will be very difficult to follow the ZW path. Education and awareness are thus the first aspects of working towards ZW. The second crucial aspect is the industrial transformation of product design and manufacturing. Without sustainable production processes in which products are designed to be disassembled at the end of life, the overall ZW goals will not be possible to accomplish. Finally, the role of global citizens is one of the most important aspects in ZW because ZW is not about managing the waste but mainly about not creating waste in the first place during the consumption process. Therefore, without responsible global stewardship, the visionary ZW goals can never be achieved.

Based on the survey findings and strategic directions, three fundamental strategic action plans that need to be implemented simultaneously for moving towards ZW societies are suggested as follows: (i) sustainable production through a C2C design and product stewardship, (ii) collaborative and responsible consumption of natural resources, and (iii) ZW management through conservation of resources. In addition, a constant evaluation of progress towards ZW goals is also required. Achieving ZW goals requires a holistic, long-term waste management strategy; thus, it may not be possible to solve waste problems overnight or within a short period of time.

Conclusion

A strategic ZWF is essential for initiating major activities to achieve ZW goals. This study tried to identify the key guiding principles for the development of a strategic ZWF based on a consensus analysis of waste experts. The key elements of the ZWF are identified in the literature focusing on waste prevention and avoidance, waste management and treatment, and monitoring and assessment.

The expert survey identified 18 strategic elements as important guiding principles for the development of a holistic ZWF. The study acknowledged that all the strategic elements may not be feasible in all countries, especially in the developing countries where appropriate infrastructure and regulatory policies are not available and for developed countries where associate waste management costs are very high. A further study could be conducted to identify and explain the elements that are appropriate for different economic contexts (developed and developing). It is expected that by considering the local circumstances, such as local waste management priority, waste market, and economic condition, the proposed elements would work as guiding principles for achieving the ZW goals.

The fundamental transformation of existing systems is required, and the study concluded that the ZW goals may not be achieved without a closed-loop production system in place, wide application of responsible consumption practices, conservative WMS, and continuous improvement through monitoring and assessment of waste management performance. The findings of this study are important and can contribute to the knowledge of ZW management. Therefore, it would be beneficial for local authorities to consider the proposed strategic elements while developing the local and national ZWS.

References

Braungart, M., McDonough, W., & Bollinger, A. (2007). Cradle-to-cradle design: Creating healthy emissions: A strategy for eco-effective product and system design. *Journal of Cleaner Production, 15*(13–14), 1337–1348. doi:10.1016/j.jclepro.2006.08.003

Connett, P. (2013). Zero waste 2020: Sustainability in our hand. In S. L. R. Crocker (Ed.), *Motivating Change: Sustainable Design and Behaviour in the Built Environment.* London: Earthscan.

Cossu, R., & Masi, S. (2013). Re-thinking incentives and penalties: Economic aspects of waste management in Italy. *Waste Management, 33*(11), 2541–2547.

Cox, J., Giorgi, S., Sharp, V., Strange, K., Wilson, D. C., & Blakey, N. (2010). Household waste prevention—A review of evidence. *Waste Management and Research, 28*, 193–219.

Dahlén, L., & Lagerkvist, A. (2010). Pay as you throw: Strengths and weaknesses of weight-based billing in household waste collection systems in Sweden. *Waste Management, 30*(1), 23–31.

DEFRA. (2013). *Consultation on the Waste Prevention Programme for England.* Retrieved June 12, 2014, from https://consult.defra.gov.uk/waste/waste_prevention/

European Commission. (2012). *Preparing a Waste Prevention Programme: Guidance Document.* Paris: European Commission.

Gillwald, A., Anyango Tocho, J., & Mwololo Waema, T. (2013). Towards an e-waste management framework in Kenya. *Info, 15*(5), 99–113.

Gilg, A., Barr, S., & Ford, N. (2005). Green consumption or sustainable lifestyles? Identifying the sustainable consumer. *Futures, 37*, 481–504.

Hansen, W., Christopher, M., & Verbuecheln, M. (2002). *EU Waste Policy and Challenges for Regional and Local Authorities.* Berlin, Germany: Ecological Institute for International and European Environmental Policy.

Hoornweg, D., & Bhada-Tata, P. (2012). *What a Waste: A Global Review of Solid Waste Management.* Knowledge papers no. 15. U. d. series. Washington, DC: World Bank.

IWMB. (2005). A Comprehensive Analysis of the Integrated Waste Management Act Diversion Rate Measurement System. California Environmental Protection Agency and IWMB California. California, California Environmental Protection Agency and Integrated Waste Management Board (IWMB).

Jackson, T. (2005). *Motivating Sustainable Consumption: A Review of Evidence on Consumer Behaviour and Behavioural Change* (T. Jackson, Ed.). Surrey, UK: Sustainable Development Research Network.

King, Sue. (2004) Strategic Framework—The Foundation of an Effective Planning Process. CIDM. Retrieved from http://www.infomanagementcenter.com/enewsletter/200411/third.htm

Lang, J. C. (2005). Zero landfill, zero waste: The greening of industry in Singapore. *International Journal of Environment and Sustainable Development, 4*(3), 331–351.

Liao, C.-H., & Chiu, A. S. F. (2011). Evaluate municipal solid waste management problems using hierarchical framework. *Procedia: Social and Behavioral Sciences, 25,* 353–362.

Lu, W., & Yuan, H. (2011). A framework for understanding waste management studies in construction. *Waste Management, 31*(6), 1252–1260.

Mack, N., Woodsong, C., Macqueen, K. M., Guest, G., & Namey, E. (2005). *Qualitative Research Methods: A Data Collector's Field Guide.* Durham, NC: Family Health International, New York.

Ogden, J., & Lo, J. (2012). How meaningful are data from Likert scales? An evaluation of how ratings are made and the role of the response shift in the socially disadvantaged. *Journal of Health Psychology, 17*(3), 350–361.

Pallant, J. (2013). *SPSS Survival Manual.* UK: McGraw-Hill Education.

Ramesh, V., & Kodali, R. (2012). A decision framework for maximising lean manufacturing performance. *International Journal of Production Research, 50*(8), 2234–2251.

Rogers, R., & Botsman, R. (2010). *What's Mine Is Yours: The Rise of Collaborative Consumption.* New York: HarperBusiness.

Seltenrich, N. (2013). Incineration versus recycling: In Europe, a debate over trash. Environment 360: Opinion, Analysis, Reporting & Debate, from https://e360.yale.edu/features/incineration_versus_recycling__in_europe_a_debate_over_trash.

Sentime, K. (2013). The impact of legislative framework governing waste management and collection in South Africa. *African Geographical Review, 33*(1), 81–93.

Seyfang, G. (2005). Shopping for sustainability: Can sustainable consumption promote ecological citizenship? *Environmental Politics, 14*(2), 290–306.

Schmidt, Marcus. (2012). "Retail shopping lists: Reassessment and new insights." *Journal of Retailing and Consumer Services, 19,* 36–44.

Treiblmaier, H., & Filzmoser, P. (2011). *Benefits from Using Continuous Rating Scales in Online Survey Research.* Vienna: Vienna University of Economics and Business.

UNEP/GRID-Arendal. (2006). A history of waste management. Retrieved May 10, 2011, from http://maps.grida.no.go/graphic/a-history-of-waste-management

Usapein, P., & Chavalparit, O. (2014). Options for sustainable industrial waste management toward zero landfill waste in a high-density polyethylene (HDPE) factory in Thailand. *Journal of Material Cycles and Waste Management, 2014*(16), 373–383.

Yang, H.-L., & Innes, R. (2007). Economic incentives and residential waste management in Taiwan: An empirical investigation. *Environmental and Resource Economics, 37*(3), 489–519.

Zaman, A. U. (2015). A comprehensive review of the development of zero waste management: Lessons learned and guidelines. *Journal of Cleaner Production, 91,* 12–25.

Zaman, A. U. (2017). A strategic framework for working toward zero waste societies based on perceptions surveys. *Recycling, 2*(1), 1.

Zotos, G., Karagiannidis, A., Zampetoglou, S., Malamakis, A., Antonopoulos, I. S., Kontogianni, S., & Tchobanoglous, G. (2009). Developing a holistic strategy for integrated waste management within municipal planning: Challenges, policies, solutions and perspectives for Hellenic municipalities in the zero-waste, low-cost direction. *Waste Management, 29*(5), 1686–1692.

ZWIA. (2004). *Zero Waste Definition Adopted by Zero Waste Planning Group.* Retrieved July 16, 2010, from www.zwia.org/main/index.php?option=com_content&view=article&id=49&Itemid=37

ZWSA. (2013). *South Australia's Kerbside Three-Bin System Waste Report.* Retrieved October 29, 2015, from www.zerowaste.sa.gov.au/upload/resource-centre/publications/local-government/ZWSA%20Kerbside%20report%202015%20DE_02.pdf

10
SMART ZERO-WASTE TRACKING SYSTEM

The role of smart technologies in WMS

Smart technologies and devices have been the core components of the smart city lifestyle. The application of smart devices has increased significantly in recent years to ensure security and safety of people and to mine big data to deliver smart city services and identify any emerging challenges through cloud computing (Hashem et al., 2016). The Internet of Things (IoT), or smart technologies, plays a vital role in our urbanized modern society; however, the application of smart technologies in the waste industry is very limited. In recent years, a number of studies have been conducted to integrate IoT technologies in the WMS.

Smart recycle bins and solar-powered waste bins in compaction facilities have been tried in a number of cities, such as Melbourne in Australia. Bins with sensors can inform the waste management authority when they become full (Wahab, Kadir, Tomari, & Jabbar, 2014), and bins with compaction technology can compact the waste to increase its storage capacity, which is very useful for the waste authority for developing an effective and efficient waste collection system.

The radio frequency identification (RFID), load cell sensor, imaging, and weighing technology can be employed for not only bringing down waste management costs but also to facilitate automating and streamlining WMSs (Chowdhury & Chowdhury, 2007). The barcode reading device, imaging, machine learning, and web-based, cloud-computing technologies make real-time tracking system of waste possible from its point of consumption (buying), creation, recycling, and collection to the final treatment. Therefore, the application of smart technologies could be very vital in overall performance of the WMS. Figure 10.1 shows the solar compactor bins used at the Curtin Campus in Western Australia.

The GPS-equipped waste collection truck has been used in many developed countries for an effective and efficient fleet management system. Integrating the imaging and weighing technology will enable us to assess the waste characteristics in realtime to make better decisions in determining the fate of the waste (recycling vs. disposal).

FIGURE 10.1 Solar compactor bins at Curtin Campus, Western Australia

Smart resource tracking system

Our lives have been transformed by and evolved around smart gadgets and technologies in recent times due to rapid innovation and development in the ICT sector. From personal diet monitoring to household energy or household security to country protection, smart devices have become a vital part of the urban system. Smart devices not only deliver vital services to us but also provide digital data, which was once not available for common use. Big data mainly sourced from various smart devices, such as mobile phones, traffic cameras, and so on, is often considered the next gold mine. Despite its potential, smart tracking systems have not yet been implemented widely in the waste sector. The waste sector, in fact, is one of the least developed sectors when it comes to reliable and accurate data.

We need a long-term plan and mass participation to achieve ZW goals. The strategic plan can extend for the next 10–20 years, which means without considering the next generation, it is not possible. The 'heads down generation' spends more time looking at smart device screens than interacting with other human beings. Although the intention of smart devices or social networks is to connect with other people, this generation seems to be the most disconnected and isolated generation ever. Yet there is no way we can or should ignore their potential, and that's why we have seen teenage kids become instant millionaire celebrities as a result of their mobile application or entrepreneurial skills. Our next generation may not be on board to move towards ZW unless we provide the platform equipped with smart devices. Without appropriate tracking and monitoring systems, we may not be able to achieve the expected ZW goals.

Challenges of waste tracking

Waste management is a complex and dynamic system and involves a wide range of stakeholders, and thus it possesses a number of challenges (DEFRA, 2018), such as

- Waste characteristics and composition always changes;
- A diverse range of waste types in which mis-interpretation can occur;
- Due to process/moisture loss, mass balance of waste input and output cannot be done;
- Similar waste can be generated in different sources, which impacts the categorization of waste;
- Involves a large number of operators and vendors, which makes data tracking more challenging; and
- Lacks centralized and systematic reporting systems.

Available smart tracking devices

Studies have already been conducted to measure the resource flow at the household level to the city scale to understand the urban metabolism. For example, Harder et al. (2014) quantified household consumption and waste generation, and Shahrokni, Lazarevic, and Brandt (2015) quantified individual resource metabolism and urban metabolism using smart devices.

Smart devices, such as RFIDs, sensors, GPS trackers, imaging, and videos have been implemented in security, fleet management, marketing, resource management, and many other sectors. There is an opportunity to apply the smart devices to track household resources and waste flows to generate big data on waste, which was not possible without using the innovative technologies that are available today.

Despite being threatened by climate change and the global warming phenomena, the world is still divided on the debate regarding whether the north should decrease its pollution and the south should continue to increase GHG emissions in the next decades. Smart resource tracking systems will enable us to understand our contribution to conservation or depletion of resources in each and every resource consumption and supply-chain stage. This will allow not only a better understand of the resource flow but also bring transparency to the transboundary movement of hazardous waste from OECD to non-OECD countries (Breivik, Armitage, Wania, & Jones, 2014).

Recently, the e-waste watchdog BAN used GPS trackers to trace the journey of electronic equipment in Australia. It was found that the electronic equipment in reality ended up in Thailand and Hong Kong, which under the current Basel Convention is unethical and irresponsible according to BAN (2018). Since waste is not considered as vital and important as many other commodities, the industry lacks a comprehensive data collection and reporting system.

The integrated smart ZW tracking system

The integrated smart zero-waste tracking system (ISZTS) is a system in which waste is not only monitored at the end-of-life phase from the bin to recycling or temporary disposal but also tracks back through the production and consumption to inform both producers and consumers about the problematic practices. To make zero disposal and burning a reality, we need to travel a long way with the utmost dedication and strong economic policy to support ZW practices with the support of the community. We need to resolve issues and challenges that hinder the achievement of ZW goals while considering disposal and WTE as interim provisions.

The ISZTS will bring all relevant stakeholders to a single platform to scrutinize each other's practices and improve their performances. Figure 10.2 shows a schematic diagram of the ISZTS. At first, we need to understand our shopping and consumption behaviour. A customized mobile application equipped a with bar scan reader will assist households with capturing their shopping habits by analysing the shopping receipts or monthly bills (energy, water, groceries, etc.). This will allow the consumer to track his or her consumption habit and identify any problematic issues in relation to his or her shopping habits. The data from shopping will allow us to record product types, packaging, and almost every detail of the products and inform the consumer if the packaging is recyclable or not. Although various packaging is

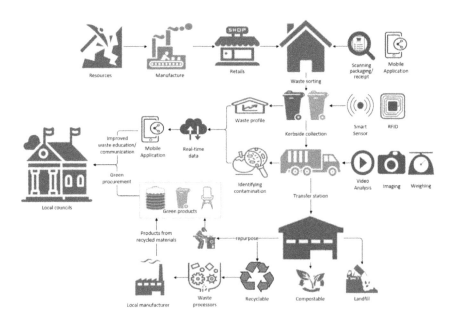

FIGURE 10.2 The schematic diagram of the ISZTS system

certified as recyclable/compostable, often, they don't get recycled or composted, so this problematic packaging will be identified at this stage. From the recycling and waste management practices, we can identify which packaging creates problems and cannot be recycled.

The Australian government has taken the 100% waste packaging target, which is achievement of 100% recyclable, compostable, and reusable packaging by 2025. However, this target alone is not enough because we need a follow-up target, such as a 100% recycling of the packaging by 2030 (Zaman, 2018). We have PET bottles, which are 100% recyclable; unfortunately, we are not recycling 100% of the PET bottles and that is the problem. Given this background, it is reasonable to say that innovative technology using smart devices can address some of these packaging issues.

The 'amazon effect' is a packaging issue that the waste industry is facing globally due to increasing online shopping practices. In the USA, it has been seen that certain problematic packaging is coming from online shopping, which does not comply with the local waste and recycling infrastructure. We need to understand the packaging of local as well as overseas products that are coming through online shopping. Without appropriate data capture, it may not be completely understood why, despite having modern equipment and technology in place, we are not achieving the expected level of performance due to the problematic packaging or design issues. The data on the problematic packaging or design will be shared with the relevant manufacturers and retailers so that they can improve their product design. In addition, individual households would be able to analyse their consumption and waste management data and compare their behaviour with their peers to motivate themselves.

After analysing household consumption behaviour, we need to know what the household waste profile is in the context of recycling practices (i.e. accuracy and efficiency).

Using RFIDs and sensors with all waste bins and weighing all bins during collection will allow the household to understand how much waste was generated and what goes in which bins to complete a more accurate household waste profile. This can be used for 'bill by weighing' system what we called pay as you throw (PAYT). PAYT is not a new system; it has been implemented in many countries in Europe and the Americas.

In addition, the photograph of the waste analysing the machine learning technique will allow us to identify the level of contamination of certain bins in certain areas. The level of contamination can be reduced by developing and offering a customized recycling programme for the target group/community.

All data will be available in the cloud system to synchronize the waste data from the generation point to the end-of-disposal point for validation and monitoring of littering and public use. The whole database can be synchronized with the national database, such as the Australian Bureau of Statistics.

This database will allow not only us to see the real-time waste management practice but also forecast the future trend and the necessary policy and infrastructure requirements.

The key characteristics of the ISZTS

One of the key objectives of integrating smart technologies in the WMS is to mine as much data as possible. In the waste industry, securing quality data is very challenging, as the sector involves multiple stakeholders. The key characteristics of the ISZTS are given next:

- It acquires data from both generators and stakeholders.
- The system applies a data-driven approach.
- It provides real-time accurate/reliable data.
- The data is accessible for public use.

References

Basel Action Network. (2018). *Illegal Export of e-Waste from Australia: A story as told by GPS Trackers.* Retrieved from http://wiki.ban.org/images/7/7c/Australian_e-Waste_Report_-_2018.pdf

Breivik, K., Armitage, J. M., Wania, F., & Jones, K. C. (2014). Tracking the global generation and exports of e-waste: Do existing estimates add up? *Environmental Science & Technology, 48*(15), 8735–8743.

Chowdhury, B., & Chowdhury, M. U. (2007). *RFID-based real-time smart waste management system.* Paper presented at the 2007 Australasian Telecommunication Networks and Applications Conference.

DEFRA. (2018). *SBRI GovTech Catalyst: Smart Waste Tracking Supplementary Information Pack.* Retrieved from https://assets.publishing.service.gov.uk/government/uploads/system/uploads/attachment_data/file/723436/smart-waste-tracking-supplementary-info.pdf

Hashem, I. A. T., Chang, V., Anuar, N. B., Adewole, K., Yaqoob, I., Gani, A., Chiroma, H. (2016). The role of big data in smart city. *International Journal of Information Management, 36*(5), 748–758.

Harder, R., Kalmykova, Y., Morrison, G. M., Feng, F., Mangold, M., & Dahlén, L. (2014). Quantification of goods purchases and waste generation at the level of individual households. *Journal of Industrial Ecology, 18*(2), 227–241.

Shahrokni, H., Lazarevic, D., & Brandt, N. (2015). Smart urban metabolism: Towards a real-time understanding of the energy and material flows of a city and its citizens. *Journal of Urban Technology, 22*(1), 65–86.

Wahab, M. H. A., Kadir, A. A., Tomari, M. R., & Jabbar, M. H. (2014). *Smart recycle bin: A conceptual approach of smart waste management with integrated web based system.* Paper presented at the 2014 International Conference on IT Convergence and Security (ICITCS).

Zaman, A. U. (2018). *The New 100% Recyclable Packaging Target Is No Use If Our Waste Isn't Actually Recycled.* Retrieved from https://theconversation.com/the-new-100-recyclable-packaging-target-is-no-use-if-our-waste-isnt-actually-recycled-95857

11

MEASURING TOOL
FOR ZERO-WASTE

The need for a zero-waste tool (ZWT)

SWM requires integrated planning and design strategy. Integrated WMSs manage waste from generation to collection, recycling, treatment, and disposal to landfills. The success of sustainable WMSs often relies on the success of each component of an integrated waste management strategy. To measure the success and failure of waste management strategies, an accurate and reliable tool is needed.

WMSs consist of various socio-economic, environmental, and technological issues and involve multiple stakeholders, including the community, local government, business organizations, research institutes, etc. Therefore, waste management always attracts a diversity of interest groups. Depending on the interest of the particular group, the waste management assessment tool can vary. Waste management assessment tools can be integrated to assess the performance of social, economic, or environmental benefits.

Most of the currently available tools for assessing the performance of WMSs are based on the concept that waste is generated by and managed at the last phase of the production and consumption process (Timlett & Williams, 2011; Zorpas & Lasaridi, 2013). This study, however, defies the traditional concept of waste by putting forward the suggestion that waste is an intermediate phase of production and consumption. Waste that is generated from the production and consumption process should be recirculated to production processes through reuse, recycle, reassemble, resell, redesign, or reprocess.

The primary elements that are used in the production process are natural resources in the form of materials, energy, and water. A number of other elements are also involved in the process, such as knowledge, money, manpower, technology, and infrastructure. Therefore, the creation of waste and its disposal to landfills results in the loss of materials, energy, and money. In addition, waste disposal not only depletes natural resources but also imposes various negative impacts on the environment. An effective waste management evaluation tool should consider the amount of resources that are recovered and conserved by the WMS.

As a closed-loop urban metabolism in a CE ensures that we can refurbish, remanufacture, and recycle waste products to recover and conserve resources, the ZWT should evaluate waste management performance by measuring the resources gained and environmental degradation avoided in the context of GHG emissions. Presently, waste diversion is widely used as a benchmark of a city's performance on ZW management systems. Achieving a 100% diversion rate (one of Adelaide's and San Francisco's ZW targets is to achieve a 100% waste diversion) is considered a ZW goal, but this is not truly justified and is not the core concept of ZW philosophy. This study is interested in developing a tool that can assess the overall performance of the current WMSs to monitor progress towards a CE in the context of materials, energy, water, and environmental benefits.

The purpose of this chapter is to formulate the waste management performance evaluation tool. This chapter presents the key criteria, mathematical formula, and data set used in developing the ZWT. Finally, the proposed ZWT is applied to evaluate the waste management performance of the four case study cities.

Limitations and scope of the proposed ZWT

According to the ZWIA (ZWIA, 2004), the key goal of the ZW movement is to guide people in changing their lifestyles and practices to emulate sustainable natural cycles in which all discarded materials are designed to become resources for others to use. Hence, ZWSs ensure a circular material flow in urban systems and conserve and recover all resources. However, many cities (including Adelaide and San Francisco) have developed their ZW goal to achieve 100% waste diversion from landfills. The waste diversion rate is used as an indicator and progress towards ZW systems. This study argues that the waste diversion rate can only be used as a milestone, as it does not capture the degree to which a WMS can be evaluated as successful in approaching ZW.

As ZW combines resource consumption behaviour, conservation, flow, recovery, and depletion within the urban system, a ZW evaluation tool should capture all these aspects while measuring the performance of WMSs in developing ZW cities. The ZWT provides a quantitative numeric value reflecting the state (progress) of the WMSs. The proposed ZW evaluation tool only considers resource flow in urban systems in regard to resource conservation.

There are various types of waste depending on material composition and source of generation (EPA, 2010). All these waste types require different management approaches and treatment technologies. This study analyses only household waste with a selected number of materials in the waste – i.e. organic, plastic, paper, metal, glass, and mixed waste composition are used in developing the ZWT. The study excludes nutrient recovery from organic waste, so the ZWT considers generic compost recovery from organic waste instead of recovering nutrients' value in compost materials. The ZWT has been developed by considering eight fundamental assumptions, and it aggregates different factors (resource substitution from various treatment methods) into a single value – i.e. ZWI, which may not always reflect the whole scenario. It provides a quantifiable indication of progress towards the goods of ZW.

Development of the ZWT

The products that we consume every day are primarily produced using virgin materials, energy, and water. From resource extraction to waste generation, consumption depletes the environment by contributing GHG to the atmosphere. One of the main aims of this study is to conceptualize ZW based on material flow analysis and develop a measurement tool to account for the performance of WMSs in cities. In addition, the tool will forecast the potential amount of virgin materials, energy, water, and GHG emissions that can be substituted by the WMSs. Therefore, the study proposes the ZWI as an innovative tool to measure waste management performance.

The nine steps undertaken in the development and application of the ZWT are given next:

i   Characterization of MSW (types, composition, and generation of household waste in the case study cities);

ii   Identification of waste management techniques (waste management methods, such as recycling, composting, incineration, and landfills, used in the case study cities);

iii   Identification of design variables (that were considered in the development of ZWT);

iv   Define system boundaries based on the scope of the ZWT;

v   Design criteria of the ZWT;

vi   Design the formulation of the ZWT (formula or equations used in quantifying the ZWI);

vii   Development of a database for the resource substitution factor of virgin materials, energy saving, water savings, and GHG emission offsets for different waste management techniques;

viii   Quantify the ZWI by accounting for resource gains in the WMSs using resource substitution factors; and

ix   Application of the ZWT in evaluating waste management performance in the case study cities.

The key concepts used in the ZWT

MSW

Definitions of MSW vary between countries. Generally, MSW is defined as 'waste generated by households and waste of a similar nature generated from commercial and industrial process' (UN-HABITAT, 2010). Based on the source of generation, MSW can be divided into domestic, industrial, and hazardous waste categories (Hartlén, 1996). MSW is composed of broad categories of organic and inorganic waste. However, for the formulation of the ZWT in this study, MSW refers to the common solid waste generated by households, excluding electronic waste, household hazardous, and hard waste.

Reverse resource flow

Reverse resource flow means the resource recovery process in which resources are recovered from the 'end-of-life' waste phase and recirculated to the production process. Currently, resources are used and consumed in an almost linear way, and thus only a fraction of the recoverable resources are recirculated to the production process. Reverse resource flow ensures an optimum resource recovery and effective utilization of natural resources.

Resource substitution factor

The resources used in production are transformed as waste after consumption. But in sustainable WMSs, resources can be recovered from waste and used in the production process. The amount of resources recovered from waste will eventually meet the demand for new or additional resources for the production of products, and these recovered resources will serve as substitutes for new ones. Hence, resource recovery efficiency is called resources substitution factor in this study. For example, if the resource substitution factor of paper is 0.9, it means that the maximum resource that can be recovered from 1 kg of paper waste is 900 gm of paper materials, and this 900 gm of paper materials is assumed to be able to substitute for the demand for 900 gm of virgin paper materials. This study acknowledges that material recovery from waste would be different for various types of waste. In addition, the repetitive recycling would not be possible for all types of waste – for example, resource recovery of metal would be greater, and it can be recovered on multiple occasions (repetitive), but it would not be similar to paper. The proposed ZWT assumes the first round of resource recovery of waste; thus, the resource recovery efficiency in a repetitive occasion is not considered in this study.

The geo-administrative boundaries

The geo-administrative boundary is very important in this study. Due to globalization, materials from one part of the world are used in another part. Similarly, waste that is generated is transferred to other places. Waste that has a high economic value, such as e-waste, metal, plastic, or paper, is at the top of list of trans-boundary wastes traded. Depending on the WMS, waste can be exported and imported beyond the geo-administrative boundary of the country. Hence, the study acknowledges the factors and challenges associated with the geo-administrative boundary and considers the export and import of waste in the tool's design.

Settings and system boundaries

Waste is a part of our everyday life. Very few of us, as the creators of waste, think about the flow of waste in real-world scenarios. Waste follows a very complex path of management systems from the point of generation to the end of disposal. To develop a waste management assessment tool, researchers need to consider all the variables and boundaries associated with waste. However, in the assessment tool, it is not possible to consider all socio-economic, environmental, political, institutional, or technical issues. Hence, it is very important to set a boundary and design variables for the tool. The ZWI was developed by limiting the scope of the study by considering MSW within six broad categories: organic, paper, plastic, metals, glass, and mixed MSW. Table 9.1 shows the variables that have been considered in designing the ZWT.

The ZWI

The ZWI is a tool to measure the potency of virgin materials to be offset from the ZW management system, as well as energy, water, and GHG savings. One of the main goals of the ZW concept is zero depletion of natural resources. The ZWI is a performance assessment tool for ZW cities. Therefore, measuring the performance of ZW cities would measure the resources that are extracted, consumed, wasted, recycled, recovered, and, finally, substituted for virgin materials and offset resource extraction by the WMSs. By introducing the ZWI globally, we could measure the virgin material offset potentiality and the potential depletion of natural resources. The ZWI is also a useful tool because it allows us to compare different WMSs in different cities, and it gives a broader picture of the potential demand for virgin materials, energy, carbon pollution, and water in the city. The ZWI can measure the performance of WMSs from the household to country scale.

One of the key benefits of the ZWI is it incorporates four different key performance indicators (KPIs) such as material substitution, energy saving, avoided carbon emission and water savings, which are not considered in the traditional waste management performance measurement technique such as waste diversion rate or recycling rate. The recent climate emergency and global climate strike movement initiated by Greta Thunberg, urges to cut global GHG emissions inclusive of waste management. Thus, the proposed ZWI would be a useful tool to measure the performance by considering both materials as well environmental performances.

Design variables

The ZWT considers a number of variables, such as source of waste, composition, waste, management, treatment, and final disposal. In addition, geo-administrative boundaries and socio-economic and environmental benefits are also considered in the ZWT. Trans-boundary issues are very important in globalized systems where waste can be generated in one part of the world and managed in other parts of the world. Thus, trans-boundary factors are also considered in the ZWT. However, in the application of the ZWI in the case study cities, the trans-boundary factor is not considered due to a lack of detailed waste management data from the cities. This is a recognized limitation noted in the interpretation. The list of design variables in Table 11.1 was considered in the ZW evaluation tool. The design variables were considered to enhance the scope and applicability of the ZWT.

TABLE 11.1 Design variables used in the ZWT

Characteristics	Typical Common Variables	Variables used in ZWT
Sources of waste	MSW	√
	C&D	×
	Commercial/institutional	×
	Industrial non-hazardous	×
	Hazardous waste	×
	Other	×
Types of waste	Organic	√
	Paper	√
	Plastic	√
	Metal	√
	Glass	√
	Textile	×
	Leather	×
	Electronic waste	×
	Mixed MSW	√
	Other	×
Waste management/geo-administrative boundaries	Premise level	×
	Neighbour level	×
	City level	√
	Country level	×
	International	×
	Others	×
Waste quantity	Volumetric quantity (m³)	×
	Weighted quantity (kg/ton)	√
	Quantity at the point of generation	×
	Quantity at the point of management	√
	Other	×
Waste management and treatment technologies	Reuse	√
	Recycling	√
	Composting	√
	Incineration	√
	Gasification	×
	Pyrolysis	×
	Sanitary landfill	√
	Landfill	√
	Open dumping	√
	Other	×

Characteristics	Typical Common Variables	Variables used in ZWT
Socio-economic and environmental benefits	Social stewardship	√
	Economic benefit	√
	Material recovery	√
	Energy recovery	√
	Water savings	√
	GHG savings	√
	Environmental stewardship	√
	Other	×
Trans-boundary movement of waste	Export	√
	Import	√

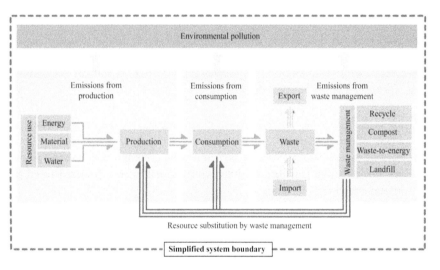

FIGURE 11.1 A schematic diagram of the ZWT's system boundary

System boundary of the ZWT

The metabolism of cities has been studied by several researchers (Baccini & Brunner, 2012; Boyden, Millar, Millar, & O'Neil, 1981; Kennedy, Cuddihy, &Engel-Yan, 2008; Peter, 1999). The system boundary of these studies was different and was based on the scope and focus of the studies. A simplified system boundary is used for the ZWT. The basic concepts of the tool are to measure the resource substitution potentiality (i.e. virgin material substitution, energy, water, and GHG savings) of WMSs. Figure 11.1 shows a schematic diagram of the system boundary of the proposed ZWT. The production process of creating consumer products and services primarily uses energy, materials, and water and emits GHG into the environment. The consumption of products and services results in the depletion of natural resources and generation of waste. The waste which has a resource value needs proper management to recover the resources in it.

Unsustainable waste management not only fails to recover resources from waste but also poses a danger to the environment. In the traditional WMSs, an extended knowledge gap is observed between the input (resources used in production) and output (resources recovered from waste). The gap between input and output can only be minimized by reducing resource use and maximizing resource recovery from waste. Hence, the ZWT is developed to measure the resources recouped (via reuse, recycling, or recovery from WMSs (output), which substitutes the demand of natural resources in the production and consumption phases (input).

Design criteria

The ZWI tool was designed by considering the life-cycle data of resources recovered from waste. As the life cycle of waste is complex, the design criteria have been limited by a set of assumptions. The following design criteria and key assumptions were considered when creating the ZWI:

i   Six broad categories (organic, paper, plastic, metal, glass, and mixed waste) of MSW were considered.
ii   Various waste treatment systems, such as recycling, composting, resource recovery (incineration, gas from landfills), and disposal were considered based on resource recovery efficiency.
iii Material recovery, energy, water, and GHG savings were considered.
iv   Export and import of waste between cities and countries were considered.

The following eight assumptions were considered for the ZWI:

i   Waste is an intermediate phase of the production and consumption process in the closed-loop city metabolism.
ii   Materials can be recovered from waste through reusing, recycling, treatment, and sanitary disposal.
iii Virgin materials can be substituted by the materials recovered from waste.
iv   Recovered materials would potentially reduce the demand for extraction of virgin materials.
v   Energy, water, and GHG emissions can be offset by the resources recovered from waste.
vi   Socio-economic and environmental benefits from WMSs are significantly affected by the local context.
vii The amount of materials recovered from waste is assumed to be substituted for the extraction of virgin materials, resulting in energy, water, and GHG savings.

viii As site-specific data may vary, the outcome of the ZWI may also vary on different sites. However, in this study, site-specific data variations are not considered due to the unavailability of data in those contexts.

Design formulation

The ZWI is the ratio of the substitutable amount of virgin materials from waste, and the total amount of waste managed. Substitution values for material, energy, water, and GHG emissions have been extracted from the life-cycle database of several life-cycle assessment tools and databases. The amount of materials and resources substituted is positively related to the development of technology used in the material recovery process; therefore, the substitution value varies for different materials and different WMSs.

The process of quantifying resource recovery from waste involves several complex steps, starting with sorting and progressing through collection, transportation, treatment, recovery, and final disposal. Different waste categories (six categories for this study) are managed by different waste management processes. Based on the waste categories and management systems, the efficiency of the resource recovery process can be measured. A simplified formula for resource substitution in the six waste categories is given in Equation 11.1.

Waste categories used in the ZWI:

Equation 11.1: Total amount of waste managed

Total amount of MSW managed = Organic (OR) + Paper (PA) + Plastic (PL) + Metal (ME) + Glass (GL)+ Mixed (MX) + Other (OT)

Substitution factor used in the ZWI

Equation 11.2: Substitution factor for WMSs

Substitution factor for waste reuse = SF_{reuse}
Substitution factor for waste compost = $SF_{compost}$
Substitution factor for waste recycle = $SF_{recycle}$
Substitution factor for waste incineration = $SF_{incinerate}$
Substitution factor for waste landfill = $SF_{landfill}$

Resource substitution from organic waste

Substituted amount of resources from organic waste by reusing = $OR_{reuse} \star SF_{reuse}$
Substituted amount of resources from organic waste by composting = $OR_{compost} \star SF_{compost}$
Substituted amount of resources from organic waste by recycling = $OR_{recycle} \star SF_{recycle}$

Substituted amount of resources from organic waste by incineration = $OR_{incinerate} \star SF_{incinerate}$

Substituted amount of resources from organic waste by landfill = $OR_{landfill} \star SF_{landfill}$

Substituted amount of resources from organic waste by other = $OR_{other} \star SF_{other}$

Total amount of resources substituted from organic waste =

$\Sigma\ (OR_{reuse} \star SF_{reuse} + OR_{compost} \star SF_{compost} + OR_{recycle} \star SF_{recycle} + OR_{incinerate} \star SF_{incinerate} + OR_{landfill} \star SF_{landfill} + OR_{other} \star SF_{other})$

Resource substitution from paper waste (PA)

Substituted amount of resources from paper waste by reusing = $PA_{reuse} \star SF_{reuse}$

Substituted amount of resources from paper waste by composting = $PA_{compost} \star SF_{compost}$

Substituted amount of resources from paper waste by recycling = $PA_{recycle} \star SF_{recycle}$

Substituted amount of resources from paper waste by incineration = $PA_{incinerate} \star SF_{incinerate}$

Substituted amount of resources from paper waste by landfilling = $PA_{landfill} \star SF_{landfill}$

Substituted amount of resources from paper waste by other = $PA_{other} \star SF_{other}$

Total amount of resources substituted from paper waste =

$\Sigma\ (PA_{reuse} \star SF_{reuse} + PA_{compost} \star SF_{compost} + PA_{recycle} \star SF_{recycle} + PA_{incinerate} \star SF_{incinerate} + PA_{landfill} \star SF_{landfill} + PA_{other} \star SF_{other})$

Resource substitution from plastic waste

Substituted amount of resources from plastic waste by reusing = $PL_{reuse} \star SF_{reuse}$

Substituted amount of resources from plastic waste by composting = $PL_{compost} \star SF_{compost}$

Substituted amount of resources from plastic waste by recycling = $PL_{recycle} \star SF_{recycle}$

Substituted amount of resources from plastic waste by incineration = $PL_{incinerate} \star SF_{incinerate}$

Substituted amount of resources from plastic waste by landfilling= $PL_{landfill} \star SF_{landfill}$

Substituted amount of resources from plastic waste by other = $PL_{other} \star SF_{other}$

Total amount of resources substituted from plastic waste =

$\Sigma\ (PL_{reuse} \star SF_{reuse} + PL_{compost} \star SF_{compost} + PL_{recycle} \star SF_{recycle} + PL_{incinerate} \star SF_{incinerate} + PL_{landfill} \star SF_{landfill} + PL_{other} \star SF_{other})$

Resource substitution from metal waste

Substituted amount of resources from metal waste by reuse = ME_{reuse} ★ SF_{reuse}
Substituted amount of resources from metal waste by composting = $ME_{compost}$ ★ $SF_{compost}$
Substituted amount of resources from metal waste by recycling = $ME_{recycle}$ ★ $SF_{recycle}$
Substituted amount of resources from metal waste by incineration = $ME_{incinerate}$ ★ $SF_{incinerate}$
Substituted amount of resources from metal waste by landfilling = $ME_{landfill}$ ★ $SF_{landfill}$
Substituted amount of resources from metal waste by other = ME_{other} ★ SF_{other}

Total amount of resources substituted from metal waste =
Σ (ME_{reuse} ★ SF_{reuse} + $ME_{compost}$ ★ $SF_{compost}$ + $ME_{recycle}$ ★ $SF_{recycle}$ + $ME_{incinerate}$ ★ $SF_{incinerate}$ + $ME_{landfill}$ ★ $SF_{landfill}$ + ME_{other} ★ SF_{other})

10.1.1.1.1. Resource substitution from glass waste

Substituted amount of resources from glass waste by reuse = GL_{reuse} ★ SF_{reuse}
Substituted amount of resources from glass waste by composting = $GL_{compost}$ ★ $SF_{compost}$
Substituted amount of resources from glass waste by recycling = $GL_{recycle}$ ★ $SF_{recycle}$
Substituted amount of resources from glass waste by incineration = $GL_{incinerate}$ ★ $SF_{incinerate}$
Substituted amount of resources from glass waste by landfilling = $GL_{landfill}$ ★ $SF_{landfill}$
Substituted amount of resources from glass waste by other = GL_{other} ★ SF_{other}

Total amount of resources substituted from glass waste =
Σ (GL_{reuse} ★ GL_{reuse} + $GL_{compost}$ ★ $SF_{compost}$ + $GL_{recycle}$ ★ $SF_{recycle}$ + $GL_{incinerate}$ ★ $SF_{incinerate}$ + $GL_{landfill}$ ★ $SF_{landfill}$ + GL_{other} ★ SF_{other})

Resource substitution from mixed waste

Substituted amount of resources from mixed waste by reuse = MX_{reuse} ★ SF_{reuse}
Substituted amount of resources from mixed waste by composting = $MX_{compost}$ ★ $SF_{compost}$
Substituted amount of resources from mixed waste by recycling = $MX_{recycle}$ ★ $SF_{recycle}$
Substituted amount of resources from mixed waste by incinerate = $MX_{incinerate}$ ★ $SF_{incinerate}$

Substituted amount of resources from mixed waste by landfill = $MX_{landfill} \star SF_{landfill}$

Substituted amount of resources from mixed waste by other = $MX_{other} \star SF_{other}$

Total amount of resources substituted from mixed waste =
$\Sigma\ (MX_{reuse} \star SF_{reuse} + MX_{compost} \star SF_{compost} + MX_{recycle} \star SF_{recycle} + MX_{incinerate} \star SF_{incinerate} + MX_{landfill} \star SF_{landfill} + MX_{other} \star SF_{other})$

Total amount of substituted virgin materials

Total amount of substituted virgin materials from waste is calculated by Equation 11.3.

Equation 11.3: Total amount of substituted virgin materials

Total substituted amount of resources from glass waste =
$\Sigma\ (GL_{reuse} \star SF_{reuse} + GL_{compost} \star SF_{compost} + GL_{recycle} \star SF_{recycle} + GL_{incinerate} \star SF_{incinerate} + GL_{landfill} \star SF_{landfill} + GL_{other} \star SF_{other})$

ZWI of MSW

The ZWI of MSW is measured by the Equation 11.4.
Equation 11.4: ZWI

$$ZWI = \frac{Total\ amount\ of\ resources\ substituted\ by\ the\ MSW}{Total\ amount\ of\ MSW\ managed}$$

$$= \left(\sum \left[(amount\ of)\ paper\ managed \times substitution\ factor + \ldots + amount\ of\ mixed\ waste\ managed \times substitution\ factor \right) \right)$$

$$/ \left(\sum (amount\ of\ paper + \ldots + amount\ of\ mixed\ waste\ managed) \right)$$

$$= \frac{\sum OR \times SF + PA \times SF + PL \times SF + ME \times SF + GL \times SF + MX \times SF)}{\sum (OR + PA + PL + ME + GL + MX)}$$

$$= \frac{\sum_{1}^{n} MSWij \times SFij}{\sum_{1}^{n} MSWi}$$

MSW_{ij} = Amount of waste stream i (I = 1, 2, 3 . . . n = paper, plastic, metal, etc.) managed by system j (j = 1, 2, 3 . . . n = amount of waste avoided, recycled, treated, etc.)

SF_{ij} = Substitution factor for the amount of waste stream i (i = 1, 2, 3 . . . n = paper, plastic, metal, etc.) managed by system j (j = 1, 2, 3 . . . n = amount of waste avoided, recycled, treated, etc.)

MSW_i = Total amount of MSW managed (i = 1, 2, 3 . . . n = paper, plastic, metal, etc.)

Now, considering the geo-administrative boundaries, the ZWI can be expanded as

$$ZWI = \frac{amount\ of\ \left(waste\ generated - waste\ export + waste\ import\right) \times Substition\ Factor}{Total\ amount\ of\ MSW\ managed\ locally\ \left(local\ waste - export + import\right)}$$

$$= \frac{\sum_1^n \left(MSWlocal - MSWexport + MSWimport\right)ij \times SFij}{\sum_1^n MSWi}$$

Database development

Life cycle assessment (LCA) is one of many tools that are used to analyse the environmental burdens and benefits of certain products and services. A number of studies (Carlsson, 2005; Erses Yay, 2015; Laurent et al., 2014; Slagstad & Brattebø, 2012) have been conducted in the area of waste management using an LCA tool. However, the outcome of the individual LCA studies have largely depended on the choices made in their assumptions, most specifically the ones concerning energy use and generation and forestry (Villanueva & Wenzel, 2007). ZW is a new concept and a new motivation for sustainable WMSs. Thus, despite using a formal LCA tool, this study applies LCA inventory data (material substitution offset and burden allocation) to develop a new ZWT which can be easy to interpret and easy to apply in the waste industry.

The substitution values for material, energy, water, and GHG emissions have been extracted from the life-cycle inventory database of different life-cycle assessment tools and database sources, including SimaPro and EASEWASTE software. The amount of materials and resources substituted is positively related to the development of technology used in the material recovery process. Therefore, the substitution value varies for different materials and different WMSs. Even though waste prevention is one of the core components in ZW concept, a quantitative measurement of waste prevention by behaviour change has not been considered in this research due to limited quantitative data. The primary substitution efficiency and data table is developed from the evidence of resource substitution potentiality of WMSs used in life-cycle models. Life-cycle databases use 'offset' values in the inventory data based on potential benefits or burdens from WMSs. Similar principles and data are used in the ZWI, primarily concentrating on resource substitution factors.

The substitution factor for the ZWI

The composition of MSW varies widely, both within and between countries and between different seasons of the year (UN-HABITAT, 2010). Depending on the consumption pattern, waste categories vary in different households, neighbours, cities, or countries. Waste treatment technologies are also diverse in different areas. However, this study considers the most common MSW categories: paper, plastic, metal, glass, organic, and mixed waste residue.

Efficiency of 'virgin material substitution' for recycling material from waste is one of the most important aspects of SWM. Globally, consumption of natural resources has increased significantly since industrialization and the finite and rare-earth materials from nature are now being extracted more than at any other time in human history (Sagoff, 2001). From the resource point of view, there is an imminent risk of rapid supply shortfall of rare materials. By recovering materials from waste, the pressure of continuous extraction and depletion of natural resources can be reduced by substituting the recycling materials. In this study, the ZWT developed by considering the amount of virgin material substitution by the amount of material recovered from waste simply refers to the 'material substitution efficiency'. However, the material substitution factors used in the ZWT do not address what leverage points are likely to lead to greater resource extraction from current waste streams.

In this study, the material substitution efficiency is considered for six common waste categories available in MSW, such as paper, plastic, metal, glass, organic, and mixed waste. It is important to acknowledge that the material substitution efficiency will not be the same for each waste category, and the material substitution efficiency rate will decrease for certain waste categories for their repetitive use. For instance, material substitution efficiency of metal and paper would be different, and metal can be used repetitively, but after a certain number of times being recycled, paper material would not be practical to use. Despite this variation, it is important to measure the total material recovery potential from WMSs, because then it will be ideal to measure current waste management performance and to guide the future direction of WMSs.

After considering the virgin materials' substitution efficiency, Table 11.2 shows substitution factors for the ZWI that have been developed based on life-cycle data. Data are extracted from different sources, mostly from SimaPro and the EASE-WASTE LCA database. These data are usually used in LCA analysis when the model considers allocation of burdens.

In a cradle-to-grave life-cycle concept, waste is considered the last phase of life for a product, and disposal is the ultimate destination for waste. But in a C2C life cycle, a resource is used again and again through recycling and recovery from waste. Hence, the recovered resources meet the demand for additional virgin materials.

Thus, the ZWI quantifies solid waste flows and measures the extent to which materials may be reused as substitutes for virgin materials. In addition to the overall percentage of material recovery and substitution, the approach calculates other

TABLE 11.2 Substitution factor in different waste streams and management options

WMSs	Waste category	Virgin material substitution efficiency (tonnes)	Energy substitution efficiency (GJLHV/ tonne)	GHG emissions reduction (CO₂e/ tonne)	Water saving (kL/tonne)
Recycling	Paper	0.84–1.00	6.33–10.76	0.60–3.20	2.91
	Glass	0.90–0.99	6.07–6.85	0.18–0.62	2.30
	Metal	0.79–0.96	36.09–191.42	1.40–17.8	5.97–181.77
	Plastic	0.90–0.97	38.81–64.08	0.95–1.88	−11.37
	Mixed	0.25–0.45	5.00–15.0	1.15	2.0–10
Composting	Organic	0.60–0.65	0.18–0.47	0.25–0.75	0.44
Incineration	Mixed MW[a]	0.00	0.972–2.995[b]	0.12–0.55	0.00
Landfills	Mixed MW[a]	0.00	0.00–0.84[c]	(−)0.42–1.2	0.00

a Average composition of municipal waste
b Heat capture efficiency of WTE technology 15%–30%
c Energy from the landfill facility. A positive value represents the savings, and a negative value represents the demand or depletion

'savings' made, including energy saved, GHGs avoided, and water savings (regarding the water use within material supply chains). Table 11.2 uses data from several life-cycle studies (Clean Energy Future, 2011; DECCW, 2010; DTU-Environment, 2008; Grant & James, 2005; Grant, James, Lundie, & Sonneveld, 2001; Larsen, Merrild, & Christensen, 2012; Massarutto, Carli, & Graffi, 2011; Metro Vancouver, 2010; Morris, 1996; US-EPA, 2006; Van Berlo, 2007; Zaman, 2010; Zaman & Lehmann, 2011) and shows the substitution factor waste streams for different WMSs.

Economic benefits of resource recovery

Recycling and resource recovery activities are often driven by the market economy, and thus an economic evaluation of the resource benefits from the case study cities are necessary. This is important to acknowledge that despite globalization and its effects on the global economy, recycling markets depend on and are affected by local commodity (material) prices. However, in this study, a generalized market price of various recycled/recovered materials is considered to understand the overall waste management performance in the context of economic benefits. Table 11.3 shows the unit market price of the selected raw materials.

Data limitations and future development

The substitution factors are drawn from life-cycle databases of previous research. The scope of the studies varies and hence the data quality and reliability also vary. A simplified system boundary is used in this study so that the proposed tool is able

TABLE 11.3 The unit market price of various virgin materials

Materials	Unit price (US$)	Average price (US$)	Reference
Paper	80–875/t	477	(Indexmundi, 2015; WRAP, 2015)
Plastic	139–300/t	219	(WRAP, 2015)
Glass	15–41/t	28	(WRAP, 2015)
Metal	186–1589/t	887	(Indexmundi, 2015; WRAP, 2015)
Mixed	–	104	Minimum average price
Compost	100–410/t	255	(Alibaba, 2015)
Energy (GJLHV)	20.3/kWh	55.6	(EUC, 2015)
GHG (CO_2e)	1–14/tonne	7.5	(APH, 2013)
Water (kL)	0.92/m^3	0.92	(ELD, 2010)

to test and compare different WMSs in different cities. The outcome and reliability of the ZWI depends on the accurate and comprehensive categorization of different waste streams. Due to data limitations and various waste management options being available in different cities, six waste categories and four waste treatment options are considered in the ZWI. Hence, there is an opportunity to expand the data categories by including hazardous, non-hazardous, electronic waste, and so on and by considering various waste streams, such as industrial and commercial waste sources. A comprehensive set of data on vigorous waste categories and WMSs will make the tool more accurate, reliable, and transparent to decision makers and other potential users.

References

Alibaba. (2015). *High Quality Biological Compost*. Retrieved from www.alibaba.com/product-detail/high-quality-biological-compost_2022139935.html?spm=a2700.7782932.19987 01000.2.72GJCQ

APH. (2013). *Emissions Trading Schemes Around the World*. Retrieved from www.aph.gov.au/About_Parliament/Parliamentary_Departments/Parliamentary_Library/pubs/BN/2012-2013/EmissionsTradingSchemes

Baccini, P., & Brunner, P. H. (2012). *Metabolism of the Anthroposphere: Analysis, Evaluation, Design* (2nd ed.). Cambridge and London: MIT Press.

Boyden, S., Millar, S., Millar, K., & O'Neil, B. (1981). *The Ecology of a City and Its People: The Case of Hong Kong*. Canberra, Australia: Australian National University Press.

Carlsson, R. M. (2005). Economic assessment of municipal waste management systems: Case studies using a combination of life cycle assessment (LCA) and life cycle costing (LCC). *Journal of Cleaner Production*, *13*(3), 253–263. http://dx.doi.org/10.1016/j.jclepro.2004.02.015

Clean Energy Future. (2011). *Emissions from Landfill Facilities, Fact Sheet*. Retrieved from www.cleanenergyfuture.gov.au/wp-content/uploads/2011/10/FactSheet-Emissions-from-landfill-facilities.pdf

DECCW. (2010). NSW government report on environmental benefits of recycling. *NSW*. Retrieved from www.environment.nsw.gov.au/resources/warr/1058BenefitsOfRecycling. pdf

DTU-Environment. (2008). *EASEWASTE 2008 Database (Environmental Assessment of Solid Waste Systems and Technologies)*. Retrieved May 6, 2012, from Copenhagen: www. easewaste.dk

ELD. (2010). *The Cost of Water*. Retrieved from http://everylittledrop.com.au/knowledge-center/the-cost-of-water/

EPA. (2010). *Municipal Solid Waste in the United States: 2009 Facts and Figure*. Retrieved from https://nepis.epa.gov/Exe/ZyPURL.cgi?Dockey=P100A0NX.TXT

Erses Yay, A. S. (2015). Application of life cycle assessment (LCA) for municipal solid waste management: A case study of Sakarya. *Journal of Cleaner Production*. http://dx.doi.org/10.1016/j.jclepro.2015.01.089

EUC. (2015). *Global Electricity Prices*. Retrieved from http://energyusecalculator.com/global_electricity_prices.htm

Grant, T., & James, K. L. (2005). *Life Cycle Impact Data for Resource Recovery from Commercial and Industrial and Construction and Demolition Waste in Victoria*. Retrieved from VIC: www.sustainability.vic.gov.au/resources/documents/Life_Cycle_Impact_Data_for_Resource_Recovery_from_CI_and_CD_Waste_in_Vic.pdf

Grant, T., James, K. L., Lundie, S., & Sonneveld, K. (2001). *Stage 2 Report for Life Cycle Assessment for Paper and Packaging Waste Management Scenarios in Victoria*. Retrieved from VIC: www.ecorecycle.vic.gov.au/resources/documents/Stage_2_Report_for_Life_Cycle_Assess_for_Packaging_Waste_Mg.pdf

Hartlén, J. (1996). Waste management in Sweden. *Waste Management, 16*(5–6), 385–388. doi:10.1016/s0956-053x(96)00085-2

Indexmundi. (2015). *Commodity Agricultural Raw Materials Index Monthly Price*. Retrieved from www.indexmundi.com/commodities/?commodity=wood-pulp

Kennedy, C., Cuddihy, J., & Engel-Yan, J. (2008). The changing metabolism of cities. *Journal of Industrial Ecology, 11*(2), 43–59. doi:10.1162/jie.2007.1107

Larsen, A. W., Merrild, H., & Christensen, T. H. (2012). Assessing recycling versus incineration of key materials in municipal waste: The importance of efficient energy recovery and transport distance. *Journal of Waste Management, 2012*(32), 1009–1018.

Laurent, A., Bakas, I., Clavreul, J., Bernstad, A., Niero, M., Gentil, E., & Christensen, T. H. (2014). Review of LCA studies of solid waste management systems: Part I: Lessons learned and perspectives. *Waste Management, 34*(2014), 573–588.

Massarutto, A., Carli, A. D., & Graffi, M. (2011). Material and energy recovery integrated waste management systems: A life-cycle costing approach. *Waste Management, 2011*(31), 2102–2111.

Metro Vancouver. (2010). *Metro Vancouver Response to Environmental Life Cycle Assessment of Waste Management Strategies with a Zero Waste Objective*. Retrieved from www.metrovancouver.org/services/solidwaste/planning/ContraryOpinions/SoundResourceManagementReportandResponse.pdf

Morris, J. (1996). Recycling versus incineration: An energy conversion analysis. *Journal of Hazardous Materials, 47*, 277–293.

Peter, W. G. N. (1999). Sustainability and cities: Extending the metabolism model. *Landscape and Urban Planning, 44*(4), 219–226. doi:10.1016/s0169-2046(99)00009-2

Sagoff, Mark. 2001. "Consumption." In Dale Jamieson, Ed., *A Companion to Environmental Philosophy*. London: Blackwell Publishers Ltd.

Slagstad, H., & Brattebø, H. (2012). LCA for household waste management when planning a new urban settlement. *Waste Management, 32*(7), 1482–1490. http://dx.doi.org/10.1016/j.wasman.2012.03.018

Timlett, R., & Williams, I. D. (2011). The ISB model (infrastructure, service, behaviour): A tool for waste practitioners. *Waste Management, 31*(6), 1381–1392.

UN-HABITAT. (2010). *Solid Waste Management in the World's Cities: Water and Sanitation in the World's Cities* (Earthscan Ed.). London: Earthscan.

US-EPA. (2006). *Solid Waste Management and Greenhouse Gases: A Life Cycle Assessment of Emissions and Sinks.* Retrieved from Washington, DC: http://epa.gov/climatechange/wycd/waste/downloads/fullreport.pdf

Van Berlo, M. A. J. (2007). Value from waste: Amsterdam's vision. *4th Generation Waste-to-Energy, Seminar Presentation.* Retrieved from www.bioenergytrade.org/downloads/rovan-berlo.pdf

Villanueva, A., & Wenzel, H. (2007). Paper waste: Recycling, incineration or landfilling? A review of existing life cycle assessments. *Waste Management, 27*(8), S29–S46. http://dx.doi.org/10.1016/j.wasman.2007.02.019

WRAP. (2015). *Data Sources.* Retrieved from www.wrap.org.uk/content/data-sources-0

Zaman, A. U. (2010). Comparative study of municipal solid waste treatment technologies using life cycle assessment method. *International Journal of Environmental Science and Technology, 7*(2), 225–234.

Zaman, A. U., & Lehmann, S. (2011). Urban growth and waste management optimization towards "zero waste city". *City, Culture and Society, 2*(4), 177–187. http://dx.doi.org/10.1016/j.ccs.2011.11.007

Zorpas, A. A., & Lasaridi, K. (2013). Measuring waste prevention. *Waste Management, 33*(5), 1047–1056.

ZWIA. (2004). *Zero Waste Definition Adopted by Zero Waste Planning Group.* Retrieved from www.zwia.org/main/index.php?option=com_content&view=article&id=49&Itemid=37

12

APPLICATION OF THE ZERO-WASTE INDEX

Introduction

The proposed ZWI as a performance measurement tool has been applied to the four case study cities. These four cities represent varied socio-cultural, economic, geographic, and environmental settings. The UN-HABITAT (2010) study on WMSs is considered a core waste data source for the cities of Adelaide, San Francisco, and Dhaka. The composition and WMS in Stockholm is developed from different secondary reliable data sources. The brief section that follows describes the waste composition and WMSs in the four cities. Resource substitution and other environmental benefits listed in Chapter 11, Table 11.2, are potential resource recovery values because the case studies assumed that all waste generated in the cities examined are managed locally, which may not be the real scenario for all cities. This assumption is made because no data were available on how much waste is exported to other regions. So the ZWI provides the potential benefits from WMSs, which might in the future be corrected by generating or accessing field data.

ZWIs in case study cities

The ZWIs have been calculated by considering the virgin material substitution factor of waste in Table 11.2 using Equation 11.4. Table 12.1 presents the waste data composition, management substitution value and hence the overall energy, GHG, and water savings from waste. Despite local WMSs and the efficiency of waste treatment technologies, the substitution value may vary in the four cities. However, in the performance analysis given in Table 12.1, the substitution and resource savings factors have been considered unchanged for the four cities due to data unavailability in the local context. Table 12.2 shows the potential substitution of resources in the selected cities according to the ZWI. It is important to acknowledge that this study

TABLE 12.1 Substitution values for the ZWI[1]

Case study cities	WMSs	Waste category	Total waste managed in the city (tonne)	Virgin material substitution efficiency (tonne)	Energy substitution efficiency (GJLHV/tonne)	GHG emissions reduction (tonne CO_2e/tonne)	Water saving (kL/tonne)
Adelaide	Recycling	Paper	23,918	0.84–1.00	6.33–10.76	0.60–3.20	2.91
		Glass	17,084	0.90–1.00	6.07–6.85	0.18–0.62	2.30
		Metal	17,084	0.79–0.96	36.09–191.42	1.40–17.8	5.97–181.77
		Plastic	17,084	0.90–0.97	38.81–64.08	0.95–1.88	–11.37
		Mixed	266,521	0.25–0.45	5.00–15.0	1.15	2.0–10
	Composting	Organic	59,424	0.60–0.65	0.18–0.47	0.25–0.75	0.44
	Landfill	Mixed MW[2]	341,692	0.00	0.00–0.84	(−)0.42–1.2	0.00
San Francisco	Recycling	Paper	121,997	0.84–1.00	6.33–10.76	0.60–3.20	2.91
		Glass	15,096	0.90–0.99	6.07–6.85	0.18–0.62	2.30
		Metal	20,332	0.79–0.96	36.09–191.42	1.40–17.8	5.97–181.77
		Plastic	55,915	0.90–0.97	38.81–64.08	0.95–1.88	–11.37
		Mixed	50,830	0.25–0.45	5.00–15.0	1.15	2.0–10
	Composting	Organic	101,665	0.60–0.65	0.18–0.47	0.25–0.75	0.44
	Landfill	Mixed MW	142,331	0.00	0.00–0.84[3]	(−)0.42–1.2	0.00
Stockholm	Recycling	Paper	36,552	0.84–1.00	6.33–10.76	0.60–3.20	2.91
		Glass	10,083	0.90–0.99	6.07–6.85	0.18–0.62	2.30
		Metal	3,781	0.79–0.96	36.09–191.42	1.40–17.8	5.97–181.77
		Plastic	8,823	0.90–0.97	38.81–64.08	0.95–1.88	–11.37
		Mixed	66,805	0.25–0.45	5.00–15.0	1.15	2.0–10
	Composting	Organic	4,065	0.60–0.65	0.18–0.47	0.25–0.75	0.44
	Incineration	Mixed MW	239,891	0.00	0.972–2.995[4]	0.12–0.55	0.00

Dhaka							
Informal Recycling	Paper	116,800	0.84–1.00	6.33–10.76	0.60–3.20	2.91
	Glass	23,360	0.90–0.99	6.07–6.85	0.18–0.62	2.30
	Metal	11,680	0.79–0.96	36.09–191.42	1.40–17.8	5.97–181.77
	Plastic	23,360	0.90–0.97	38.81–64.08	0.95–1.88	−11.37
	Mixed	34,807	0.25–0.45	5.00–15.0	1.15	2.0–10
Composting	Organic	233	0.60–0.65	0.18–0.47	0.25–0.75	0.44
Landfill	Mixed MW	51,3920	0.00	0.00–0.84	(−)0.42–1.2	0.00
Uncollected waste	Mixed MW	44,3840	0.00	0.00	(−)0.42–1.2	0.00

1 Site-specific data may vary; the final outcome of the ZWI may also vary at different sites. However, in this study, site-specific data variations are not considered due to the unavailability of data in the site-specific context.

2 The average composition of municipal waste.

3 Energy from landfill facility. A positive value represents the savings and a negative value represents the demand or depletion.

4 The heat capture efficiency of WTE technology is 15%–30%.

TABLE 12.2 Comparative ZWI in case study cities

City	ZWI
Adelaide	0.23
San Francisco	0.51
Stockholm	0.17
Dhaka	0.14

did not consider how economic benefit influences in the development of regulatory policy and overall resource extraction processes by the WMSs. The total economic benefits of the substituted virgin materials can be measured by using the unit price of the virgin materials, which has been considered and measured in this study.

The ZWI was used to measure the four cities' waste management performance. San Francisco performed best, scoring 0.51, meaning that around half of its municipal waste materials were recovered and, therefore, had the potential to replace the demand for virgin materials. Adelaide scored 0.23. Stockholm, however, scored just 0.17 despite having the most advanced waste regulations and waste treatment technologies. Surprisingly, Dhaka scored 0.14, which is very impressive as a developing city without an effective WMS in place compared to the city of Stockholm. The core reason for a low ZWI in Stockholm is because of its high use of incineration, which means that it loses large amounts of raw materials. Table 12.2 shows the ZWIs of the WMSs in the four cities.

A comprehensive analysis of the resource recovery, virgin material substitution, and overall ZW performances has been done for the case study cities and is presented in Table 12.3. In addition, the study analysed the economic benefits in terms of monetary gain from resource recovery from waste. The comparative economic benefits are measured in Table 11.3 using the unit cost of resources showed in Table 12.3. It is important to acknowledge that the economic benefits significantly vary on both global and local market conditions. This study provides an approximate monetary value, which could be different if the local context were considered.

Comparative ZWIs in case study cities

The comparative analysis is not to rank the cities but to analyse their performances based on their resource recovery and WMSs. The comparative study is done by considering (a) the substitution of virgin materials from waste, (b) energy savings, (c) avoided GHG emission, and (d) water savings. Although Stockholm, produces less waste per capita, its high use of incineration means that it loses large amounts of raw materials. San Francisco also achieved far greater energy and GHG savings, as well as greater water savings, than the other cities. As a performance evaluation tool, the ZWI provides a single value, and thus to measure the total benefits of the WMSs in all four categories, such as potential materials recovery, energy saving, water savings, and avoided GHG emissions, need to be considered.

TABLE 12.3 Potential substitution of resources according to the ZWI

Cities	WMS (ii)	Waste category (iii)	Total waste managed in the city (tonne) (iv)	Potential total virgin material substituted (tonne) (v)	Total energy substituted (GJLHV)	Total GHG emissions reduction (tonne CO₂e)	Total water saving (kL)	ZWI (ZWI = v/iv)
Adelaide	Recycling	Paper	23,918	20,091	204,260	45,444	69,601	0.23
		Glass	17,084	15,375	110,362	6,833	39,293	
		Metal	17,084	13,496	1,944,159	164,006	1,554,644	
		Plastic	17,084	15,375	878,800	23,917	−194,245	
		Mixed	266,521	66,630	2,665,210	306,499	159,9126	
	Composting	Organic	59,424	35,654	19,609	29,712	26,146	
	Landfill	Mixed MW	341,692	000	000	−143,510	000	
	Total value		742,807	166,621	3,157,190	421,901	3,094,565	
	Benefits (person/year)		681 kg	153 kg	2.9 GJ	387 kg	2.8 kL	
San Francisco	Recycling	Paper	121,997	102,477	1,041,854	231,794	355,011	0.51
		Glass	15,096	13,724	98,508	6,099	35,072	
		Metal	20,332	16,062	2,313,781	195,187	2,760,212	
		Plastic	55,915	50,323	283,691	78,281	−635,753	
		Mixed	50,830	12,707	508,300	58,454	304,980	
	Composting	Organic	101,665	60,999	33,549	50,832	44,732	
	Landfill	Mixed MW	142,331	000	000	−59,779	000	
	Total value		508,323	256,292	4,279,683	560,868	2,864,254	
	Benefits (person/year)		609 kg	307 kg	5.1 GJ	672 kg	3.42 kL	

(Continued)

TABLE 12.3 (Continued)

Cities	WMS (ii)	Waste category (iii)	Total waste managed in the city (tonne) (iv)	Potential total virgin material substituted (tonne) (v)	Total energy substituted (GJLHV)	Total GHG emissions reduction (tonne CO_2-e)	Total water saving (kL)	ZWI (ZWI = v/iv)
Stockholm	Recycling	Paper	36,552	30,703	312,154	69,448	106,366	0.17
		Glass	10,083	9,074	65,136	4,033	23,190	
		Metal	3,781	2,987	426,863	36,297	344,071	
		Plastic	8,823	7,940	453,855	12,352	-100,317	
		Mixed	66,805	16,701	668,050	76,825	400,830	
	Composting	Organic	4,065	2,439	1,341	2,032	1,788	
	Incineration	Mixed MW	239,891	000	477,383	80,363	000	
	Landfill	Mixed MW	36,596	000	000	-1,536	000	
	Total value		406,596	69,844	2,404,782	279,814	775,928	
	Benefits (person/year)		480 kg	79 kg	2.83GJ	330 kg	0.92 kL	
Dhaka	Recycling	Paper	116,800	107,456	998,056	221,920	48,888	0.14
		Glass	23,360	22,075	150,905	9,344	46,720	
		Metal	11,680	10,220	1,328,658	112,128	1,096,401	
		Plastic	23,360	21,841	1,201,755	33,054	-265,603	
		Mixed	34,807	12,182	348,070	40,028	208,842	
	Composting	Organic	233	145	75	116	102	
	Landfill	Mixed MW	513,920	0.00	000	(-) 215,847	0.00	
	Uncollected waste	Mixed MW	443,840	0.00	0.00	(-) 186,412	0.00	
	Total value		1,168,000	173,919	4,027,519	416,590	1400,953	
	Benefits (person/year)		167 kg	25 kg	0.58 GJ	60 kg	0.2 kL	

Virgin material substitution

Virgin material substitution by reusing and recycling is one of the main goals of the ZW concept. Current trends of hyper-consumption deplete an enormous amount of natural resources every day. Hence, substituting resources available from the waste that is produced every day would be the ultimate goal for achieving ZW. As Figure 12.1 shows, San Francisco recovered 51% (307 kg) of the MSW that is produced by each person every year. Adelaide and Stockholm recovered around 23% (153 kg) and 17% (79 kg), respectively, from the municipal waste that is generated every year. Despite having an informal recycling system in Dhaka, it recovered around 15% (25 kg) of substituted resources. This finding is also supported by a previous study which asserted that informal recycling provides significant resource and economic benefits. The ZWI for Dhaka appeared to be high because of per capita less waste generation rate compared to the other cities. This also indicated that low resource consumption, which leads to the generation of less waste, would have a higher ZW performance.

Energy savings

One of the important resources that is depleted by waste is energy. Sometimes, more energy is used to produce a product than when the product is used. Hence, recovering resources from waste potentially saves an enormous amount of energy. Comparing the energy savings in the three cities, San Francisco substituted the highest amount of energy demand from the resources recovered in WMSs. The average person in San Francisco substituted around 1,417 kilowatt hours (kW-h) of energy demand in a year. In Adelaide and Stockholm, the energy demand substitution

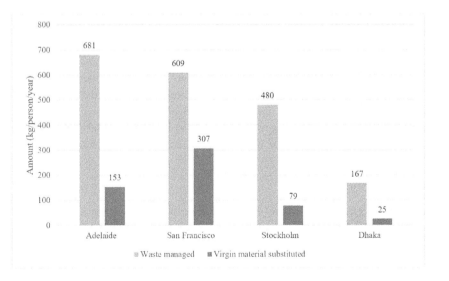

FIGURE 12.1 Virgin material substitution in case study cities

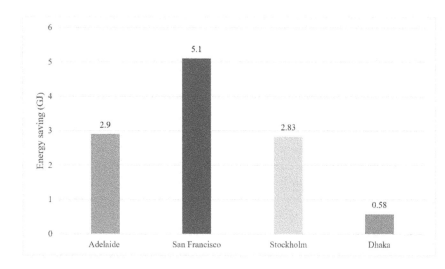

FIGURE 12.2 Energy savings from WMSs in case study cities

value was 805 kW-h and 786 kW-h, respectively. Even though the ZWI for Stockholm was 0.17, which was lower than San Francisco (0.51) and Adelaide (0.23), overall energy saving was significantly higher in Stockholm. The key reason for the high energy savings from the WMS in Stockholm was the energy generation from incineration of MSW. The WMSs in Dhaka saved around 0.58 GJ or 160 kW-h per person by substituting resources from waste. Figure 12.2 shows the comparative energy savings in Adelaide, San Francisco, Stockholm, and Dhaka.

GHG emissions

One of the major environmental impacts from waste is GHG emissions to the atmosphere, which intensifies global warming and climate change. Landfills are the main source of methane and other GHG emissions from WMSs. Resource recovery from waste eventually limits the emissions that would otherwise reach the atmosphere if waste is managed by landfills. Each person in Adelaide, San Francisco, Stockholm, and Dhaka saved 387 kg CO_{2e}, 672 kg CO_{2e}, 330 kg CO_{2e}, and 60 CO_{2e} of GHG each year, respectively, from the WMSs. Figure 12.3 shows the GHG savings.

Water savings

Water is not an abundant resource anymore; rather, it is already a scarce natural resource in many parts of the world. The relationship between water and waste is significant at the point of resource recovery because a significant amount of freshwater is used to process raw materials to produce goods and services. Therefore, substituting virgin materials can save water. Figure 12.4 shows the per capita water saved in the four cities. Adelaide, San Francisco, Stockholm, and Dhaka saved around 2,800 litres, 3,420 litres, 920 litres, and 200 litres of water per person per year, respectively.

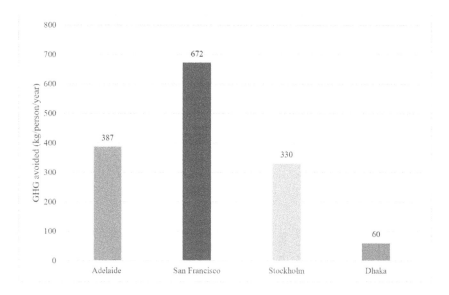

FIGURE 12.3   GHG savings from WMSs in case study cities

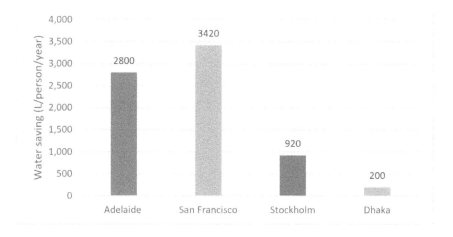

FIGURE 12.4   Water savings from WMSs in case study cities

Comparative economic benefits in the case study cities

The economic benefits of the WMSs (as shown in Table 12.4) depend on the types of resource gain from the WMSs. The condition of a local waste market is a vital factor for the overall monetary gain. Figure 12.5 shows that Adelaide has the highest monetary gain for avoiding or saving energy of $297 (person/year) and San Francisco has the highest gain from the resource recovery of $110 (person/year). It

TABLE 12.4 Economic benefits of the WMSs

Cities	WMS	Waste category	Economic benefits of MS	Economic benefits of energy savings	Economic benefits of GHG savings	Economic benefits of water savings
Adelaide	Recycling	Paper	9,583,407	11,356,856	340,830	64,033
		Glass	430,500	6,136,127	51,247.5	36,150
		Metal	11,970,952	108,095,240	1,230,045	1,430,272
		Plastic	3,367,125	48,861,280	179,377.5	−178,705
		Mixed	6,929,520	148,185,676	2,298,742.5	1,471,196
	Composting	Organic	9,091,770	1,090,260	222,840	24,054
	Landfill	Mixed MW	0	0	−1,076,325	0
	Total economic benefits (US$)		41,373,274	323,725,440	3,246,757.5	2,847,000
	Benefits ($/person/year)		38	297	3	3
	Total benefits ($/person/year)		341			
San Francisco	Recycling	Paper	48,881,529	57,927,082	1,738,455	326,610
		Glass	384,272	5,477,045	45,742.5	32,266
		Metal	14,246,994	128,646,224	1,463,902.5	2,539,395
		Plastic	11,020,737	15,773,220	587,107.5	−584,893
		Mixed	1,321,528	28,261,480	438,405	280,582
	Composting	Organic	15,554,745	1,865,324	381,240	41,153
	Landfill	Mixed MW	0	0	−448,343	0
	Total economic benefits (US$)		91,409,805	237,950,375	4,206,510	2,635,114
	Benefits ($/person/year)		110	285	5	3
	Total benefits ($/person/year)		403			

Stockholm	Recycling	Paper	14,645,331	17,355,762.4	520,860	97,857
		Glass	254,072	3,621,561.6	30,248	21,335
		Metal	2,649,469	23,733,582.8	272,228	316,545
		Plastic	1,738,860	25,234,338	92,640	−92,292
		Mixed	1736904	37,143,580	576,188	368,764
	Composting	Organic	621,945	74,559.6	15,240	1,645
	Incineration	Mixed MW	0	26,542,494.8	602,723	0
	Landfill	Mixed MW	0	0	-11520	0
	Total economic benefits (US$)		21,646,581	133,705,879.2	2,098,605	713,854
	Benefits ($/person/year)		26	158	2	1
	Total benefits ($/person/year)		188			
Dhaka	Recycling	Paper	51,256,512	55,491,913.6	1664,400	44,977
		Glass	618,100	8,390,318	70,080	42,982
		Metal	9,065,140	73,873,384.8	840,960	1,008,689
		Plastic	4,783,179	66,817,578	247,905	−244,355
		Mixed	1,266,928	19,352,692	300,210	192,135
	Composting	Organic	36,975	4,170	870	94
	Landfill	Mixed MW	0	0	-1,618,853	0
	Uncollected waste	Mixed MW	0	0	-1,398,090	0
	Total economic benefits (US$)		67,026,834	223,930,056.4	107483	1,044,522
	Benefits ($/person/year)		10	32	0	0
	Total benefits ($/person/year)		42			

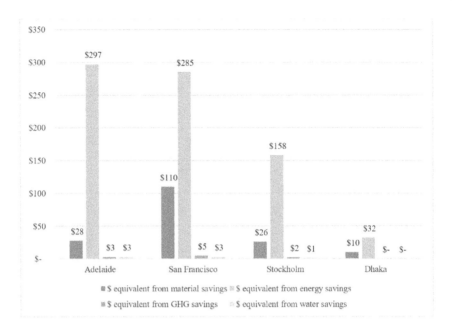

FIGURE 12.5   Per capita economic benefits in case study cities

is important to note that the economic benefits that influence the global and local market conditions vary in different countries. For instance, there is an influence on the local recycling material market, particularly for plastic and metal recycling, as oil and iron prices have significantly declined in the global market. Due to low commodity prices, recyclers would receive a lower financial value of their recycling materials, which eventually affects the overall waste recycling activities. The overall recycling performance would vary due to the global market conditions.

Implication of the ZWI

This study tries to better understand the interactions between consumption of resources, resource flow, and WMSs in cities. Therefore, the ZWI proposed in this chapter measures the amounts of resources recover from waste which can offset the need for raw materials and meet the demand for virgin materials at the resource extraction phase. Subsequently, offset virgin materials can save energy and water use and avoid GHG emissions to the atmosphere. One of the key benefits in applying the ZWI in evaluating a city's progress towards ZW goals is that the ZWI provides a wide picture of resource gain, and it also relates the resources gained to the resource consumption process, which is not possible in widely used waste diversion measurement tools.

Another possible implication of the ZWI is to measure the resource recovery potential at the global scale. The Waste Atlas (supported by D-Waste) for instance, is a collaborative initiative to visualize MSW management, data across the world for comparison, and benchmarking purposes (Waste Atlas, 2018). Therefore, by applying the ZWI, it is possible to measure the benefits of WMS (substitute materials, waste, and energy savings and avoided GHG) at a global scale which would be beneficial for comparing and benchmarking overall waste management performances.

At this stage, the practical use of the proposed ZWI is limited to MSW of six waste categories (organic, paper, plastic, metal, glass, and mixed waste) and four waste treatment technologies (recycling, composting, incineration, and landfill). The ZWT can be implemented and useful to apply to a broad range of waste types by developing a comprehensive database of substitution factors for different types of waste (C&D, electronic, mining, etc.) and treatment technologies (AD, pyrolysis, gasification, etc.). By quantifying the potential substitution of virgin materials, resources, and GHG offsets from WMSs, cities can be helped to monitor their resource consumption and resource recovery and measuring their progress towards a state of ZW. The real implication of the ZWI is very important in evaluating the progress of WMSs, and thus it is essential to improve the proposed tool in future iterations.

Key findings from the waste evaluation tool

This chapter presented an innovative waste management performance evaluation tool called the 'ZWI'. In addition, the chapter presented the application of the ZWT in the case study cities by evaluating and comparing their WMSs. The proposed ZWI measures reverse resource flows by considering virgin material substituted by resources recovered from waste to the production process. In addition, the ZWI measures the energy savings, GHG emissions avoided, and water savings from the materials substituted.

The ZWI is applied to measure the performance of WMSs in the case study cities. One of the key findings from the comparative analysis of the ZW performance in the case study cities is a reflection of true progress towards the ZW goals. The ZWI tool measures the potential amount of virgin material substituted through various WMSs in Adelaide, San Francisco, Stockholm, and Dhaka. In addition, the ZWI also measures total energy, water, and GHG savings from waste.

In regard to the ZW performance of the case study cities, San Francisco performed the best, followed by Adelaide, Stockholm, and Dhaka. Surprisingly, waste management performance in Dhaka is quite remarkable despite its informal waste recycling and inefficient WMSs. The reasons are (i) the volume of waste generated is low compared to the other cities and (ii) resource recovery in Dhaka's WMS is highly effective due to resource scarcity and low labour costs despite having a formal waste collection system.

Waste diversion rate is widely used as an indicator for progress towards ZW. Waste diversion rates in the case study cities are 46% in Adelaide, 52% in San Francisco, 32% in Stockholm, and 18% (informal) in Dhaka. Through the waste diversion rate, it is hard to measure the true benefits and progress in WMSs. By contrast, the ZWI provides a better picture of resources recovered from waste than the waste diversion rate does. The ZWIs in the case study cities are 0.23 in Adelaide, 0.51 in San Francisco, 0.17 in Stockholm, and 0.14 in Dhaka. An elaboration of the ZWI in Adelaide shows that the amount of resources that are recovered from the waste in Adelaide can potentially replace approximately around 23% virgin materials. By substituting for these virgin materials, Adelaide would save energy and water and avoid GHG emissions into the atmosphere. Hence, the ZWI helps us to add resource values by measuring the true contribution in regard to resource recovery, energy, and water savings and avoiding GHG emissions to the atmosphere.

The ZWI is an effective tool to assess the performance of a ZW management system in a city. Even though the proposed ZWI is limited to six waste categories, the tool captures a bigger and more detailed picture of WMSs compared to the traditional diversion rate. The 100% diversion rate is used as a goal for achieving ZW in many cities, but the diversion rate fails to capture the total resource recovery and environmental benefits of WMSs. Hence, the ZWT could be a more effective and reliable tool for decision makers. Although the ZWT is a relatively simple tool, this study illustrates its potential to enrich our understanding of urban metabolisms in our pursuit of ZW cities.

References

UN-HABITAT. (2010). *Solid Waste Management in the World's Cities: Water and Sanitation in the World's Cities* (Earthscan Ed.). London: Earthscan.

Waste Atlas. (2018). *Waste Atlas: Waste Management for Everyone.* Retrieved from www.atlas.d-waste.com/

CONCLUSION

Steve Jobs said, 'If you define the problem correctly, you almost have the solution', and this is also very true for waste management. We often failed to understand the core problem of our waste challenges. Managing waste is not the core problem; rather, 'not creating waste' (waste avoidance) through innovative design and circular urban system is the biggest challenge. In the classical economy and urban metabolic system, waste has been considered a valueless material that needs to be discarded of sustainably. ZW concept challenges the very core notion of waste, it refers to waste as a 'misallocated resource' or 'resource in transition' which is produced during the intermediate phases of production and consumption activities, and thus it should be recirculated to product supply chain through reuse, recycle, reassemble, resell, redesign, or reprocess (Zaman, 2016).

Realizing the core change and the potential opportunities in the ZW concept, are we going to achieve the ZW goals soon? The answer to this vital question would be 'no', at least under the current design philosophy (designing waste-ready product) and linear economic urban system, achieving ZW goals would be very difficult. ZW requires a whole transformation of our 'take-make-disposal' system to a circular system and to do that we need to transform our economic system. The very core of our economic system is grounded on the principle of constant ownership of new products and goods, most of them often not being used at all. Since environmental costs mostly ignore the pricing mechanism, we often overlook how our irresponsible production and consumption lifestyle impact our environment which may not continue to provide services the same way to our next generation, the way we inherited it from our ancestors.

Sustainable production and responsible consumption are the underpinning principles of the ZW philosophy. As stated in Chapter 3, we need to consider the whole life phase of waste from resource extraction-production-consumption to the final fate and not just from the point of generation, collection to landfill. The problematic marketing strategy such as planned obsolescence must be omitted by embracing the C2C design practice. The need to 'accesses' of the necessary goods and 'excess' unsustainable consumption of global resources should be minimized through design-led collaborative consumption (Crocker & Lehmann, 2013). There is an influx of research on the necessary behaviour change of our throwaway society and its impacts on the planet. Experts believe that the current trend of consumption is unsustainable and irresponsible and it cannot continue forever as we can't grow infinite due to our ecological limit (Meadows et al., 1972). Do we actually need to own every single product and service in our society? We need to move from an ownership-based economic system to a service-based economic system where consumers will use product services rather than own the product itself. The sooner we embrace the new economic system, the better we can execute the ZW solution.

As an aspiration, ZW needs the global market for recycling materials with the option for domestic use of recovered material instead of heavily relying on an overseas market. For example, the waste industry in Australia is currently facing significant challenges since China's waste ban in 2018 and is looking for a way out of this crisis. As an urgent response, the government has promised to spend more money to hold off council rate rises (Pash, 2018).

The Australian governments have set a 100% packaging targets which means that any packaging needs to be recyclable, compostable or reusable by 2025. Although a number of waste experts believe that only packaging targets is not enough and a follow-up on recycling targets are necessary (Zaman, 2018), which has been integrated on the "working draft" of the 2018 National Waste Policy.

The revised national waste policy sets 2030 targets to achieve 10% waste reduction, 80% waste diversion from landfill, 30% average recycled content across all goods, phase-out problematic plastic waste and halve the volume of organic waste sent to landfills (Topsfield, 2018).

Despite these initiatives, the challenges remain the same and there are practically no changes in the waste economy. The biggest challenges that the waste experts have identified to resolve the crisis are (i) lack of marketable waste economy due to cheap virgin materials, (ii) absence of local use and high dependency on the overseas market, and (iii) high contamination of the recyclable materials.

Australia alone may not control the price of virgin materials which often influence to overturn the use of recyclable materials over virgin materials. However, the biggest opportunities lie under creating a local waste market and using recyclable waste locally under stricter policies. The lobbying by Australian officials and politicians to get China to overturn the ban (Pash, 2018) shows how desperately Australia needs to offshore their problems to overseas countries. It would not have been a crisis if the level of contamination of the recyclable waste was under 0.5% threshold, which is not an easily achievable goal. San Francisco one of the global leaders in waste recycling and after investing around US$30 million in 2016, they have reduced the waste contamination from 5% to 3% in 2017 and still adapting new strategy to reduce contamination.

How have the European countries like Germany reduced their landfill dependency to almost zero, whereas in Australia, even the recyclable waste collected from the yellow bins are sent to landfills? This is utterly a wrong practice and it shows our incompetence in prioritizing and setting the correct strategy.

Since the China waste ban in 2018, WTE option has been considered a quick solution for Australia. Despite public protests, the option is still under consideration and in-progress in a number of Australian regions (Kilvert, 2018). However, this could be a bigger problem if proper consideration such as industrial symbiosis is not been taken to acquire the benefits of the technology; otherwise, it could become a very expensive exercise for Australia.

There is no quick way out from the current crisis and without a long-term plan, the crisis will worsen both economically and environmentally. The sooner we create a true CE to retain the value of materials the better. The revised national waste policy seems promising; however, the policy would remain ineffective without local community's active engagement in correct recycling and a lack of proper producer's responsibility, along with local solutions and markets for waste.

The data availability is also an important issue which is often ignored when it comes to SWM. We need a robust and reliable data capture mechanism so that we can act, develop and update our waste management policy and plans based on the real-time reliable data. We need to apply suitable measurement techniques to complete a comprehensive waste profile from household to national level. There is no doubt that by using smart technologies in the WMS, we can find our way out from the current crisis not only in Australia but around the globe. Finally, we need to identify and develop appropriate technologies to transform our valueless waste into valuable resources.

References

Crocker, R., & Lehmann, S. (Eds.). (2013). *Motivating Change: Sustainable Design and Behaviour in the Built Environment*. Oxfordshire: Routledge.

Kilvert, N. (2018). Waste-to-energy incineration should be "last resort" as Josh Frydenberg flags expansion, published by the ABC News on 27 April. Retrieved from www.abc.net.au/news/science/2018-04-27/waste-incineration-last-resort-experts-warn-frydenberg/9702490

Meadows, D. H., Meadows, D. H., Randers, J., & Behrens III, W. W. (1972). *The Limits to Growth: A Report to the Club of Rome (1972)*. New York: Universe Books.

Pash, C. (2018). Australian state governments will spend vast amounts of money to hold off council rate rises stemming from China's recyclable waste ban, Briefing. *The Business Insider Australia*, published on 22 March. Retrieved from www.businessinsider.com.au/australia-recycling-crisis-waste-state-government-support-2018-3

Topsfield, J. (2018). Australia to set national targets to reduce waste, published by the Sydney Morning Herald on 26 September. Retrieved from www.smh.com.au/politics/federal/australia-to-set-national-targets-to-reduce-waste-20180925-p505w5.html

Zaman, A. U. (2016). A comprehensive study of the environmental and economic benefits of resource recovery from global waste management systems. *Journal of Cleaner Production, 124,* 41–50.

Zaman, A. U. (2018). The new 100% recyclable packaging target is no use if our waste isn't actually recycled, published by the Conversation on 4 May. Retrieved from https:// theconversation.com/the-new-100-recyclable-packaging-target-is-no-use-if-our-waste-isnt-actually-recycled-95857

INDEX

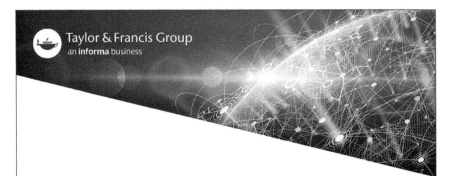

For Product Safety Concerns and Information please contact our EU
representative GPSR@taylorandfrancis.com
Taylor & Francis Verlag GmbH, Kaufingerstraße 24, 80331 München, Germany

www.ingramcontent.com/pod-product-compliance
Ingram Content Group UK Ltd.
Pitfield, Milton Keynes, MK11 3LW, UK
UKHW022306280425
457818UK00041B/136